HOW ENTHUSIASM CAN HELP
YOU TO A BETTER LIFE

In his new book, Dr. Peale brings the problems of today into focus and provides hardhitting, practical advice on how to cope with them. He shows that enthusiasm is the magic ingredient in the formula for success and explains:

> How enthusiasm sharpens your mind and improves your problem-solving abilities

> How enthusiasm kindles the powerful motivation that makes things happen

> How enthusiasm develops and maintains the quality of determination that helps you overcome fear and builds self-confidence

ENTHUSIASM MAKES THE DIFFERENCE

Norman Vincent Peale

FAWCETT CREST • NEW YORK

Grateful acknowledgment is made to the following: Doubleday & Company, Inc. for permission to quote from **The Executive Breakthrough** by Auren Uris, © 1967 by Auren Uris, Horatio Alger Awards Committee of the American Schools & Colleges Association, Inc., for permission to quote from **Opportunity Still Knocks,** Tenth Edition, 1965. Guideposts Associates, Inc. for permission to quote from **Guideposts,** September 1962, April 1964, © 1962, 1964 by Guideposts Associates, Inc. Prentice-Hall, Inc., for permission to quote from **How I Raised Myself from Failure to Success in Selling** by Frank Bettger, © 1949 by Prentice-Hall, Inc.; **The Secret of Successful Selling** by John Murphy, © 1956 by Prentice-Hall, Inc.; **Let Go and Let God** by Albert E. Cliffe, © 1951 by Prentice-Hall, Inc.; **Success Through A Positive Mental Attitude** by W. Clement Stone and Napoleon Hill, © 1960 by W. Clement Stone & Napoleon Hill. The Reader's Digest Association for permission to quote from "Sing-Out, America!" by Clarence W. Hall. The **Reader's Digest,** May 1967, © by The Reader's Digest Association, Inc. Simon & Schuster, Inc., for permission to quote from **The American Diamond** by Branch Rickey with Robert Riger, © 1965 by Branch Rickey and Robert Riger.

A Fawcett Crest Book

Published by Ballantine Books

ISBN 0-449-20069-8

This edition published by arrangement with Prentice-Hall, Inc.

Doubleday Dollar Book Club, January 1968

Guideposts, February 1969

Christian Herald, between February 1969 & February 1971

Manufactured in the United States of America

First Fawcett Crest Edition: June 1969
First Ballantine Books Edition: June 1982

This book is dedicated
to our grandchildren
LAURA STAFFORD PEALE
CHARLES CLIFFORD PEALE
SARAH LACY PEALE
JENNIFER RUTH EVERETT
and to
JOHN, CYNTHIA, and JENNIFER ALLEN
in the hope they will learn that
enthusiasm makes the difference.

CONTENTS

INTRODUCTION

Enthusiasm—the priceless quality that makes everything different!—that is the message of this book.

Life is not all sweetness and light, not by a great deal; certainly not with its manifold difficulty, pain, and frustration. This book faces life exactly as it is. But, a creative solution is offered—a solution that works. This is an in-spite-of type of book. In spite of all the negatives you can bring forth the positives.

Interest, excitement, aliveness—that is what this book is about.

It shows that you need not have a dull, routinized, desultory existence—not at all! Never settle for such a thing. And regardless of harsh, painful, and discouraging situations you can be alive, vital, and on top of things.

You can put new spirit, new creative skill into your job. Indeed, you can do better with everything. Enthusiastic, zest-packed living is yours if you want it. And who doesn't want it?

Personally, I believe one hundred percent in the message of the book. I have seen the tremendous things enthusiasm has done for so many. Believe me it works!

Norman Vincent Peale

ONE

WHAT ENTHUSIASM
CAN DO FOR YOU

Like an enormous map, the city of New York lay sharp and clear on that bright April day. From the window of a towering downtown office building, Sandy Hook could be seen far to the south and the George Washington Bridge to the north. To the west the low hills of New Jersey retreated in mystic blue haze. The deep-throated whistle of an outward bound ocean liner came faintly from the harbor. The vast network of the world's greatest city spread out below us.

The man behind the desk was obviously worried and the concerned look on his face underscored his feelings. "Sometimes I wish I might escape my responsibility for the people in this organization," he said. "Being the executive dealing with personnel can be a headache, believe me. Often I am compelled to do things that I dislike very much. To have the future destiny of people in my hands is something I do not enjoy at all."

"But their destiny is not really in your hands," I countered. "In the final analysis every man's destiny is in his own hands. But I sympathize with your problem, for you do indeed have to make decisions concerning people that can vitally affect their future."

"And that," he replied, "is exactly why I have asked you to come here today. It's about our mutual friend,

Fred Hill. This is one of the most painful decisions I have ever had to make about the future of a man, and I need your help." I assured him that my help was available but that it was not quite clear to me how I, who knew nothing of the business problems involved, could give any practical assistance.

"But you see, it's not entirely a business problem; primarily it's a human problem. As a matter of fact, this conference may well determine what happens to a dear friend; to his wife and three sons. How effective Fred can be henceforth, not only in business but in other capacities such as the church and community, gives me great concern. You see," he continued, "there will be an opening in this organization within the next six months and from the business structural point of view, Fred is the logical choice for the job. I've wrestled with my conscience, and in all fairness to the company, I cannot recommend him. So I'm hoping you and I might figure out some way to help revamp Fred and, incidentally, I realize this is a mighty big order."

"What needs to be done?" I asked. "He seems a topnotch man. I can't imagine anything wrong with him, except perhaps that at times he seems apathetic."

"That's just it," the executive exclaimed. "Fred is well trained; he's had good experience; he has an attractive personality. He's a good husband and a fine father. But he lacks drive and vitality. Fred hasn't an ounce of enthusiasm. If we could help him acquire enthusiasm, he'd be the right man for the right job."

"In six months' time?" I asked.

"Six months," he repeated.

I was lost in thought, for this was a real problem. At last I said, "You know, it's possible that Fred has never been awakened."

My friend quickly picked up that suggestion. "You may be right. If it's so, he's not the only one. In personnel work, I see it all the time—capable people who've never been awakened. If only we could motivate them—starting with Fred. You know, I want to see him realize his potential."

As I rode home in the subway, I studied the faces of the passengers—worried faces, dull faces, unhappy faces. I counted only a few people whose countenances reflected vitality and a positive attitude toward life. Many of us too often accept the humdrum life without making a fight for a better one. We think in a downbeat way that maybe we don't deserve more.

Just then it occurred to me that one of the greatest human needs of our time is a weapon to fight mediocrity, one that will teach us how to make use of zest and vitality and the creative forces buried deep within us. What we so desperately need is the capacity for exercising enthusiasm. Then and there, I determined to write this book, *Enthusiasm Makes the Difference.* For I truly believe that enthusiasm makes the difference between success and failure.

As regards Fred Hill—in Chapter Five we will take up in detail what happened to him.

But now I want to talk about enthusiasm and its significance to you. Having carefully observed people over many years, I am convinced that the fortunate individuals who achieve the most in life are invariably activated by enthusiasm. The men who do the most with their lives are those who approach human existence, its opportunities and its problems—even its rough moments—with a confident attitude and an enthusiastic point of view. Therefore, it seems timely to stress the vital power of enthusiasm and to suggest procedures to develop and maintain this powerful and precious motivating force.

Enthusiasm can truly make a difference—the difference in how your life will turn out. Consider, for example, the vast disparity between two current types. One group consists of the optimistic, the cheerful, the hopeful. Since they believe in something, they are the dynamic individuals who set events in motion, always working for the betterment of society, building new enterprises, restructuring old society and creating, hopefully, new worlds.

MODERN YOUTH IN REBELLION

Contrast these energetic optimists with those purveyors of gloom, the rebels who defy not only their parents and teachers but their barbers. Lacking the vision and strength to help humanity by righting great wrongs, they play childish games and their rebellion shows itself in rude manners, an aversion to the bathtub, muddled thinking and a cult devoted to nothingness. Enthusiasm has never been a part of a negative cult.

So we must learn how to utilize enthusiasm in order to move into that exciting and creative segment of the human race, the achievers. You will find among them total agreement that enthusiasm is the priceless ingredient of personality that helps to achieve happiness and self-fulfillment.

Sir Edward V. Appleton, the Scottish physicist whose scientific discoveries made possible worldwide broadcasting and won him a Nobel prize, was asked for the secret of his amazing achievements. "It was enthusiasm," he said. "I rate enthusiasm even above professional skill." For without enthusiasm, one would scarcely be willing to endure the self-discipline and endless toil so necessary in developing professional skill. Enthusiasm is the dynamic motivator that keeps one persistently working toward his goal.

Voltaire once described a man as being like a warming oven, always heating but never cooking anything. Commenting on this viewpoint, Harold Blake Walker points out that many people live without zest, dragging themselves through their jobs without vitality; in a word, heating just enough to get by but never really cooking.

But amazing things do happen, he points out, when a person really catches fire and starts the cooking process. Walt Whitman said of himself, "I was simmering, really simmering; Emerson brought me to a boil." What an apt description of a personality, gifted but lacking in power until the fire of enthusiasm brought it to the boiling point. As a result, Whitman created immortal poetry. Isn't it perhaps time to stop "simmering, really simmering," and become fired by a new and vital enthusiasm? The mental and spiritual heat created by enthusiasm can burn off the apathy-failure elements in any personality and release hitherto unused, even unsuspected powerhouse qualities. Walker puts it another way: "Go beyond simmering, even to boiling, and you will discover talents and powers you never dreamed were yours."

Years ago I came across a quotation from Charles M. Schwab, one of the dynamic men who built the American industrial structure. "A man," said Schwab, "can succeed at almost anything for which he has unlimited enthusiasm." And that is an important fact, as we shall show in this book.

It is, of course, true that most outstanding achievements are accomplished over great odds. At the start of every enterprise there are invariably the negativists who darkly opine, "It just cannot be done," as they eagerly marshall all the arguments against success. The pessimist is so eager to be able to say, "I told you so." Of course such people seldom if ever are constructive, which could be the reason they hope you won't be either.

Recently, I had the pleasure of conferring an Horatio Alger Award of the American Schools and Colleges Association upon John H. Johnson, Editor and Publisher of the highly successful publication *Ebony* and other periodicals. He had an idea for a great magazine to serve the Negro community but was, as is often the case, short on money. So he was advised to "forget it."

It is some years later, and those so-called friends still cannot forget that they might have owned stock in what is now an immensely profitable enterprise. Mr. Johnson and his wife own all the stock today because he was the only one who had enthusiasm for the project. His enthusiasm bred faith, and faith stimulated action. John H. Johnson is a living example of Charles M. Schwab's declaration that "a man can succeed at almost anything for which he has unlimited enthusiasm." George Matthew Adams expresses the matter equally well: "Enthusiasm is a kind of faith that has been set afire."

But I urge you to understand that enthusiasm is related to fire in a special way. It is fire under control, which is the only kind of fire that counts. Fire must be harnessed to produce power. The world belongs to the enthusiast who can keep cool. Thinking in depth and sound action always require coolness. So the process may be described as follows: enthusiasm builds a fire within a person, but he must control his enthusiasm for an idea or a project rather than be controlled by it. He must never allow uncontrolled anticipation to run away with judgment or reason. Like any powerful force, uncontrolled enthusiasm can destroy, as controlled enthusiasm can create.

LITTLE GOALS ADD UP

As Mr. Johnson developed *Ebony* magazine, he decided not to attempt immediately the larger goals for which enthusiasm for his project inspired him. Instead, he wisely chose to set and accomplish what he called "little goals," one after the other. The attainment of one small goal gave him the feel of success and taught him technique. Then he proceeded with growing experience to tackle the next "little goal," and presently those small goals added up to an immense goal. The "little goal" philosophy is sagacious advice, especially for overheated enthusiasts who, tricked into believing the world is their oyster, attempt too much too fast, only to end up in defeat and frustration.

While warning against overheating, we must with equal emphasis also warn against becoming too cool. A high degree of combustion in the mind is required to keep enthusiasm hitting strongly on all cylinders. The super-sophisticated, who unfortunately control much of the thought-affecting media of our time, superciliously play enthusiasm down. Indeed, any emotion to them, except perhaps existential sadness, seems to be looked at askance as being corny.

My friend, Raymond Thornburg, himself an irrepressible enthusiast, in commenting upon the downgraders of enthusiasm, quoted Anatole France's wise insight: "I prefer the folly of enthusiasm to the indifference of wisdom." Or shall we call it tired-out cynicism?

Indeed, one should never hesitate to be on the warm side. Even though enthusiastic commitment may carry with it the risk of being wrong, still only those who take the chance will ever attain complete creativity. The committed person, win or lose, is the one who finds the real excitement in living.

Betty Friedan, author of *The Feminine Mystique,* makes a statement which registers. "A good woman," she says, "is one who loves passionately, has guts, seriousness and passionate convictions, takes responsibility and shapes society. I'm horrified by the word 'cool.' Coolness is an evasion of life. Being cool isn't at all. . . . I'd rather be hot and wrong. I'd rather be committed than detached." Amen. So would I. So would any do-something-about-it-person. And this is precisely why enthusiasm makes the difference. It lifts living out of the depths and makes it mean something. Play it cool and you may freeze. Play it hot and even if you get burned, at least you will shed warmth over a discouraged and bewildered world.

There are, of course, quite a few people in the "couldn't care less" category, who are neither hot nor cold. This emotionally empty crowd apparently has always been around and has never rated very high either. As a matter of fact, in Biblical times they were referred to as ". . . lukewarm, and neither cold nor hot, I will spue thee out of my mouth." That is a pretty rough evaluation and forthright treatment, but it describes a pretty innocuous lot. If we can help reduce the number of lethargic people and bring even a few of them into the creative enthusiastic class, not only will they get more out of life personally, but the world itself will be improved.

HE COULDN'T CARE LESS—HE SAID—BUT HE DID

There are many people today who pride themselves on indifference to the normal way of life. They are jaded and bored, and conceal their destructive thinking under the guise of "I couldn't care less." Perhaps it is their defense against living, because life demands total commitment and commitment is apt to bring pain as well as challenge.

Harry Simpson fell into this category. He was the most apathetic man I have ever known. He said he'd been everywhere and had seen everything, including some of the human race which didn't inspire his esteem. He announced he was fed up with the young rebels and the middle-aged stuffed shirts. As for politics, what difference did it make who was elected? In his opinion, politicians were all crooked, and no matter which party won, the people always lost. He attended baseball games, without even rooting for a team. Even in the World Series, he remained apathetic. He was a cynic and like most cynics, totally selfish and self-indulgent. He felt no obligation to participate in church or civic affairs. As for charities, his was a token gift, simply, as he put it, "to shut them up." He couldn't care less about the needy. Finally his negative attitude won him the nickname of "Les," obviously borrowed from his well-known couldn't-care-less philosophy. In spite of this he was a convivial person; a good golfer, bridge player and club member. He and his wife did considerable entertaining. He had more than average success in his professional career.

Then enthusiasm slipped into the picture and what a difference it made in Harry Simpson. It happened this way. He and his wife decided they needed a change of pace. They came to New York and went the usual round of shows, restaurants and night clubs. Mrs. Simpson enjoyed it, but Harry was unimpressed. "I couldn't care less for this junk," he growled. "Let's clear out of here."

But they had promised a business associate back home to look up a friend in New York and reluctantly Harry telephoned the man. Surprisingly a cordial invitation to dinner was extended, and more surprisingly Harry accepted. "I never knew why," he explained, ". . . until later."

There were several other couples present and it proved to be the gayest and happiest evening the Harry Simpsons had spent in years. "I can't figure those people," Harry said when they were back at the hotel. "Nobody had a drop to drink, at least as far as I could see. But how come they were all so high? And they actually made politics and world affairs interesting. Did you notice they referred to religion as though it really mattered to them? What have they got that we haven't?"

"I don't know," replied Mrs. Simpson, although she thought she did but wanted him to find out for himself. "Why don't you see our host again and ask him?"

So Harry invited his host to lunch and asked, "How come a group of metropolitan people, supposedly sophisticated, showed such effervescence and excitement?"

"Well," explained the other, "there is a history to the things you noticed. That group is pretty modern and every one of them in varying degree had gotten generally fed up. For myself, I'd about decided that life was just more of the same and I got no real interest out of living. Oh, business was going pretty well but Betty and I were on edge much of the time. The parties we went to were all dull, the same people, the same inane conversation—you know how it is."

"Yeah, I sure do," said Harry. "That description fits me like a glove. Go on."

"Well, anyway," the other man continued, "quite accidentally I ran into the minister of a New York church. In fact, he came to my place of business to make a purchase. I had never met him but had read one of his books. I asked him to step into my office. He never said a word about religion, but I found myself opening up and telling him all about my frustrations and boredom. He listened quietly until I ran down. I thought sure he would start selling me on going to church or pull out a Bible and read to me. But he didn't. He sat thoughtfully, then asked me 'What's next?'

"It seemed a queer question, but of a sudden I actually said, 'What's next? What's next?—I know what it's all about. I need God.' I was shocked to hear myself saying that—it just didn't sound like me at all.

"The minister said, 'Could be. Guess that's what we all need. We human beings do have unsatisfied hungers and the principal one is for God.' The minister rose to go, 'If you want to pursue this further give me a ring.' Before I knew it he was on his way and I sat back and smiled, saying to myself, 'Boy, what a salesman! He leaves me reaching for his merchandise. He knows I am going to buy.'

"Well, I finally went to see this minister and he introduced me to a man, saying, 'Get to know this fellow. He's got what you're looking for.' This man asked me to join him and a few others for breakfast, of all things. I looked around at the group and they certainly were a regular crowd of good guys yet I never knew men to be so enthusiastic. The atmosphere they created began to get to me. Breakfast over, they started sharing 'spiritual experiences' with each other. They told how they applied 'practical Christian strategy' to business and personal relations and I could see that these fellows were *released*. I knew then this same release was what I needed. And staying with that crowd I found it, too. That's the story. Wouldn't have told you if you hadn't asked."

"So that's it," Harry said, after a moment's silence, "just plain old Christianity in new language. But you should see the church I belong to. I seldom attend because it's dull and the minister is a kind of half-baked socialist, if you ask me. I can't abide him. Not many others can either, it seems, for only a handful show up on Sunday for services. Our minister needs what you're talking about, that's for sure."

"Well," said the other, "why don't you get it and then pass it along to your minister? Maybe he is looking for the same thing, but won't admit it. He certainly can't be happy about a dead religion."

"Don't dump that on me," Harry grumbled. "I'm not about to be a missionary to a God-is-Dead minister. I've got myself to think of." But later, he mused, "Maybe God *is* my answer. Isn't it something? I came to New York to get away from it all, but instead I've got myself into something—really into it."

Harry, puzzled though he was, made a spiritual commitment in his own way. "From now on, I'm putting God at the center of my life," he said. Naturally, he had to think and study to "get the hang of it." But the strange and reassuring phenomenon in such matters is that whenever a person consciously or unconsciously desires spiritual rejuvenation and begins working toward it on a simple and genuine basis, amazing things do begin happening. The change in Harry did not come about at once or even quickly. But a definite change did begin and it continued, and gradually people became aware of a new Harry Simpson.

"You ask me to name our local ball of fire," said one of his golfing partners some months later, "and who do you think I'll name? You've guessed it. Harry Simpson."

"And what made the difference?" I asked.

"Enthusiasm, a new and terrific enthusiasm that *made* the difference. He is no nut—far from it. In my book he is the sharpest businessman in town. But ever since he got this enthusiasm he exudes a strange sense of power and contentment. He was never like that before," he concluded pensively.

I cite Harry's case because when enthusiasm develops in depth, usually a religious factor is involved. But for that matter, any upsurge of spirit, religious or otherwise, that introduces into the personality a verve, an excitement, an outgoingness, and which raises slow simmering to a boil, will bring about the quality of enthusiasm that makes the difference. Once enthusiasm took over, Harry lost his "couldn't-care-less" attitude. The new virtue and the old fault were not compatible.

ENTHUSIASM—THE SPICE OF LIFE

I have no idea whether Mr. John Kieran, the well-known writer, is religiously inclined, but that he has avoided apathy is evidenced by some potent expressions of his on the subject of enthusiasm. "William Cowper, the English poet, is the man who handed down the opinion that 'variety is the very spice of life' but I disagree and I point in passing to the fact that Cowper was three times locked up for insanity, which only shows what too much variety can do to you," writes Kieran.

"As for me, I believe that enthusiasm is the spice of life. Emerson wrote: 'Nothing great was ever achieved without enthusiasm.' When I was a college student I heard David Starr Jordan, then president of Stanford University, tell of a man who said that the only way to make good coffee was to 'put some in.' And that was also Dr. Jordan's advice about life, given to us as students and future citizens. I can still hear him thumping on the desk and saying: 'Put some in. Whatever you attempt, go at it with spirit. Put some in!'

"I'm prejudiced in this matter," continued Mr. Kieran, "because I'm full of enthusiasm for and against persons, places and conditions. It's more fun that way. An enthusiast may bore others—but he has never a dull moment himself."

Mr. Kieran's comments are reminiscent of a statement by the historian, Arnold Toynbee, who said, "Apathy can only be overcome by enthusiasm, and enthusiasm can only be aroused by two things; first, an ideal which takes the imagination by storm, and second, a definite intelligible plan for carrying that ideal into practice." Here again are the basic elements of enthusiasm, namely, heat and intelligence and some profound motivation which drives off apathy and cynicism.

Jack London, whose books charmed many of us years ago, summed up the matter thus: "I would rather be ashes than dust. I would rather that my spark would burn out in a brilliant blaze than be stifled by dry-rot. I would rather be a superb meteor, every atom of me in magnificent glow, than a sleepy and permanent planet. The proper function of man is to live, not to exist."

That, of course, is precisely why I undertook to write this book. So very many people are not really living; so many are apathetic and unhappy; so many are failing in life rather than succeeding as they should, so many lacking dynamic motivation. The reason, and it is often a primary reason: they are short on enthusiasm.

My friend, Alfred Krebs, proprietor of the beautiful Grand Hotel Regina in Grindelwald, Switzerland, once told me: "There can be no success without enthusiasm. The secret of a full life is lots of enthusiasm, the kind that keeps you fighting and winning over all obstacles—and enjoying every minute of it."

Of course Alfred Krebs is right, for being enthusiastic is being fully alive. It is a strange, sad fact that many individuals exist, yet are not really alive. And when one is not alive, days come and go in an unending march of mediocrity. Henry Thoreau, one of the half-dozen great thinkers who set the intellectual tone of our country in its beginning, said, "Only that day dawns to which we are awake."

ENTHUSIASM REBUILDS A COLLAPSED PERSONALITY

In a city where I was scheduled to speak at a dinner meeting I was seated beside a local judge, an alert man of thirty-five. He said, "I think you might be interested to hear about the reawakening of a collapsed personality in this city."

"Please say that again, Judge," I requested.

"Yes, that's what I mean; the reawakening of a collapsed personality," he repeated.

"This man George is a police officer assigned to my court," the judge continued. "He stands six feet two inches tall and physically is strong and impressive. At first he did a good job for us. Then I began to notice a change in him. It seemed as though all interest leaked out of his mind. He just sagged; lost vitality and dragged himself through the day's work. We sent him to the doctor who, after careful examination, reported 'There is nothing wrong physically except that his whole energy and bodily function levels are down, and that goes for his mental outlook too. When the body is run down, often the mind is involved, since mind and body function together.'

"'This man must have something troubling him mentally or emotionally,' the doctor continued. 'Maybe you had better have a psychiatrist run a check on him.'

"Instead of doing that," said the Judge, "I decided to work on George myself. 'Just how do you feel?' I asked him, and he replied, 'Well, Judge, I've got some personal worries, but they shouldn't make me collapse. Seems like I just haven't got any strength left. Living has become too much for me, I guess. I'm ashamed of being such a weak character.'

" 'Look, George,' I said, 'here is a book. I'll admit that it's a religiously slanted book, but it's written in simple style—no preachy stuff in it—and I think you will be interested in what it has to say. I want you to take it home tonight. Read the first chapter and study it carefully. Then come to my office tomorrow and I will quiz you on it.' "

Every day the Judge put George through an examination on each succeeding chapter until, after two weeks, the officer had read and studied and had been examined on the total book. "I doubt that George had ever read a book in his life before." Then he asked, " 'George, give me in a few words what this book has said to you.'

"George didn't hesitate a moment. 'Judge, this book says that if a person puts his life in God's hands he can overcome his weaknesses. That's what I make out of it, although there is a lot about thinking right.'

" 'That is exactly what I have been trying to get across to you, George. Maybe you should start putting the principles of the book into operation. It could work for you as it has for others, you know. Many people have really been helped by this book.' "

"And what happened?" I asked.

"Well, George got the message. He started studying creative spiritual principles. I supplied him with other books and pamphlets which might help him. I'm glad to tell you that he has pretty well worked out of his trouble. He is certainly no longer a collapsed personality. He has a new enthusiasm that has made all the difference in the world in him, though he still has much to learn about spiritual power as a source of real living. But he is learning. The main thing is he wants to learn, and so I am confident George is on the way."

Next morning while having breakfast in my hotel room, I turned on the television and happened to tune in to a panel on which three policemen were discussing "Safety Week." One officer was a big, vital man who talked about how wonderful life is and how important safety precautions are. The way he spoke, with great enthusiasm, telling the viewers how exciting life can be, convinced me that this was the officer of whom the judge had spoken. This was the former collapsed personality come alive. It was a thrilling and conclusive demonstration of how enthusiasm had made a difference in one man once he really went all out for it.

And there will be a great deal more about enthusiasm making a difference in people. So read on if you want your life improved, for enthusiasm can make a vast difference in every area of your life, in your work, your relationship with family and friends, in your entire outlook.

TWO

ENTHUSIASM
THAT NEVER RUNS DOWN

I shall never forget the night I met Miss Nobody. After making a speech in a West Coast city, I was shaking hands with people who came up to greet me, when along came a young woman who gave me a limp handshake and said in a small timid voice, "I thought I'd like to shake hands with you, but I really shouldn't be bothering you. There are so many important people here and I'm just a nobody. Forgive me for taking your time."

I took a look at her and said, "Will you do me a favor? Please remain a few minutes. I'd like to talk with you."

In some surprise she did as I suggested. When I had finished greeting the others, I said, "Now, Miss Nobody, let's sit down and have a little visit."

"What did you call me?" she asked in surprise.

"I called you by the only name you gave. You told me you were a Nobody. Have you another name?"

"Of course."

"I thought you must have," I said. "One reason I wanted to talk with you is to find out how anybody can get the idea she's a nobody. Another reason is that referring to yourself this way is in my opinion an affront to God."

"Oh, Dr. Peale!" she exclaimed, "you can't be serious. An affront to God?"

23

"You are a child of God, created in His image. So it really bothers me, it hurts me, to hear you say you're a nobody." And I asked, "Tell me a little about yourself."

She proceeded to describe her circumstances and problems. She talked haltingly, but with evident relief at being able to confide in someone. "So you see," she concluded, "I've quite an inferiority complex and sometimes I get terribly discouraged. I came to hear you tonight hoping you might say something that would help me."

"Well," I answered, "I'm saying it to you now: You are a child of God." And I advised her to draw herself up tall each day and say to herself, "I am a child of God."

She looked at me with a lovely smile and promised to follow that advice. And she added, "Pray for me."

And I did. I prayed that the Lord would help her to acquire real enthusiasm about herself and some proper self-confidence as well.

Recently I was speaking in the same area and an attractive young woman approached me asking, "Do you remember me?"

"Have we met before?" I asked.

"Yes, we have. I'm the former Miss Nobody."

Then I remembered. And I knew that she had fared extremely well since our first meeting. I could tell it from her manner and the sparkle in her eyes even before she had time to report anything in words. She had discovered her extension powers as a child of God.

This incident underscores an important fact. You can change! Anybody can change! And even from a dull nobody to an enthusiastic somebody.

In addition to "Miss Nobody," I have seen many people change and change greatly. They cease to be defeated and unhappy people and become altogether different in nature, so they are hardly the same individuals. Less attractive qualities have given way to better ones and their personalities have been dramatically brought out and enchanced. As a result they enter upon a life so full of happiness and success and creativity that people around them marvel. And they themselves marvel. And why not? For it is a marvel.

In the years that we have taught creative living through spiritual practice, I have seen people who were literally packed full of hate changed into people equally full of love. I have watched defeated individuals shed anxiety as they absorb the amazing secret of victory. I have observed people who suffer from fear transformed into courageous, worry-free persons.

ENTHUSIASM WILL IMPROVE YOUR PERSONALITY

There is another important form of change, one perhaps more complicated, related as it is to complex moods, to the cyclic rise and fall of emotional reaction. It is the change from apathy to enthusiasm, from indifference to exciting participation; it is an astonishing personality change which sensitizes the spirit, erases dullness and infuses the individual with a powerful motivation that activates enthusiasm and never allows it to run down.

Most people acknowledge the possibility of personality change in connection with hate, fear and other common forms of conflict, but seem to doubt that they can be made over into enthusiastic persons. They argue, "Sure I would like to have enthusiasm, but what if you just haven't got it? You cannot make yourself enthusiastic can you?" This is always said in anticipation of an of-course-you-can't agreement. But I do not agree at all. For you can make yourself an optimist. You can develop enthusiasm, and of a type that is continuous and joyous in nature.

The important fact is that you can deliberately make yourself enthusiastic. Actually you can go further and develop a quality of enthusiasm so meaningful and in such depth that it will not decline or run dry no matter what strain it is put to. It has been established by repeated demonstration that a person can make of himself just about what he wants to, provided he wants to badly enough and correctly goes about doing it. A method for deliberately transforming yourself into whatever type of person you wish to be is first to decide specifically what particular characteristic you desire to possess and then to hold that image firmly in your consciousness. Second, proceed to develop it by acting as if you actually possessed the desired characteristic. And third, believe and repeatedly affirm that you are in the process of self-creating the quality you have undertaken to develop.

MAKE USE OF THE "AS IF" PRINCIPLE

Many years ago the noted psychologist, William James, announced his famous "As if" principle. He said, "If you want a quality, act as if you already had it." Try the "As if" technique. It is packed with power and it works.

For example, let us suppose you are a shy and diffident individual with a miserable inferiority complex. The procedure for change into normal extrovertism is to start visualizing yourself not as you think you are, but rather as you'd like to be, a person confident and assured, able to meet people and to deal with situations. Once the thought or image of what you desire to be is deeply imbedded in your consciousness, then deliberately start acting in a confident manner, as if you are competent to handle situations and personal encounters. It is a proven law of human nature that as you imagine yourself to be and as you act on the assumption that you are what you see yourself as being, you will in time strongly tend to become, *provided* you persevere in the process.

This law of self-assumed personal change has been demonstrated by many and diverse people. For example, the famous religious leader John Wesley was terrified in a violent storm on the Atlantic as he sailed to America in the seventeenth century. But some people aboard the wildly tossing ship were calm and confident during the storm. Wesley was so impressed by their imperturbability that he asked their secret. It proved to be simply a serene faith in God's providential care. When Wesley sadly confessed that he did not have such faith, one of them said, "It is a simple secret. Act as if you do have such faith and in time faith of that character will take hold of you." Wesley followed the advice and ultimately developed such powerful faith that he was able to overcome the most difficult situations. So therefore if you are afraid, discipline yourself to act as if you had courage. If you are tense, deliberately act as if calm and assured. Shakespeare, whose insights into human nature have scarcely ever been equalled, supports this method. "Assume a virtue if you have it not," he tells us in Act III of *Hamlet*.

Another outstanding illustration of the law of acting "As if" and as you desire to be is that of Frank Bettger, a top insurance man. In his book *How I Raised Myself from Failure to Success in Selling* * Mr. Bettger tells of his early experience as a professional baseball player on a minor league team from which he was summarily discharged. The manager regretted letting him go since Frank possessed the basic qualifications of a good player. But though competent, he was dropped for one reason only— lack of enthusiasm.

Bettger, signed by another team at a lower salary, continued to play the same desultory kind of game. Then one day he encountered a famous oldtime professional who asked, "Frank, don't you really like baseball? You have real ability, but you are totally lacking in enthusiasm, and until you get that you will never go ahead in this sport, or for that matter, in anything else in life. You must have enthusiasm. It's a primary requisite for success."

"But," complained Bettger, "what can I do? I haven't got enthusiasm. You just can't go out and buy it in a store. You either have it or you don't. I haven't, so that's it, I guess."

"You're wrong, Frank," said the older man urgently. "Make yourself act enthusiastic. It's as simple as that. Act with enthusiasm, play ball with enthusiasm, and pretty soon you will have enthusiasm. Once you're fired with conviction your natural talents will take you to the top in this sport."

Finally Frank Bettger's chance came. He was taken on by the New Haven ball club, and when he went out to play that first day he resolved to take his old friend's advice and act as though he was charged with enthusiasm. He ran like a man electrified. He threw the ball so hard it seared the gloves of other players. He swung like mad at the ball and actually made some hits. He literally burned up baselines; all this, while the temperature was over ninety in the shade.

The New Haven newspapers the next day asked where this terrific new player Bettger came from. He was a human dynamo, they reported. Soon they were calling him "Pep" Bettger. As he continued to play with such vigor he found himself feeling like a new man. And why not, for he was just that. He became such an enthusiastic player, that a scout for the St. Louis Cardinals spotted him and before long he was playing in the National League.

Later, having taken up a career in insurance, Bettger was once again plagued by apathy and he was once more courting failure. Then he recalled how he had deliberately cultivated enthusiasm, and applied the same "As if" principle to his insurance work. The result was that he rose to the top in his selling field as he had in baseball. Mr. Bettger's experiences demonstrate that enthusiasm can be cultivated and developed by deliberately thinking and acting with enthusiasm. You too can activate yourself into enthusiasm by use of the "As if" principle. What you are comes to you. This remarkable principle is thus stated by Emerson, "A man is a method, a progressive arrangement; a selecting principle, gathering his like unto him wherever he goes." So act as you want to be and you will be as you act.

MENTAL VENTILATION LETS IN ENTHUSIASM

Another practice important to the development of optimistic attitudes is that of mental ventilation. A mind full of gloomy foreboding thoughts makes difficult the cheerful and spirited quality of thinking that stimulates enthusiasm. This is true also of such dark closed thoughts as hate, prejudice, resentment and general dissatisfaction with people and world conditions. Discouragement and frustration form a heavy cloud-blanket over the mind and condition mental attitudes accordingly. Mental ventilation, then, is a highly important step in reconditioning the mind to accept the creative thought climate in which enthusiasm may develop and finally become the dominant factor.

This concept of mental ventilation was first suggested to me some years ago by Mr. A. E. Russ, an old friend who operated a drugstore on lower Fifth Avenue near Twelfth Street in New York. Mr. Russ, a member of my church, had a remarkable gift of native wisdom and insight. He was a natural philosopher, a keen and discerning thinker, a voracious reader, and a successful businessman. His spiritual life had depth, the kind which results when personal suffering emerges into understanding and victory. He knew how to help people and communicate to them a sense of meaning in life, as is evidenced by my personal experience with him.

Discouragement was once somewhat of a problem for me and it would occasionally plunge me into pretty low feelings. Though enthusiastic and optimistic by nature, I was sometimes given to depressions. During such low periods, it seemed that nothing went right. In those days I preached at Marble Collegiate Church on Sunday nights as well as Sunday mornings. (Later the morning congregations grew to such proportions that it became necessary to give the same sermon twice on Sunday morning; the evening service was handled by associates.) But at the time of which I write, I felt I had done particularly badly in my sermon one Sunday evening. Avoiding as many people as possible I plunged out into the dark misty night and walked glumly down Fifth Avenue toward my home.

Passing Mr. Russ's drugstore, I decided on an impulse to go in to see him. He was making sodas at the fountain, so I sat at the counter and watched him. "How come you are making sodas?" I asked. "Where is your regular counterman?"

"He left me, so I'm shorthanded," he replied.

"Tell you what," I said. "I preached a terrible sermon tonight. Can't imagine why I ever took up preaching in the first place. I'm a flop. How about giving me that soda jerk job?"

"Sure, why not?" replied Mr. Russ without a change of expression. "Come around the counter and make a soda for me. I want to see how good you are before taking you on." So Mr. Russ sat at the counter while I donned an apron and proceeded to put together a chocolate ice cream soda. It had a fairly good head on it, I thought. I laid a straw against it as I'd seen the experts do and put it in front of him. He took a long draw while I waited for the verdict. Removing the straw from his mouth he said, "Better stick to preaching."

Climbing down off the stool he locked the front door. "Closing time," he explained and then added, "Come into my back room and let's talk." He led me into those mysterious recesses behind the drug area to which druggists retire to compound prescriptions. There, I must say, he made up a "thought prescription" for me for which I have been grateful through the many years that have passed since that gloomy night.

Mr. Russ began to tell of his personal battles with discouragement. As I listened to his story of difficulties, reverses and sorrows, my depression seemed trifling indeed. "But I can tell you honestly," he declared, "that since I began a certain mental and spiritual practice I have never had any lasting discouragement. And I'm sure you will agree I'm on the enthusiastic side."

"I don't know a man of more genuine enthusiasm than yourself. What is this mental and spiritual practice which helped you?"

"Daily mental ventilation," he replied. "That's what did it and, I may add, still does it. Keeping the mind free of darkness is a day to day job."

He went on to emphasize the importance of the process of daily mind-emptying. "If you allow dark thoughts, regrets, resentments and the like to accumulate, your whole psychology can in time be so adversely affected that a major effort may be required to bring it back to a normal state of balance." I knew he was right, for our religio-psychiatric counseling service at the church was even then working with the pathetic problem of a man who had, as he himself put it, "accumulated a putrifying mass of old unhappiness in the mind." Weeks were required for our ministers and psychiatrists to cleanse and restore his psychological equipment to proper working order.

Since then I have used the mental ventilation system employed daily by Mr. Russ, both personally and in other cases, and with such effective results in stimulating new enthusiasm that I set it down here for the benefit of all who may read this book. He "emptied" his mind at the end of every day to prevent unhealthy thoughts from lodging in consciousness overnight, for he knew such thoughts can take root quickly if allowed to accumulate even for as long as twenty-four hours.

This mental emptying took the form of a recapitulation of unpleasant incidents that had occurred during the day; a sharp word, an insinuating remark, a hostile act by some other person. Also, a review of his own mistakes, errors or stupidities. To these he added disappointments, frustrations and every form of unhappiness that had clouded the preceding hours. He held all these in a strong mental view, deliberately drawing from them all the experience and understanding they had to give. Then he "lumped" them together and mentally "dropped" them out of consciousness, saying as he did so these therapeutic words: "Forgetting those things which are behind, and reaching forth unto those things which are before . . ." (Philippians 3:13)

Mr. Russ stated that when he first began to use his

"lumping" and "dropping" practice, the mental accumulation, as he put it, readily "lumped" but just did not "drop." However, the continued application of a determined and disciplined mental effort resulted in due time in a remarkable ability to forget the useless and unhealthy material that had previously cluttered his mind, siphoning off zest and enthusiasm. In these procedures, Mr. Russ made use of the law that one can do practically anything he wants with his thoughts, provided he consistently continues the effort.

"You cannot possibly realize until you try it for yourself what a powerful upthrust of joy surges through your being when you find that you can actually 'lump' and 'drop' those pesky enemies of a happy mind," he declared. "Ventilate—that's the answer. Ventilate. Let them go; throw them out, 'lump' and 'drop'—ventilate the mind.

"Now take yourself," he exclaimed, "you say you've had a bad evening; that you preached a disappointing sermon. All right then; analyze it carefully. Determine what you did that may have been wrong. Learn something from your analysis. Then 'lump' and 'drop'—ventilate. The old enthusiasm will bounce back."

He punched me affectionately on the chest as we said goodbye. I went home and at once started practicing Mr. Russ's mental ventilation system. It took some time and some doing over many days, but finally I got the hang of making my mind obey me. Then it was easy. Believe me, this method is a sure-fire secret of having boundless enthusiasm.

TELL YOURSELF ALL THE GOOD NEWS YOU KNOW

A vital element in developing enthusiasm is the manner in which you start the day. You can pretty well condition a day in the first five minutes after you wake up. Of course, some people are naturally slow starters and for them it takes time to become fully awake and adjusted to a new day. But even so, careful attention to the matter of setting the tone of a day in the early hours is likely to have a determinative effect.

Henry Thoreau, the American philosopher, used to lie abed for awhile in the morning telling himself all the good news he could think of; that he had a healthy body, that his mind was alert, that his work was interesting, that the future looked bright, that a lot of people trusted him. Presently he arose to meet the day in a world filled for him with good things, good people, good opportunities.

This good news technique each morning can help make your day, despite the fact that there may be disappointing news that must be faced. Still, the more good news you tell yourself, the more such there is likely to be. The practice will also help you take bad news in your stride. At any rate, that which the mind receives upon awakening tends to influence and to a considerable degree determine what your day will be.

One man whose enthusiasm is always in evidence, even when the going is rough, has his own method for beginning a day. He takes a few minutes before breakfast for what he calls a "quiet time." This consists of reading a brief spiritual or inspirational piece and is followed by three or four minutes of quiet during which he affirms and practices a quiet state of mind. Regardless of how busy his program for the day, in those few minutes no hurry or haste is permitted, even in thought.

He then pictures every person he expects to contact during that day and prays for each one. "Then I commit the day to God and get going," he says. And he really does get going. Everyone he touches is revitalized by this man whose boundless enthusiasm seems never to diminish. And a principal reason for its vitality is that his practice of spiritual motivation at the start of each day infuses him with new zest.

EVERY MORNING A NEW SET OF FACTS

Apprehension about the day ahead is characteristic of some people, particularly if they find difficult and trying problems looming ahead. They view the prospect with distaste, perhaps even fear, so they have little enthusiasm for the exciting challenge that problems present. But I do admire the attitude of a friend toward each day. He has experienced some tragic trials and reverses in his lifetime, enough in fact to completely destroy many men. But he says, "A reversal is not a disaster, merely an incident in a total business career." He approaches each day on the principle that you get a new set of facts each morning.

Then you convince yourself that you are going to take this new set of facts, be happy with it and do something constructive with it.

This man, whose enthusiasm and ability are considerable, declares, "There are only two kinds of days for me: Some days I'm happy. Other days I'm hysterically happy." The policy of taking hold of a new set of facts each morning and being happy about it seems to be a real factor in sustaining high-level enthusiasm. It has been said that every tomorrow has two handles. You can take hold of either the handle of anxiety or the handle of enthusiasm. The continued choice of handle determines the character of your multiplying days. Choose enthusiasm daily and you are likely to have it permanently.

HOW TO HAVE CONTINUING ENTHUSIASM

The problem of sustaining enthusiasm is often difficult, especially for older persons. The natural enthusiasm of youth may take a fearful battering as the years add up. Disappointments, frustrated hopes and ambitions, the drain-off of natural energy all conspire to dull excitement and enthusiastic response.

But such deterioration of your life force need not occur. In fact, it will happen only if allowed to happen. You can arrest the decline of spirit; you can be perpetually motivated by enthusiasm despite age, pain, sickness, disappointment and frustration.

I have known people who have remained enthusiastic until the end of their lives and then seemed to go out of this world with flags flying, the light of enthusiasm for life still in their eyes. Nothing could ever happen to destroy the precious gift of enthusiasm.

In thinking of such energetic and enterprising people, Huxley's insight comes to mind—that the true genius of living is to carry the spirit of the child into old age. And what is the spirit of the child, but that of wide-eyed open wonder, excitement and zest; the optimistic attitude that nothing is too good to be true, that the world is literally a wonderful place?

In Montreux, Switzerland, I met Mr. and Mrs. William P. Daggett, schoolteachers from Long Beach, California, and their children, Lucy, Cathy and Larry. Mrs. Daggett mentioned a quotation from Thoreau which hangs on her kitchen wall at home. "None are so old as those who have outlived enthusiasm." Well, believe me, that is an auspicious saying that could well be engraved on the wall of the mind. It is a fact that the oldest, saddest people are those who have outlived the enthusiasm of their youth.

That quotation from Thoreau set me thinking. I am writing these lines on a balcony of the famous Montreux Palace Hotel of which my friend Paul Rossier is general manager. My balcony looks out on an incomparable vista across the blue waters of Lac Leman (Lake Geneva) to the misty heights of the Alps towering above. Nearby and downlake at the water's edge stand the grim gray walls of the ancient Castle of Chillon, immortalized by Lord Byron.

I well recall my first visit to this old-world city and hotel forty years ago. I was very young and enthusiastic and wanted to travel to Europe and see the places I had read about in history books. Having scarcely two nickels to rub together I organized a tour party for which I earned the cost of the trip and a couple of hundred dollars besides. It was the experience of a lifetime. My mind was full of the romantic future, and I lived in perpetual excitement. Like "The Youth, who daily farther from the east must travel, and by the vision splendid is on his way attended," so I was fascinated by sights and sounds. The Montreux Palace Hotel, to my wondering eyes, was the most elegant hostelry imaginable. And I was actually looking for the first time at the Alps and Lac Leman. I just could not believe it. It was all so incredible and wonderful.

Well, four decades have passed since that first enthralling visit. The question now is: How about those youthful dreams? What has happened to that glorious excitement? What is the state of that ardent enthusiasm?

What would be your own honest answer to such reflections? Ponder well those words from Thoreau: "None are so old as those who have outlived enthusiasm." And just what have we got, you or I, if we have outlived enthusiasm? The Bible had a graphic picture of such persons. "When they shall be afraid of that which is high, and fears shall be in the way . . ." On that basis, one can be old at twenty, and some are. It is the rejuvenation of the mind that keeps enthusiasm alive and, as a matter of fact, restrains aging in spirit and mind, perhaps even in body too.

Well, what is your answer? Want to know mine? I can honestly report that the excitement and enthusiasm of forty years ago are still very much alive, only deeper and more satisfying. So I know from personal experience that enthusiasm can be perpetual; that it need never run down. And that is a fact too, a great big wonderful fact.

KEEP THE FIRES OF ENTHUSIASM BURNING UNDER YOUR GOALS

What an ingredient it is, this vital thing called enthusiasm! And a factor that keeps it perking is an irresistible goal, a fascinating objective, a consuming purpose that dominates, motivates and will not let go of you. Set yourself a goal that you've just got to reach. Then build under it the fire of anticipation and keep it burning—you will acquire enthusiasm and never lose it. That goal will keep beckoning, saying: "Come on after me." And when you reach your goal still new goals will succeed one another as each is attained. New goals, fresh objectives—these are the self-perpetuating motivators of enthusiasm.

Take my friend Paul Chow as an example. I first met Paul in Hong Kong. He had literally walked out of Red China with his family. His astonishing enthusiasm is reflected in a glorious smile and a radiant face. Paul had a dream, a goal, to come to America to raise his family. He was very poor and one of the thousands of refugees crowding into Hong Kong. But Paul had something of much more value than money. He had faith, purpose, enthusiasm.

It is a long story, but one Sunday I looked from my pulpit in New York City, halfway around the world from Hong Kong, and there amidst that huge congregation, right in the front pew, sat Paul Chow and his family. And he was smiling up at me as if to say, "We made it to New York."

Mrs. Peale and I visited his new home in a section of New York where crowding, noise and filth brought back memories of their ordeal in Hong Kong. "Not another day shall they live in this hell-hole," we agreed. We helped them move to Pawling, New York, where Paul has become a valued worker in our publishing plant at the Foun-

dation for Christian Living, and where his family has
made a real place for themselves in the community life.

Stephen Chow has become a top honor student in high
school, and Ruth and Martha Chow are leaders in their
classes. The family has made a second move to a better
house. They work hard; indeed they work like Americans
worked in the old days. Stephen cannot understand why
some young people fail to realize the tremendous privilege
and opportunity they have in schools in America.

One vivid picture I carry in mind. Mrs. Peale and I
were leaving our farm at Pawling on a beautiful July Saturday afternoon for a vacation in Europe. Paul and Stephen were painting a long white fence. They are always
working. They have a goal, so they work. The road runs
below a high bank atop which Paul, spattered with paint,
was making that fence white and beautiful as his sense of
perfection dictated. As we drove away he stood there paint
brush in hand, etched against a blue sky and a field of
waist-high corn, his face alive with a happy smile, waving
farewell to us.

As we drove down the road to the airport I marveled at
how far that Chinese refugee family had come from such
unpropitious beginnings with so many obstacles ahead.
What can possibly explain it? That's easy. It was a goal, an
objective, a purpose. It was aspiration for a better way of
life. It was enthusiasm that never weakened because it was
subject to constant renewal.

Dwayne Orton expressed a solid truth when he said:
"Every business organization should have a vice-president
in charge of constant renewal." If it is good for an industry constantly to renew itself, then surely it is important
for the individual to have an automatic self-motivator that
keeps him alive and vibrant, always alert to the dynamic
present in which he lives. In the absence of constant renewal he may fail to keep pace with changing times. Then
life races ahead of him. He becomes not a living, vital
man, but a relic who fades each day further into the dead
past. Possessed of enthusiasm one is a citizen of the present regardless of how many years he has dwelt upon earth.
Such a vitalized person cannot possibly become a *has-
been*. He is perpetually the *is-now* type.

Happy expectations make the ultimate difference in any
person. "Every man is enthusiastic at times. One man has
enthusiasm for thirty minutes—another has it for thirty

days—but it is the man who has it for thirty years who makes a success in life." So says *The Catholic Layman.*

ENTHUSIASM AND FINGER LICKIN' GOOD

Colonel Harland Sanders was sitting on his porch in Shelbyville, Kentucky, on his sixty-fifth birthday when the mailman came up the walk and handed him an envelope. It contained his first social security check. While grateful to the government for this tangible expression of concern for its older citizens, Colonel Sanders had no mind to settle down to a nonparticipation status in business. With boundless confidence despite his limited financial position, he turned his thoughts toward using that modest check to begin a new career. What an exciting experience it would be to launch a new career at an age when one is expected to start playing shuffleboard.

Sitting on his porch that day, do you know what he did? He started thinking—and ideas came to his mind. Ideas change things. He remembered the delicious fried chicken his mother used to make, crispy brown and tender. The very aroma seemed to be wafted across the years, filling him with nostalgia. The recipe for that fried chicken was imprinted indelibly in his taste buds and on his memory.

Then came the creative idea that was to change his life. Why not sell the recipe for his mother's fried chicken on a royalty basis to restaurant owners? Immediately he took action on the thought. Getting into his battered car he set out calling on restaurant owners everywhere, enthusiastically telling them of his out-of-this-world fried chicken. But no one would go for his idea. Across the country from Kentucky to Utah restaurant men maintained that their own recipes for fried chicken were good enough for them and their patrons. In Salt Lake City a restaurant owner who doubted that his northern clientele would respond to Kentucky-type fried chicken was swayed by the Colonel's enthusiasm, and finally agreed to give it a trial.

The result—people crowded his restaurant clamoring for those golden brown chicken pieces for which the positive-thinking colonel had coined the graphic selling phrase: "It's finger lickin' good."

Colonel Sanders, a striking figure in immaculate white suit and black string tie, finally sold out his interests for two million dollars, and then was hired by the new owners as goodwill ambassador at an annual salary of $40,000. His ruddy face is full of humor and intelligence; he is now over eighty years old but he still reaches out enthusiastically toward a future that calls for fresh thinking. And what is the motivation of this man and others like him? It's enthusiasm, the kind of enthusiasm that believes there is always something new and better ahead. It is creative conviction that never runs down.

Finally there is a prime factor in the maintenance of continuing enthusiasm, one that brings all other ingredients together into powerful focus. And that is a profound spiritual feeling, a faith in God, that activates a sharp awareness of life and a consuming interest in living. Age does not dull it. Pain and problems do not take the edge off of it. The blows of time and circumstance do not affect it. With this faith, a sense of confidence in life itself continues, unaffected by all the difficulties of human existence. A deep personal and vitalized faith in God is the basic factor in developing enthusiasm that never weakens. And it is vividly expressed in a statement from the Bible: "Be renewed in the spirit of your mind." (Ephesians 4:23)

I tried making a list of the most enthusiastic men I have ever known and discovered that this fundamental statement explained the enthusiasm of them all. One man on my list is an old friend, Bryson F. Kalt. One of New York's top salesmen with a phenomenal selling record, Bryson has the ability to maintain enthusiasm (without which no man can succeed as a salesman) with the help of the principle stated in those words "be renewed in the spirit of your mind."

Asked the secret of his continuing and undiminished vitality over many years, Bryson replied, "Well, it's like this. You taught me to love God and people and life and to keep my mind and spirit renewed and at a high level. I followed your positive teaching and the result has been happiness and enthusiasm that never runs down."

There you have, I believe, the basic answer to the problem of undiminished enthusiasm. Simply "be renewed in the spirit of your mind." Keep the mind perpetually renewed and you're in.

THREE

ENTHUSIASTIC
PERSUASION

There is a magic formula for success.

No enterprise can succeed without it; any enterprise can succeed with it. Indeed, it can lead to success in life itself. The formula is stated in six powerful words—short words, only three of them containing as many as four letters. They are these—and mark them well: *find a need and fill it.*

Every business enterprise that has achieved success and demonstrated outstanding performance has been predicated on that formula. The managers of such enterprises discovered a need for some service or commodity that was generally required by people. They went about filling that need, they filled it well, and so their efforts were rewarded by corresponding response.

The great men of history were those who saw a need, who became aware of some timely requirement. They proceeded to fill the need, they met the requirement, and so were leaders and benefactors of mankind. They became outstanding and successful personalities, being possessed of the great quality of timely participation. These men were need-watchers, situation-handlers, condition-rectifiers, requirement-fillers.

Success is not based on smug cleverness, sharp practice, shady promotion, or super high pressure. These may carry

39

one along for a while, but they have no substance, they don't hold up, and so presently they show through, they wear thin. Loud-talking, simulated enthusiasm that is usually coupled with high pressure is another false procedure that doesn't have what it takes to persuade and communicate and produce long-lasting results. It washes out inevitably.

But a salesman's enthusiasm based on a sincere belief that his goods or services are needed, and that such goods and services will meet people's needs with validity, is the kind of enthusiasm that does succeed, and it is entitled to do so. It will succeed if it isn't overpressed. An overpressing salesman creates resistance. But sincere enthusiasm attracts confidence.

So if you are a salesman and have something to sell, something that people really need, which when purchased will honestly fill that need, you have the makings of a successful career. But you must be certain that what you are trying to do or be is right. If it isn't right, it's wrong—not half-right, not half-wrong. It is either right or wrong and nothing wrong can ever turn out right. Unless it's good, it's bad, and nothing that is bad can be good. So get with the right—get with the good.

When you have something you really believe in, then you can put the amazing power of conviction behind your efforts. Then it is that enthusiasm is activated, develops and starts working. And when enthusiasm—real burning enthusiasm for something, for a product or a service—gets involved, then persuasion becomes a factor. Enthusiasm that persuades is perhaps the most powerful communicator on earth. It puts you in a position to reach people, to make them aware of their need and it also conveys to them that you can supply their need. You then become a vital necessary factor in their lives—and why not? You have what they need. You are essential to their happiness and welfare, and they know it.

But the strange fact about human nature is that people are not always aware of their needs. So they often resist buying that which they really need for their own best interests. This is the point at which communication and persuasion are so profoundly required. The art, skill or science of communication is the process by which you persuade another person or many persons to walk the road of agreement with you. Communication and persuasion—

these are the two absolutely essential qualities that every human being *must* have if he desires to affect the lives of other people; to get them to buy a product, accept an idea, share a conviction or walk with him toward a goal.

HOW TO BE A REAL SALESMAN

This chapter largely has to do with salesmanship. And I feel entitled to write on this subject, having spoken before many sales meetings and been closely associated with the selling profession even to the extent of making a motion picture entitled *How to be a Real Salesman*.

How do you become a real salesman? Well, this chapter will outline and illustrate some suggested methods. I want to list here an eleven-point salesmanship technique which I believe gives important elements in effective selling.

1. Find a need and fill it. It's pretty hard to sell something no one needs. Believe that you are selling what people really need.

2. Since you must sell yourself even before selling your goods, it's important to sell yourself on yourself. So believe in yourself.

3. Want to sell. Get the thrill of selling desirable goods or services.

4. Get full of enthusiasm, the kind that keeps you excited about your job and about people.

5. Don't ride enthusiasm so hard that you become offensively high pressure. All that will get you is resistance and no sale.

6. Develop the powerful motivation that comes from deep inner enthusiasm that never runs down.

7. Don't be a half-a-minder. Be an all-out, not a half-out. Give your whole mind, your whole self. That will provide the impact that achieves results—real results.

8. Concentrate—think—concentrate—think. Keep your mind working and keep your mind on your selling. Thinking produces ideas and ideas sell.

9. Learn to communicate. Develop rapport with people. Know people and like them. They will like you and buy what you have to sell.

10. Ask God to guide you in your planning. Then plan your work and work your plan.

11. Believe that being a salesman is the greatest, most

important job in the American economy. Believe that you are a trustee of free enterprise and freedom. Be proud you are a salesman.

ENTHUSIASM PERSUADES AND PERSUASION SELLS

From boyhood I have personally been fascinated by salesmanship. Always I wanted to sell—to sell something to somebody—to offer people some value. I clerked in a candy store after school and sold candy, at least that which I didn't eat. I worked in a grocery shop and got a big charge out of *selling* groceries, not merely filling orders. I sold the Cincinnati *Enquirer* and worked early and late getting new subscribers and did so in large numbers.

My selling career as a boy included selling men's clothing for my dear old friend, Emil Geiger. Years ago he operated one of the best haberdashery shops I ever knew back in Bellefontaine, Ohio. Emil was one of the most effective communicators and practicers of the art of persuasion I have ever watched in operation. He offered good quality merchandise. Actually he loved his goods. To him, they were the best; there was nothing better.

He was patient, wanting the customer to have that which was the best for him. Rather than allow a man to go out of his store with a suit that wasn't just right, Emil would tell him to look elsewhere. I have even known him to phone a competitor to supply a customer when he felt honestly he could not do it himself. People always came back to him, for they trusted him. He knew how to sell and what is perhaps more important, how to keep on selling. Honesty and integrity were the hallmark of this man who remains in my memory one of the greatest salesmen I ever knew.

He was like the late Amos Sulka, famous New York City haberdasher, who was also a friend of mine. Sulka told me that the late William Randolph Hearst, publisher of the Hearst chain of newspapers, once came to his shop to lay in a new supply of collars. Sulka felt that the style of collar worn by Mr. Hearst was entirely unsuited to him and as a matter of fact not even in good style. He suggested in his best persuasive manner another type collar. Hearst bristled, "I know what I want. Do you want to sell me that or not?"

Sulka, unruffled, pleasant and polite, still was firm. But he knew how to communicate. "Mr. Hearst," he said to the big, stern, beetle-browed publisher, "you are the greatest seller of newspapers in the world. You know what people need and you sell them what they need. I, Sulka, am the greatest haberdasher in the world. I know what people need in the way of clothing. I'm the world's expert in suiting the proper item to the man, especially the great men."

The eyes of the two strong personalities, the two supersalesmen, met. Sulka's never wavered, "I want Mr. Hearst to look Sulka's best, and that is the best."

Hearst grinned. "All right, you old egotist, put the collar on me that you think is right."

Sulka believed in his goods. He knew what was right. He couldn't compromise. And he wasn't afraid of a world-famous customer. He was no sycophant. He communicated with the other's strong mind and will. His enthusiasm, his honesty and integrity, plus undisputed preeminence in his field, made him a salesman extraordinary.

Well, to get back to Emil Geiger—he said to me one day, "You're always going to be a salesman, Norman, but it will be a system of ideas you will be selling. You will sell Christianity, for I know that you are going to be a minister. So let me give you some advice. Give people a religion that will work, one that will help people the way they need helping. And believe in it yourself. Be sincere. Then be enthusiastic about it. Be persuasive. Learn to communicate and they will buy."

Emil was of the Jewish religion, but now and then in later years he used to come to my church in New York and he would clap me affectionately on the back. "Give them the real thing, for that's what they need," he would say. "Be enthusiastic, communicate, persuade—that will sell them." And, of course, Emil was right, for the preaching and teaching of Christianity as a way of thinking and living is a form of salesmanship. By these approaches, one tries to get people to accept the message and persuade them to walk a road of agreement with him.

I SELL ALUMINUM POTS AND PANS

I learned through a selling experience years ago how enthusiasm and persuasion add up to successful communication, and bring about creative results. In those days everyone got himself a summer job, and one year I became a salesman of aluminum-ware kitchen utensils. It was a house-to-house canvassing job, with now and then a staged cooking demonstration to show the advantages of aluminum pots and pans. The idea was to persuade some popular housewife, well-known for her cooking, to invite several neighborhood women to a luncheon at which time you would give them a sales talk on the advantages of the cooking utensils.

An avid devotee of Ohio-Indiana cooking, which was strong on fried chicken, mashed potatoes and gravy, I naturally exuded enthusiasm and persuasiveness. I exclaimed over the delicious food! My zeal communicated itself to the women so compellingly that my order book bulged with sales.

But that cold house-to-house selling! Believe me, that called for extra courage, perseverance and super-enthusiastic persuasion. At that time I lived in Greenville, Ohio, and was so nervous and self-conscious that I decided to "work" Union City, Indiana, just across the state line. Hesitantly that first day I started up what appeared to be a promising street, having already passed by several on untenable excuses.

The first house was a bit run down. I said, "Those people are not progressive enough to buy aluminum ware," and passed it up. The next house was trim and neat. I reasoned, "These people are progressive and probably already have aluminum ware." By this time I was conscious of my own fear-conditioned rationalization. So taking myself in hand I mounted the steps, rehearsing the sales talk that had been given me along with my kit of merchandise. Then praying that no one would be at home, I timidly pressed the bell. The door was flung open and to my nervous gaze the biggest woman (or so she seemed) I had ever seen filled the doorway. "What do you want?" she barked, glaring at me.

"You don't want any aluminum ware, do you?" I said in a weak voice.

"Of course not," she snapped and banged the door shut.

Abjectly I dragged myself and my case of aluminum ware back home. But not liking to take a licking, I went to see a friend named Harry. "Have you ever sold aluminum ware?" I asked. When he replied in the negative, I shouted, "What? You've never sold aluminum ware? Why, that's the greatest business in the world." My enthusiasm swept him off his feet and in no time at all I had sold him a half interest in the business. I gave him the sales talk to study and told him that we would get started early the next morning for a day of selling to Union City.

Next day we got off the streetcar at the scene of my ignominious failure of the previous afternoon. "Shall we sell on this street?" asked Harry.

"No," I replied, "let's skip this one. I worked it yesterday."

Approaching the next street I felt a strange new sense of enthusiasm and confidence, inspired no doubt by the presence of my friend. "You take that side. I'll work this one," I directed, "and listen—don't take *no* for an answer. Be enthusiastic—persuasive. She needs this merchandise, so make her realize it."

I walked up to the door, full of the joy of salesmanship. I was going to persuade a woman to buy something she needed which would be of lasting satisfaction to her. It was positively thrilling. As I pressed the bell Harry gave me a wave of the hand. "Sell her, old boy," he shouted.

The door opened and a little wisp of a woman appeared (at least she looked little to my confident gaze). Soon I was in her kitchen, actually drying dishes for her, extolling the virtues of my aluminum ware. I positively raved about it. "My, my, but you are an enthusiastic young man. Just how can you get so worked up about cooking utensils?" This opened a flood gate of scientific information about cooking that had the lady's mouth open wide in astonishment. She signed the order and thanked me all the way to the door.

This woman was my friend until she passed away, and once years later when she came to hear me preach she said, "You sell the Gospel with the same enthusiasm and persuasion that you sold me those pots and pans. And," she added, "I'm still using a couple of them. They were as necessary to me as you said."

"Yes," I replied, "and so is the Gospel that I'm now advocating."

"Oh, I bought that long ago," she smiled.

Enthusiasm and persuasion—formula extraordinary—add up to successful communication.

ENTHUSIASM AND THE GOOD LIFE

Everyone can make use of enthusiastic persuasion in making a better and more successful life for himself and his loved ones. My mother has been gone for over twenty-five years, but I am very conscious that whatever I am doing today of a creative nature has its roots in her enthusiastic persuasion during my boyhood. And the same can be said by the children of every good and alert parent.

Actually my mother was a saleswoman and she had something to convey. She was thrilled by people and their personalities and potential abilities. She was always selling young people on what they would become. She was one of the greatest experts I ever knew in building fires in people's minds, fires that got them moving. And of course the effect of her vibrant spirit on her own children was profound. A meal at our house was always an exciting experience. Mother talked about all the wonderful things not only in our town, but all over the world.

She was in charge of women's missionary activities for a big denomination and she received letters from missionaries everywhere. She was in touch with events and movements in many countries. And she traveled the world over, her adventures even taking her through bandit-infested territory of China and into war-ravaged areas. All this she brought to the dinner table and used it in trying to persuade her three boys to make something of themselves and to contribute something worthwhile to the world. She could sell anyone on an idea because her ideas were good and she put behind them the motivational power of enthusiasm.

Mothers and fathers are salespeople, their job being to sell vibrant, creative life to their children. If they do not sell it to them, then some long-haired, sad misfit may sell their children the big lie: that the United States and life itself are flops and turn them to the LSD route or some other dead-end failure pattern.

The wife of Ramsay MacDonald, onetime Prime Minister of Great Britain, on her deathbed said to her husband, "Whatever you do, put romance and enthusiasm into the lives of our children. With those qualities their lives will be good."

Enthusiastic persuasion is a real happiness producer. It

has the power to invest the prosaic, if not with romance, perhaps at least with exciting interest and meaning. We are living in a time when many of those who have been favored with education and opportunity, beneficiaries of the wealth and culture produced by centuries of sacrifice and toil, have now concluded that life is meaningless and devoid of value. And as for enthusiasm, the mere mention of the word would cause bewilderment to flit across their uncomprehending faces. So we must admit that this isn't the most propitious era in which to advocate enthusiasm. Or maybe because of the circumstances it *is* the most propitious. At any rate, enthusiasm is not the most widely used commodity of our time. In fact, any reference to enthusiasm would be considered in some circles as unsophisticated, if not actually downright corny.

James Dillet Freeman, who writes potently, says: "We live in a time of revolt against reason. Revolt against beauty. Revolt against joy. Artists dribble paint out of paint cans onto canvas. Sculptors weld together pieces of old iron and concrete they have scavenged from a junkyard. Musicians blow klaxons and bang tire irons for symphonies. Poets babble trivial obfuscations. Philosophers prove by reason that reason can prove nothing."

And he continues, with not so much gentility as one might expect of a philosopher, "Life stinks, people say. Especially the intellectual people say this. Sophisticated people. Educated people. The people who read books— even more the people who write them—the artists and scientists and teachers and scholars. For them," says Mr. Freeman, "life stinks." Well, now, isn't this inspiring? We have come to a day and age when seemingly to be erudite you must take a dim view of enthusiasm and settle for life that is putrid.

TAKES GUTS TO PRACTICE ENTHUSIASM

Recently at luncheon I was seated by a distinguished woman, Judge Mary Kohler, who has done notable work among the underprivileged, especially children, in the ghettos of New York City. Though white of hair, she is an eternally youthful type; her face has an indefinably attractive radiance. She laughs out of sheer exuberance of spirit.

She is a respected scholar too. Pleasantly she asked what extra thing I was doing now. "Writing a book," I said.

"Oh, isn't that interesting! And what is the title?"

"Enthusiasm Makes the Difference."

"What do you know about that," she exclaimed. "Why, I think you are wonderful! I congratulate you on your audacity and courage, that you would actually write a book on enthusiasm in a day like this."

Well I was surprised to know that this required courage and audacity. Since then I've concluded that it does rather run contrary to the mainstream or present-day so-called American intellectual thought. But I'm not writing to the intellectuals, I'm writing to the mass of American people whose simple faith is that life can be good.

ENTHUSIASM EQUALS LOVE

And how does one have enthusiasm in life? Actually, it is as simple as this: Cultivate the ability to love living. Love people, love the sky under which you live, love beauty, love God. The person who loves becomes enthusiastic, filled with the sparkle and the joy of life. And then he goes on to fill it full of meaning. If you're not enthusiastic, begin today to cultivate the love of living. Like Fred, for example.

It happened in Detroit one cold winter night. It was about nine-thirty when I checked in at my hotel and since I hadn't had dinner I asked a bellboy, "Is there a restaurant in this hotel where I can get a sandwich and cup of coffee at this hour?"

"There's room service," he suggested, and handed me a menu.

Now I'm a frugal soul, and when I saw that the cheapest sandwich on the menu was two dollars and fifty cents and coffee thirty-five cents I asked, "Isn't there a lunch counter around here?"

"Yes, up the street there's a place called Fred's," he said. "It doesn't look like much, but the food is very good."

So I walked several blocks to Fred's. And the bellboy was right; it wasn't much on the outside, nor even on the inside. Seated at the counter were some seedy-looking old men (and when I sat down that made one more!). The man behind the counter was a big fellow, with sleeves rolled up revealing great hairy arms. He had a big apron tied around him. There was no style to this place whatsoever, but I liked it at once.

Resting a big hand on the counter, the man in the apron asked me, "Okay, brother, what'll you have?"

"Are you Fred?"

"Yep."

"Over at the hotel they told me you have good hamburgers."

"Brother, you never ate such hamburgers."

"Okay, let me have one."

Along the counter was an old man who looked extremely miserable. He was sitting there with his fingers shaking. Whether it was a nervous condition or delirium tremens, I wouldn't know, but after big Fred had put my hamburger in front of me he went over and put his hand on that of this old fellow. "That's all right, Bill," he said. "That's all right. I'm going to fix you a bowl of that nice hot soup that you like. How'll that be?" Bill nodded gratefully.

Then a minute or two later another old man got up and shuffled over to pay his check. Fred said to him, "Mr. Brown, watch out for the cars out there on the avenue. They come pretty fast at night. And have a look at the moonlight on the river. It's mighty pretty tonight."

I looked at the man in admiration—his love, roughly given, which is sometimes the greatest kind of big-hearted love, was sort of tender. It was really touching. And he was a salesman, too. He said to me, "You oughtn't to end up without a piece of this marvelous pie, brother. Just look at it; isn't that beautiful? Mary baked it right here on the premises."

"That is surely beautiful, but I have what's known as willpower."

"That's the trouble with some of you people. How do you expect us to stay in business?" But he gave me a big smile as he said it.

When I paid my check I couldn't help remarking, "You know something, my friend? I like the way you spoke to those old men. You made them feel that life is good."

"Why not?" he asked. "I love living myself. And they're pretty sad old guys and our place is sort of like home to them. Anyway, I kind of like 'em."

As I walked back to my hotel that night I had a new spring in my step. I felt happy—because in a rough place I had met a marvelous thing, the spirit of a man who loved life—a genius in enthusiastic persuasion, making people feel that life is good.

So don't depreciate life by enumerating all the things that are wrong with it. Things *are* wrong, and something has to be done about them. But focus mentally upon all that is right about life; life is mighty good, a lot better than not having it, I should think. A lifetime on this wonderful earth doesn't last very long, either. It is here today and gone tomorrow. So love it while you can, and be full of enthusiasm.

HE HAD PSYCHOSCLEROSIS!!

One day with two other men I took a taxi in New York City and had a most enlightening experience. As we got into the cab we greeted the driver affably commenting on the weather (which we thought was good) and asked him how he felt and how business was. To each of these genial inquiries he responded with a glum and depressing grunt. I had noticed that this youngish-looking man had a dark, dismal look on his face. He was obviously in a depressed and pessimistic frame of mind.

In our conversation the two men repeatedly called me "Doctor." This seemed to interest the driver. He looked around several times. Apparently he concluded that he had in his cab a doctor of medicine and saw a chance to get a little free medical advice. During the lull in our conversation he said, "Doc, I wonder if you'd give me a little advice."

"What advice do you want?" I asked.

"Well," he said, "I've got a pain in my back and I've got another pain in my side and I don't sleep well and I'm tired and I just don't feel good. What do you suppose is the matter with me? Can you give me something to help me feel better?"

"Well," I replied, falling in with the physician myth, "I must tell you, my friend, that I seldom practice in taxicabs or give prescriptions in this manner, but since we're here, I'll be glad to advise you as best I can. While I don't like to give an off-the-cuff diagnosis, it does seem that you have the symptoms of psychosclerosis."

Whereupon he nearly ran up onto the sidewalk. I guess it sounded like an extraordinarily formidable disease. "What is this psychosclerosis?" he wanted to know with some apprehension.

I wasn't too sure myself, but I continued, "You've heard of arteriosclerosis, haven't you?"

"Well," doubtfully, "I guess so. What's that?"

"Arteriosclerosis is hardening of the arteries. Any kind of sclerosis is a hardening—either of arteries or of tissues. Now what you seem to have is psychosclerosis, hardening of your thoughts, of your attitudes. It is a loss of the flexibility of spirit. And," I said, "that is a terrible disease and is no doubt one reason you have those aches and pains. How old are you?" And he told me he was thirty-five. "Nobody should have such aches and pains at thirty-five," I said. "Yours undoubtedly come largely from your psychosclerosis."

Psychosclerosis—I coined the word myself—aptly describes the condition of a great many people who have lost their interest and whose thinking has become hard and fixed. And one of the greatest antidotes to this disease of the spirit is enthusiasm.

When a child is born Almighty God builds enthusiasm into him. As he emerges from infancy into childhood, he is filled with excitement; with the wonder and the glory of life. To him everything is fresh, new and fascinating. But as he grows older, if he becomes sophisticated and cynical and his viewpoint hardens, he loses one of the finest elements of human nature—enthusiasm. Huxley said that the secret of genius is to carry the spirit of childhood into maturity. That is, it's important to preserve natural, God-given enthusiasm. A physician told me, "I have actually seen people die for lack of enthusiasm. Of course, I can't write that on the death certificate, but the person without enthusiasm can lose the will to live."

Lots of people fail in selling, in management, indeed, in any kind of leadership because they are victims of psychosclerosis, hardening of the thoughts. New methods, progressive ideas, adjustment to changing times and situations just cannot break through rigid old patterns.

Of course I informed the taxi driver that I was not a medical doctor but rather one who specializes in state of

mind and condition of spirit. But I assured him that many
medical doctors find important health connections between
mind, spirit and body.

I sent this man a copy of my book *The Power of Positive Thinking.** He faithfully practiced the mental and spiritual procedures presented in it. He came one day with a
grin to give me the good news that his "psychosclerosis"
was a lot better. "When I got my thinking straightened
out, it's surprising how different I felt." He actually
showed some signs of enthusiasm, which I am sure had to
do with his obviously improved condition.

Enthusiastic persuasion, to be effective, must have direction; it must be slanted toward definite purposes and objectives. Just to be enthusiastic in a vague general way
may possibly produce a bright and attractive personality,
but still not result in that communication in depth which
makes desired things happen.

John Bowles, Vice-President of Beckman Instruments,
told me of a salesman who called on a customer regularly
every Tuesday morning for six months. Homer would
come in, sit around, project his enthusiastic personality,
talk excitedly about sailing and golf and finally wind up by
saying, "Guess you don't want anything, do you?"

Sam, the proprietor, became quite fond of salesman
Homer. The two became golfing companions on Saturday
afternoons and occasionally Sam went out in Homer's
small sailboat. Always Homer exuded enthusiasm about
everything and was real good company.

One day, relaxing in the clubhouse after a round of
golf, Homer said, "You know, Sam, I don't get it. I've
called on you every week for six months and we have become good friends, but—doggone it—you've never bought
anything of me."

"That's not hard to figure," replied Sam. "You've never
told me what you're selling. You never really asked me to
buy."

Think of all that enthusiasm, all that persuasion gone to
waste. "You don't want anything, do you?" never told the
customer what he sold. Seems incredible but it is representative of so much desultory, no-objective effort that can
only result in futility. One thing is for sure; nobody ever
raised money, sold goods, helped anyone to a better life or

* © 1956, Prentice-Hall, Inc., Englewood Cliffs, N.J.

got a wife, who did not ask. The Bible says, "Ask, and ye shall receive." Even enthusiastic persuasion will never persuade unless and until the objective is definitely sought. Direction-purpose-objective—these are the qualities that measure success. And you've got to be all-out, too.

DON'T BE A HALF-A-MINDER

I had a curious encounter a couple of years ago in the Hotel Sherman in Chicago. After speaking to a convention I was in my room when a woman called on the phone and forthwith announced that she was bringing her husband to see me. Her tone was so firm I had no alternative but to agree. When they arrived, the woman's look was firm, too. Addressing her husband as Charley, she told him to sit down—and Charley sat. And Mabel was half his size.

"Now," she said to me, "I want you to do something for Charley." As if to say that as far as she was concerned she had worked with Charley for years and had given it up.

Charley seemed a nice, easy-going, likeable fellow, but as I later discovered, he was undisciplined, undirected, actually pretty much a failure in his sales job. His firm had been unusually patient with him. I met with him at intervals over some months and got to know him very well. He rather baffled me. Finally I noticed that he had one stock phrase that he used continuously. It was so repetitive that it gave the same impression as a phonograph needle stuck in a groove. Charley would be talking about something and he would say, "You know, I have half a mind to do something about that." Or, "I've half a mind to investigate that." And once when I was urging him to think positively, he said, "You know, I've half a mind to do that."

Finally I said, "I know what's wrong with you, Charley. You're a half-a-minder. Everything you think of doing you have half a mind to do. But you had better realize no one in this world ever got anywhere with only half a mind. Most of us need more than we've got. We certainly need all we do have. A half a mind just isn't enough."

It wasn't until Charley began to employ all his mind that he really began to get results in life. When he did, his ability to achieve developed amazingly. When he started giving his job all he had, his natural talents eventually put him into the top-producer category.

To be a success requires the giving of your whole self, your whole mind. In so many instances men who do give their whole mind to the job demonstrate not only the enthusiasm that makes the difference, but extra efficiency as well. A friend of mine, John Imre, is superintendent of our farm on Quaker Hill in Dutchess County, New York. He has made it a place of beauty, and keeps it running well because it receives his complete interest and concern. He studies every problem carefully and so his ratio of right conclusions is very high.

Refugees from Hungary, John and his wife Maria recently became citizens and have gained the respect of the community. He is successful in his work because he is a whole-minder, not a half-a-minder. As a well-known athletic coach remarked, "It's the all-out, not the half-outs, who become top performers."

There is another point at which enthusiastic persuasion is very much needed. To approach it another way, just about the greatest selling job you will ever have is to sell yourself on yourself. To bring yourself to an enthusiastic acceptance of yourself is one of the biggest feats of all. How to make yourself believe, really believe, in yourself, in your abilities, talents, capacities, requires the most enthusiastic persuasion.

It is tragic how many people are conditioned not by a normal, realistic and objective appraisal of themselves which brings the facts about their abilities into focus, but by an inferiority concept that distorts the proper self-image. True, there are some blatant egotistical self-worshipers, but they are infinitesimal in number by comparison with the many who struggle always against self-doubt and feelings of inadequacy. The market for selling people on themselves, believe me, is very great indeed. But when you get a person to apply enthusiastic persuasion to himself, it is remarkable how he can be sold on a proper realization of his own worth.

AIRPLANE WASHROOM EPISODE

This is perhaps the strangest experience in personal counseling of my entire career. I was on a jet airplane between New York and Chicago and every seat was occupied, including those in the lounge. I went forward to the washroom and as I was entering I felt someone behind me also trying to get into the room. I stepped back to let this man go ahead, but to my surprise he said, "I want to talk with you privately, and since the plane is crowded maybe we could talk in the washroom."

Well, I was a bit suspicious that I might have some kind of oddball on my hands and I left the door ajar in case a getaway seemed indicated. "What's on your mind?" I asked, half perched on the sink.

"Oh, I'm miserable and low. I just don't feel adequate to my job. I have no faith in myself. I feel like crawling into a hole and pulling it in after me. I've got a great big whopping inferiority complex." So ran his gloomy self-appraisal.

Trying to get a further line on my strange visitor, I asked, "What business are you in?"

"Oh, I'm just a peddler, a plain ordinary peddler," was his self-deprecatory reply.

"And in what form of salesmanship are you engaged?"

His answer rocked me. "Well, you see, my bosses send me around the country to make inspirational speeches at sales meetings."

"Well, your bosses must be pretty stupid to send out a gloom artist to try to inspire other fellows to believe in themselves and their products."

"My bosses aren't stupid. They're the smartest men in the business!" he declared with the first show of spirit.

"If that is the case, and I do not doubt it, they must see some qualities in you that you do not see yourself. That is to say, your bosses believe in a man who does not believe in himself. In the few minutes we've been talking you have depreciated your profession and yourself."

"My profession?" he asked in surprise.

"Yes, your profession. You wrote yourself off as 'only a peddler,' downgrading one of the greatest professions in this country, that of salesmanship—the process by which a vital product or service is made available to people who need it to enjoy better living for themselves and their families. What do you mean 'a peddler'? You are a salesman and more than that, a teacher and inspirer of salesmen.

"And moreover, you are a self-downgrader. Do you know who made you? Who gave you those extraordinary abilities of leadership that your keen-eyed bosses see in you? Come on, tell me, who created it all?"

"Well, I suppose you mean God," he mumbled doubtfully.

"Precisely. I do mean God. And here you are running God down by casting aspersions on His workmanship. Boy, you sure do have your thinking messed up."

"Gosh, I never saw it in that light before. Sounds different the way you work it out." He grinned slightly for the first time.

"Now look, another thing I noticed about you—you slump. You have a good height of about six feet."

"Six foot two," he corrected.

"Well, you're using only about five foot ten of it. So stand up straight. Try to touch that wall with as much of your body as possible. Carry your head high. Reach for the ceiling with it."

"This is a strange procedure," he commented.

"That's nothing. The whole setting of this conversation is strange. But let's not allow that to interfere with doing a job on you.

"Now hold that straight-up position and repeat after me the following—'I am a salesman, the greatest profession in the world. I am a vital part of the American free-enterprise system. I help make available goods and services to people who need them. Without men like me the economy would wither on the vine. I am an important trustee of free civilization.'"

"You actually want me to say that?"

"I sure do, so let's get going." Hesitantly he repeated the words, but as he got into it he began to show some evidence of feeling. "O.K.," I said, "that's good. Now let's pray." A dead silence fell. "Well go on," I prompted.

"Me pray? I was waiting for you to offer a prayer. I never prayed in public in my life."

"This is hardly in public," I commented, "so go on and pray."

That was some prayer of his, memorable and unforgettable. Of course, I did not record it and have to repeat it from memory, but as best I can recall it went something like this: "Lord, I need reorganizing. Please reorganize me. Help me to get outside myself. Yeah, Lord, that's it—help me to get outside my tied-up self. Help me to be a real salesman and amount to something. Amen."

"That was a real prayer," I said, "because you meant it.

And I'm sure that God heard it too, for he rides the airways."

Later we shook hands at the airport and he went his way, but I hear about him from time to time, and from all I gather he is going strong with a new emphasis on enthusiastic persuasion. For this man enthusiasm made the difference, a huge creative difference. He sold himself on himself, which is an important thing for anyone to do. For when an individual does that, provided he keeps some humility, he is on his way.

CHAMPION GOLFERS AND POSITIVE THINKING

Many of our great athletes use self-persuasion in their preparations for an athletic event. Here, too, enthusiasm plays a vital role. For instance, Gay Brewer called upon positive thinking and enthusiasm to help him in the 1967 Masters' Tournament and his skillful performance brought him victory. The gallery, watching enthralled, had no idea that Gay Brewer had played through tournaments without indication of potential greatness. Yet he always felt the inner resources were there. But they seemed to be shut up inside of him. So he took inventory and found on the debit side a lack of faith and enthusiasm. How could he perform like a champion when inwardly he felt like a loser? His very attitude was conspiring against him.

Then by good fortune—and because he'd begun a real search for self-help—Gay found the writings of men who had fought and won over their feelings of inadequacy; men who out of their own experiences had devised practical rules for constructive, enthusiastic living. Gay Brewer tried these suggestions and to his amazement they worked for him. The results showed not only in his golf game but in his entire way of life. As a result, he was calm yet aggressive in the Masters' Tournament. He played an offensive game with a positive attitude. He wanted to win, he concentrated, he believed in himself and he thought positively. He played champion golf because he had equipped himself mentally as well as physically to become a champion.

Gary Player, the great South African golfer, one of only four men who have won the "grand slam" of golf,

the U.S. Open, British Open, the Masters' and the
U.S.P.G.A. title, recently told me of his experiences.

"As you know, we golfers live under continual strain.
Now this can get under your skin and make you tense. I'd
like to tell you how I overcame it when I played Arnold
Palmer and Jack Nicklaus in the World Match Champion-
ship in London.

"This golf course happened to be particularly suited to
the talents of my opponents. Most people doubted that I
could win over these great players. But I didn't allow the
pessimistic opinion of press and public to influence me.
Nor would I let myself grow tense. I remembered one of
the quotations from *The Power of Positive Thinking* and I
knew that 'in quiet and confidence would be my strength.'
I knew also, Dr. Peale, that I would do my best 'through
Jesus Christ Who strengthens me.'

"Then when I played in the U.S. Open, I again called
on the suggestions from the same book. I visualized, I
prayerized, I actualized—and won the U.S. Open.

"Since the Bible is our greatest source of inspiration and
energy, and since your writings, Dr. Peale, have brought
the Bible closer to our everyday lives, I always recommend your books, particularly to young people, for constant reading. As a result of your influence, I base my own
life on these Big Three: Faith, education and physical fit-
ness."

FOUR STEPS TO ACHIEVEMENT

And here is another great formula for successful living.
It is by William A. Ward. He calls it Four Steps to
Achievement. It might be called the Eight P Plan: Plan
purposefully. Prepare prayerfully. Proceed positively. Pursue persistently.

So do believe in yourself. Practice the principles of enthusiastic persuasion. Make yourself believe that you can
be better than you think you are. And remember—if you
think you can, you can! Bring bona fide enthusiasm to
your life style—for enthusiasm always makes the difference.

FOUR

HOW ENTHUSIASM
CANCELS FEAR AND WORRY

"Killed by thirty years of thought!"

So a London newspaper headlined its report of the strange death of a woman tennis star. This woman, as a small girl thirty years before, had watched in terror as her mother had died suddenly of a heart attack while being treated by a dentist. The traumatic experience so profoundly affected the child that in the thirty years that followed, she absolutely refused any dental treatment. The mere suggestion of going to a dentist terrified her. And this, despite the realization that the dentist to whom her mother had gone had no responsibility for her mother's death. It was merely a coincidence that the heart attack which caused her death occurred in a dentist's office.

Finally dental work became so necessary that the woman was compelled to have it done in spite of her terror. She insisted, however, that her physician accompany her to the dentist's office. But it was to no avail. As she sat in the dentist's chair, just like her mother had thirty years before, she was suddenly seized with a heart attack and died.

Thirty years of thought had indeed killed her—thirty years of a killing fear thought. Consider how thirty years of faith thoughts, thirty years of enthusiastic thoughts, might have changed the life of this woman.

But let me tell a human story of another sort, one with a much happier outcome. It concerns a man who suffered from fear until he was around fifty years of age. Then he got fed up with his state of mind, did something about it and got over it; in fact, he got so completely over it that he was never bothered by fear again. How was this remarkable deliverance accomplished? By enthusiasm. He hit upon the wonderful fact that enthusiasm powered in depth can cancel fear and worry. And just how does enthusiasm accomplish this astonishing feat? That question I intend to answer in this chapter.

The fears and anxieties of this man seemed to have begun in childhood and took many forms. Whenever he had a pain, which occurred frequently, he was sure it was cancer or some other fatal malady. When any of his children were out late at night he feared a phone call would bring news of an accident. Shyness activated by fear made him timorous with other people. Accordingly he did not show up well in personal relationships.

But despite his fear problems, and this is often a curious phenomenon in such cases, he was efficient in business. He had worked up to a position of top leadership. His associates who respected him highly would have been astonished had they known the full extent of his inner struggle and misery. They would not have believed or understood his deep inner conflict. But the fact that his trouble did not show on the surface indicated a basic strength, which suggested that if ever he made up his mind to do something about his fear he could get release and relief.

That is precisely what he did. It came about in this way: I chanced to be speaking one noonday to some two thousand men in the ballroom of the Conrad Hilton Hotel in Chicago. During the talk I dealt with the terrible effect of fear and worry on the human mind and described how through the efforts of our American Foundation of Religion and Psychiatry, people had been healed of anxiety. Following the luncheon, a man whom I had met earlier at a reception given by the officers of this outstanding business association, made some sort of pleasant reference to my speech, but instead of passing on he hesitated—"I don't suppose you might have a moment to speak with me?" He rather shyly added, "Something you said in your talk is pretty important to me."

Something about the man, some intensity, almost desperation, communicated itself and we went to my room for a talk. No sooner had the door closed than he began talking. It was highly nervous talk as though he was driven by some inner compulsion. Presently he stopped. "I'm embarrassed. I've never gone on like this before or told anyone of the hell I've lived in all my life. But your speech about fear has started me off, I guess."

"Go on and talk it out," I said. "Say everything. You must completely open your mind if you expect to exorcise the mass of fear imbedded in your consciousness. If you close up now and it freezes in, you may never again have opportunity to empty it out. So let's deal with this problem now, right down to bedrock. Keep talking."

He talked for an hour recounting one fear experience after another, many of them going back to his boyhood. It amounted to a complete mental housecleaning. Finally almost spent, he sighed with relief. "I sure do feel better. Thanks for letting me ramble on like this. I know it will do me a lot of good." I reminded him that while such mind-emptying does make one feel better, to leave the matter there would mean that the basic cause of his fear psychosis had been only temporarily eased up. The mind would in time fill up again with anxiety and worry.

I suggested that he come to New York for some intensive counseling at our American Foundation of Religion and Psychiatry. I explained that while an initial process in the cure of fear might well be such mind-emptying and relief as he had experienced, the next step was to gain insight into the basic cause of fear. Finally, constructive steps would be taken to teach him how to recast his thinking to eliminate such attitudes as were causing these irrational anxiety reactions.

He came for counseling with our psychiatric-pastoral team and proved so cooperative that his anxiety began to lose its dominant hold on him. The roots of fear, running back to childhood, were clipped. I do not have space here to deal with the psychiatric counseling process conducted by our professionally trained staff, except to say that it was extremely thorough and scientific, and fortunately proved effective.

The clinic staff reported that while a longer counseling program was recommended, the prognosis was such that he seemed ready for another step, the spiritual healing procedure. So I informed our patient that on Sunday

mornings at Marble Collegiate Church it is our custom to
have a period we call "creative spiritual silence," and I
suggested that he come to church and participate. Actually
this is a form of group therapy, though hundreds of people are involved.

THE POWER OF CREATIVE SPIRITUAL SILENCE

On Sunday morning I explained as usual to the congregation the healing power of creative silence, stating that
any person who consciously let go his problem, dropping
it into the "pool" of spiritual silence created when hundreds focus in prayer and spirit, would be relieved and
through their faith be healed.

An amazing thing happened. Some might perhaps call it
a miracle, but not I. For over many years I have seen so
many astonishing personal changes take place as a result
of creative spiritual silence, that to me it is not at all a
miracle, but rather the scientific operation of spiritual law
at work in personality. I had previously outlined to this
man the amazing principle of "Let go and let God," urging him consciously and volitionally to "let go of his fear
and let God take it." This seemed "a queer sort of thing
he had never heard of before," but I reminded him that
undoubtedly there were many vital things in spiritual practice that he had never heard of before. And to the extent
that he took hold of fresh techniques hitherto unknown to
him he could achieve the new personal qualities he so desired.

In the silent period with spiritual mood and atmosphere
deepening, the man experienced, so he declared, "an overwhelming sense of the presence of God." His fear "seemed
small in that tremendous Presence." Then, for the first
time, the unbelievable thought flashed up that he could
throw off fear, not in the future but now, immediately,
and for good and all. Accordingly, in the silent period he
said, speaking directly to the Lord, "I *now* let my fear go;
I now give it to You. Please take it now and take me too.
I'm Yours forever. Thank you, Lord, for healing me
now," and he underscored the now.

A powerful new motivation following his sense of release so excited him that he came literally charging into
my private office. "He heard me! He really heard me! The

fear was lifted from me. I gave it to Him. It's all gone. I've never been happier in my life."

He stopped, flushed with embarrassment. "Don't be embarrassed," I said. "It's wonderful, isn't it? That is how God sometimes works. Usually, release from a long-held fear comes more gradually, but sometimes it does eventuate dramatically as in your case, and both experiences of renewal are equally valid." At any rate, this man was delivered from the old fear he had suffered so long. He became full of enthusiasm about his business, his church, his Rotary Club, his community. He developed an intense interest in all aspects of life. Such is the quality and vitality of his spiritual and intellectual enthusiasm that every residue of his old fear seems to have been eliminated. It has not returned with passing of time. This case proved what can happen when one deeply *wants* something to happen and when enthusiasm is given a chance to *make* it happen.

FEAR IS REMOVABLE

A primary fact to know about fear is that it is removable. Do you, for example, have the tendency to become angry? Anger is removable. You can get over it. Do you tend to become depressed? Depression is removable. Anything disruptive to human happiness and well-being, anything that fastens itself adversely onto the human spirit, is removable. Not without difficulty, but still removable. And fear, one of the worst of all enemies of human personality, is removable. Fix that fact firmly in mind. Hold it tenaciously. No matter how many worries and anxieties harass you, remember always that they are removable. Enthusiasm with its immense mental and spiritual power can cancel out all fear.

Do not give in to the notion that you must live with fear all your life. You need not. It is removable. Do not assume that because your father or your mother, or your grandparents had fears and anxieties that you must have them also. You need only have what you are willing to have. If you are willing to live with fear, you probably will. And once a person knows fear is removable and decides, with God's help, to remove it, then comes the process of removal. This involves the steps outlined above and also another factor which perhaps is not popular with this generation of Americans, namely, self-discipline. Don't overlook this fact, that you can do positively anything with yourself that you deeply desire *if* you have what it takes to discipline yourself accordingly. And deep within you the power of self-discipline exists, waiting only to be used.

In former days this powerful capacity, widely known as willpower, was highly regarded in the United States. Depreciation of willpower threatens now to produce a generation of Americans in which incidence of neurotic states will likely reach a new high. Apparently Americans were formerly more normal psychologically. One primary reason may be that they were taught to practice self-discipline. They believed that any enemy of personality is removable, and so with God's help they simply proceeded in disciplinary fashion to remove it. This is not to say that they had no worries. Of course they did.

Therefore, a good method of canceling out worry is the deliberate assiduous use of enthusiasm plus self-discipline. As I pointed out earlier, in order to have enthusiasm, simply act enthusiastic. Similarly, substitute enthusiasm for worry, eliminating the destructive emotion in favor of a constructive one. A direct frontal attack on a personality weakness such as worry may be effective, especially if faith is emphasized. But in most cases an oblique attack in the form of a substitute procedure or a psychological bypassing, is likely to get surer results.

Let us illustrate this anti-worry method with the history of a man who consulted me regarding an anxiety problem. His anxiety, judging from his dramatized description of himself, while seemingly extreme to him, appeared to me as something less than deep. For one thing he had developed a kind of rabbit's foot approach designed to assure opposite outcomes. He was like the avid baseball fan who always bet against his favorite team, believing that in so doing he would cause them to win. I got the impression that this man's anxiety had within it a considerable dash of self-manufactured hysteria. But even so his suffering was real and he was entitled to relief.

He was extraordinarily negative in comment and seemed to expect the worst to happen. Yet even this negativism seemed to have a false ring, for there was evidence that he did not really expect things to turn out badly. Here again was that curious quirk of thinking, that if one talks negatively, the opposite is more likely to occur. So in this man's mind was a strange, conflicting mixture of anxiety tinged ideas, which he feared yet didn't believe in. But he did believe in them enough to be dominated by them. The result not only caused unhappiness, but also an enormous leakage of mental energy that might have been employed for constructive purposes.

I decided to prescribe the oblique method for attacking worry. Rather than encouraging him to stand up to his anxiety, hitting it straight on as he bravely talked about doing, I said, "No, no, let's not do that. Let us outsmart your worry by coming at it from its blind side. If your fear is really strong the straight-arm approach may send you reeling back in defeat, and that could discourage you. So rather let us be like the prizefighter who dances away from his opponent, keeping out of range, but hitting unexpectedly when the other's guard is down."

I outlined a daily regimen, assuring him that if used as directed he could change from a consummate worrier into a practicing enthusiast. "And then," I promised him, "you will become happier than you ever thought of being. Your job will become child's play. You will do it so easily."

FIVE-POINT PROGRAM FOR ATTACKING WORRY

Specifically the method outlined was thus: *First* he was to carefully practice listening to himself. He was to note and study with meticulous attention every comment he made, so that he might become fully conscious of the amazing number of doleful and negative remarks he was constantly uttering.

"Never talk without listening, appraising, dissecting your remarks," I suggested. "You are not going to enjoy this for it will be a ruthless self-revelation and not a pleasant one, but it will be a primary step. Listen with your ears and your whole mind to the depressing stuff you are articulating all day."

Second, he was to start being absolutely honest so that when he heard himself making a negative statement he was to ask himself: "Now look, do I honestly believe what I am saying or am I actually mouthing negativisms that I do not really believe at all? If I want the Mets to win, why don't I start believing they are going to win and say so? And skip the infantile practice of betting against them on the stupid assumption that it can help them to win by an absurd reverse procedure."

Third, he was to adopt the practice of saying exactly the opposite of what he usually said, and he was to note how much better the new utterances sounded. He might regard himself as a hyrocrite in so doing, but hypocrisy would be nothing new. Actually had he not been saying what he did not mean for a long time?

As he continued in this new procedure, it would grow ever more exciting to hear words and ideas full of life and hope and expectancy coming from his mouth instead of the old defeatist remarks. He would soon discover that something really exciting was happening to him, namely an upsurge of dynamic enthusiasm. As he worked on this advice he would realize the value of the honest, analytical listening. new-style talking element in his process of personal change.

Fourth, he was to keep track of everything that happened as he worked in his new procedure, carefully noting and computing even the smallest results. If he had been, for example, in the habit of saying glumly: "Things aren't going to go well today," now (since he was no longer mouthing negativisms) he was to note that things were much better, as they usually are. He was to admit honestly that he had in fact expected them to go well, but now he was no longer lying to himself concerning his expectations. He wasn't afraid any longer to expect the best.

Fifth, he was to practice putting the best connotation on every person and every action each day. This is one of the most exciting of all personal development practices. I first came upon it through the late Harry Bullis, a leading figure in the flour-milling industry in Minneapolis. Harry was a genuinely enthusiastic man, so much so, that being impressed I asked for an explanation of his happy nature. "I decided long ago," he said, "to put the best possible connotation on the words and actions of every person and every situation. Naturally I was not blind to the realities, but I always tried first to emphasize the best connotation, for I believe that such practice actually helps stimulate a good outcome. This best connotation resulted in enthusiasm for people, for business, for church and other interests, and greatly added to the joy of life, and it certainly helped oust worry from my mind. In fact, I have not wor-

ried since I began practicing this enthusiasm-producing technique."

I ALMOST WALK OUT OF A CHURCH

I have myself often had occasion to put this principle of Harry Bullis's into operation. Only recently I attended a Church of England Sunday morning service in Europe. The clergyman conducting the service was a regular man who gave a solid rugged message, and I liked him immensely. It is a custom upon occasion for a layman to read the lesson. The congregation was composed mostly of English people, and I had been observing the many vigorous young men present. Then to my astonishment a young man who resembled a beatnik rose to read the lesson. Not only did his hair hang in long ringlets, but a thick beard circled his face.

I could hardly take it, to listen to this character read publicly out of the greatest Book in the world! For once in my life, I actually thought of walking out of church and could easily have done so, being in the last row of seats near the door. But Harry Bullis's principle came to my mind, and I decided that the Scripture read by anyone, even by one who seemed an offbeat character, might just possibly do me good. And I had to admit that overcoming an antipathy would be spiritually therapeutic. It was then I noticed that this fellow had a pleasing masculine voice and grudgingly I had to admit that he read the immortal words impressively, with feeling and reverence. Seeking further to put the best connotation on the matter I decided that maybe that rector had a better strategy going than I did; that if we could get young rebels involved in the Church, perhaps they might be made into real men after all. Anyway, this exercise of the best connotation principle left me in a better state of mind, and helped to escalate my feelings of enthusiasm for people in general.

Let us return to the man for whom I outlined a five-point procedure for attacking his worry problem. He did succeed because he was sold on the plan and conscientiously put the suggested principles into operation. However, this did not come easily, representing as it did an almost complete reversal of old mental habits. He related later that his struggle to achieve a normal worry-free state of mind was "really painful. But the more I tried, the more clearly I saw the possibility, at long last, of getting worry off my neck. And each time I achieved one small victory over myself, I got such a kick out of it that I went eagerly after another victory—until finally, I did begin to change."

Some months later, I happened to go to his city to make a speech and he met me at the airport. It was a dark overcast day, but the clouds seemed to dissipate in the presence of this revitalized man. He insisted on taking time off to show me the sights of the town. Then he drove me out to his house to meet his wife, whom he evidently adored. She seemed to adore him, too, for they greeted each other with an enthusiastic embrace. By this time, he had inspired me with such enthusiasm that instead of shaking hands, I kissed her, too.

Before we left for my hotel—where I had not yet had the opportunity to check in—his wife asked gently, "Might the three of us have a prayer to thank God for the wonderful change in my husband? He is a new man and life is so different." So we joined hands in prayer, giving thanks to God for this man whose fears and anxieties had been canceled. It was a most moving experience. Later, as we drove downtown, he said, "The thing that really gets me is the miracle of change."

DON'T BE AFRAID OF OTHER PEOPLE

If you keep enthusiasm up, especially enthusiasm for human beings, another weakness that will cease to bother you is the fear of people, and this is a big worry to many, though maybe few will admit it.

When I was a young reporter on the old Detroit *Journal* my editor, Grove Patterson, took a kindly interest in me, a young man fresh out of college and working on a metropolitan newspaper.

He was a man of keen, perceptive insights. One day he called me to his office. He could always make one feel at ease, even though he was top man on the paper and his visitor in this case was the lowliest.

"Norman," he said, "I sort of get the feeling that you have a lot of fear and anxiety in your system. You must get rid of it. Just what in the world is there to be afraid of anyway? Why should you or I or anybody go skulking through life like a scared rabbit? The good Lord told us that He will be with us and help us. So why not just take that at face value, hold up your head, look the world in the face and hit it real hard? And for heaven's sake, don't be afraid of anything or anybody!"

I remember the scene in the old Detroit *Journal* office on Jefferson Avenue as though it were yesterday.

"But," I said, "that's a pretty big order. How can anyone possibly go through life afraid of nothing or of nobody?"

He sat, feet on his desk, and leveled a long, inky finger at me. There always seemed to be ink on Grove's finger, and when he pointed that finger and looked at you with those piercing eyes, you listened.

"Listen," he said, "I'll tell you how. 'Be strong and of a good courage; be not afraid . . . for the Lord thy God is with you whithersoever [you go].' Just hang onto that promise," he added, "and don't forget that it's made by Someone who never lets anybody down."

That was sound advice and I needed it, for since early boyhood I had been afraid of people. In fact, I was absolutely awestruck by some.

My father was a minister, and in his denomination ministers frequently changed churches. In fact, every fall, along in September, the church voted whether or not to invite the minister to remain for another year. It was customary for a pastor to be appointed by a bishop for only a one-year term. This one-year system put the minister's security at the whim of the congregation whose support might easily turn to hostility, especially if it was engineered by someone who wanted to manipulate things. And occasionally, in fact more than occasionally, that was the case.

As a result of this climate of insecurity, I was awestruck by some of the leading members of the church, watching them apprehensively for any sign of approval or disapproval of my father's leadership. I remember sitting in the pew on Sunday mornings studying certain faces to see whether they liked his sermon. My father, an urbane sort of man, did not worry about these local big shots, but I did. And for years this anxious concern about the attitude of other people had a strong effect on me. But, I got over it in due course. As a boy, however, I was afraid of Mr.

So-and-so or Mrs. So-and-so. Therefore I built up quite a fear of people.

My father had a habit, too, that certainly did not help me in overcoming my fear of people. When we moved to a new community, he would, in introducing me to prominent church members, say, "He's a big banker," or "He's a big lawyer," or "He's a big grocer in this town." That gave me the pathetic idea that I must tremble in the presence of these "big" characters. So my hypersensitive fear of people was always being accentuated.

In school, also, I was awed by overbright, cocky, loud-mouthed students who seemingly could talk glibly on any subject. As for myself, I was shy and reticent and rather inarticulate for the most part. I knew the subject matter but expressed it poorly. If any other student laughed or smiled as I spoke, I froze immediately. So I gave way in my own thoughts before these smug fellow-students who cockily acted as if they had all the answers. I believed they were all far ahead of me in ability, and so I was afraid of them. From the vantage point of later years I wonder where these students are now. Actually I have even forgotten their names. For the most part none of them have ever been heard of since. Apparently they shot their little bolts in school.

But this fear was indeed difficult for me to overcome; that awestruck fear of the prominent or well-known or those with money or position. I felt inferior and inadequate in the presence of anyone who threw his weight around. So when Grove Patterson confronted me with the undeniable fact that I must rid myself of inordinate fear of people, he was hitting on a very sore nerve. Our conversation in the newspaper office really made me resolve to reorganize myself so that no longer would I tremble before any human being.

Even while I have been writing this book, however, I had a personal experience which shows that I need to practice more faithfully the fear-of-nobody principle. My wife Ruth and I drove one day from our farm in Pawling, New York, up to Syracuse, New York, where I was to speak to the Mutual Agents Association Convention. It is a trip of about two hundred and fifty miles up the Taconic Parkway and the New York Thruway.

On the Thruway we stopped at a gasoline station and

were waited on by a very authoritative young man. Even in his comments about the weather he somewhat flattened me by asserting that I was entirely wrong in my weather prognostication. I didn't think it was worth arguing about and I didn't continue the discussion. While he was filling the gasoline tank, he put up our car hood to check the oil, water and battery. "Oh brother," he exclaimed, "something has to be done about that fanbelt and two other belts in there."

Now one thing I know absolutely nothing about is what is under a car hood. "What is the matter with them?" I asked, alarmed.

"Why," he said, "look at that frayed place on that belt. I have seen cars come in here off the Thruway with these belts wrapped around them so tight that it took us a couple of hours to get them off. Those belts of yours have got to come off immediately."

I looked at the belts. For the life of me I couldn't see anything wrong with them, but he was so authoritative that I began to feel awestruck and tongue-tied. Assuming that he seemed to know what he was talking about, I gave in. He pulled the car over to the side and started taking all belts out. I noticed another car alongside and the belts were being removed from that one also. I was hesitant and doubtful; abjectly I asked the man inside the station, "Does this young man know what he is doing?"

"Oh, yes," he said, "he knows exactly what he is doing."

"Well," I said, "the belts look all right to me."

"If he says the belts aren't right, then the belts aren't right," he replied. At which I completely folded.

Then my wife came over and inquired what was going on, and I told her. She asked, womanlike, "What's wrong with the belts?" Now, my wife is a very clear-minded thinker and she does not let people overawe her.

I said feebly, "This young man knows all about belts and these belts, he says, have to come off. He says cars come in here off the Thruway with belts wrapped all around the engine. We have to have new belts put on."

She saw that he had two of the belts off already. She examined them, and she said, "There is nothing wrong with these belts. This is a racket. Please put the belts right back on."

Well, I was embarrassed by this plain talk and walked

away to buy a newspaper. By this time my wife had three of the four gas-station men around her and she proceeded to inform them in a very polite but firm tone that it was a racket. Well, the old belts in our car have been running just beautifully ever since; in fact, ten thousand miles since. This assertive, cocky and, shall we say, "shady" young man actually did almost succeed in selling me the unneeded belts because of the belligerent, superior manner in which he exercised his authority. Awed by him and his know-it-all attitude, my old fear of people reappeared. But my wife was not impressed in the slightest by his manner; only by facts. That is why when one keeps his thinking rational and is impressed only by facts, his fear of people vanishes.

So never be afraid of anyone; of your husband, or your wife, or (heaven help you) your children; or the boss, or the loud so-called big shot. And, of course, the best procedure for doing this is to love people and always see the best in them. Enthusiasm for them will grow in you and as it does, it will cancel out your shyness, your fear of others and your worry about what they think of you. And then, as you forget about yourself, your heartening relationship with people will add to your enthusiasm for life itself.

Careful study of worry-fear sickness will reveal in many cases an abnormal preoccupation with self. Worry presupposes an acutely sensitive self-reference in which apprehension exists concerning one's self and those close to him. The more ingrown one is, the sharper the worry is likely to be. Therefore any cancellation of the worry habit must of necessity involve getting outside of one's self.

It is this fact that makes enthusiasm so terribly important, for it is one of the most effective mechanisms for developing an outgoing personality. The ingrown individual has little concern for the world around him. Nervously he scans the daily paper and is invariably sure that everything is going wrong. But his interest in matters of social significance is only passing, tenuous and vague. His principal concern is how things may affect him personally. So he gives only fragmentary attention to outside conditions and continues to stew and fret in a self-conditioned worry mess which agitates his mind. And given enough of such worry the result can be actual strangulation of personality.

WORRY, AND YOU CHOKE AND STRANGLE

The word worry derives from an old Anglo-Saxon verb *wyrgan* meaning to choke or strangle. If someone were to grasp you around the neck with two hands, pressing as hard as possible, and thereby cutting off your air supply, he would be doing to you dramatically what you gradually do to yourself as a confirmed worrier. Through worry you are actually strangling your creative powers. In an early Anglo-Saxon illustration, worry is graphically depicted as a huge angry wolf with teeth in a man's neck.

Relief from worry is what this book is endeavoring to provide. Even more than relief, it offers a positive cure in the form of vital enthusiasm which can actually cancel worry.

The power of enthusiasm to perform so is illustrated in the case of a widow whose worry habits tended to remain minor during her husband's lifetime. After he died, however, anxiety took over. Soon she was in the grip of a severe fear reaction. Her husband had left her moderately provided for, enough to care for her comfortably if she was prudent. She was frightened of making decisions since hitherto they had been almost altogether made by her husband. She had been dependent on him for everything involving judgment. She told me she was sick with worry. I believed her, for worry can indeed make one sick.

I counseled with her in an attempt to shift her mind from the dependence she had always had on a strong husband to dependence upon a strong God. But while she was a believer of sorts, she did not seem able to muster a faith realistic enough to overcome her fears. Therefore she sank deeper into a pervasive worry state.

One noonday, passing through the lobby of the Commodore Hotel in New York City, enroute to the weekly meeting of the Rotary Club, I noticed her sitting near the entrance of the Rotary dining room. She was staring moodily ahead. In answer to my inquiry she said she came every Rotary day because, "Bill never missed a meeting and I just sit here in the lobby outside the Rotary meeting room and think about him. But, oh, Dr. Peale, whatever will I do? I am so worried. Nothing matters any more. Life is all over." And again the dull complaint, "I'm sick with anxiety."

"Look, Mary," I said, "we're going to do something about you, so just sit here until this meeting is over. Then you and I are going to have a talk. I am not going to stand by and let a strong, intelligent woman like you continue being panicky with worry. Also, I am going to tell you exactly what Bill would say to you. I know you pretty well and I knew Bill even better. So just wait for me."

All through the Rotary meeting I turned the problem over in my mind. This woman had energy and not a little capacity for enthusiasm. I decided to try a treatment of enthusiasm to heal her fear, feeling that it might stimulate her capacity to have faith, which had become stultified since her husband's death.

At Rotary I happened to notice a man, head of one of the great sociological service agencies dealing with the poor and infirm. I asked him, "Jerry, do you need more staff in your work?"

"We surely do; we are very shorthanded. But we've already used up our budget and I cannot take anyone else on."

"Well, could you use a capable, intelligent, though untrained woman of about fifty, who will work for free?"

"Yeah, I know the kind: a couple of hours per week between bridge games to give herself a sanctimonious feeling. No thanks."

But I assured him that this woman would give a full half-day, five days a week from nine to one o'clock. Rather grudgingly he said, "Well, O.K., send her along. But if she won't work regular hours I won't keep her. I want people who are on the job, not the bleeding hearts who get their kicks out of thinking they are doing good."

Returning to the lobby where Mary waited, I said, "Now, please come to my office at Marble Collegiate Church. I will see you there in an hour. But I want you to walk to the Church. No taxi or bus. And see if you can figure a pace of about four miles an hour, which means you will have to walk vigorously. This is the rate Dr. Paul White advocates for those who walk to avoid heart attacks."

"But I'm not used to walking," she exclaimed in surprise. "And whatever difference does it make how I get to your office?" I assured her that there was a very good reason in my request and extracted a promise that she would walk.

An hour later she arrived and for the first time there was good color in her cheeks. "Why, I actually feel good, better than in months," she said. "This crisply cool day and the blue sky overhead and the colorful shop windows are really wonderful."

"You didn't stop to look in those shop windows, did you? I wanted you to keep that vigorous four-miles-an-hour pace," I said. She resolutely claimed she had done so.

WALK YOUR WORRIES AWAY AND BUILD ENTHUSIASM

"Why did you insist on my walking?" she asked. I told her of an old friend of mine, the late Dr. Henry C. Link, a practicing psychologist. When a worry-ridden patient came to him, before beginning the interview Dr. Link often asked that person to walk vigorously around the block three times. Three times around the block was about half a mile. Dr. Link explained that the brain has an upper and lower section and that we worry with the upper brain while the lower controls motor reaction. "So," he said with a grin, "if I can get the patient to practice walking, he uses the lower brain which works the legs and thus relieves the upper from the strain of worry thoughts." He felt that it was easier in this way to "float the worries off."

My friend Ernest Zingg of Berne, Switzerland, with whom I have often walked in the high Swiss Alps, gave me a paper entitled *Walking—as a Cure* by Dr. Felix Oesch, medical commissioner of the city of Berne. It says in part: "Walking not only activates circulation of the blood, it also speeds up and intensifies respiration and enables greater absorption of oxygen . . . The body of the walker is absolutely free, the feet only are put periodically on the earth and rolled off. In no other position . . . will blood circulation be nearly as free . . . Walking, in addition, brings a whole orchestra of large and small muscles into action and to an accord . . . Their 'eurythmic' . . . sends the blood towards the heart as the valves of the heart only allow this direction . . . Walking has a healing influence and balances large and small psychical troubles and conflicts . . . With the distance from home one also gains distance more easily from the miseries of the world. Perspectives, the 'blue horizons' enable personal grievances to be put in a better proportion to the sorrow rucksack of the world . . . a walk taken in harmony with nature very often replaces the psychiatrist."

"So, Mary," I said, "one recommendation for you is more physical activity and I suggest walking. But when you walk do not stroll; really walk. And make it a daily practice, rain or shine."

I suggested a further technique which many have found extremely helpful, one that I often use personally. It is to punctuate vigorous walking with the saying of certain Bible texts. Breathing deeply, say, for example, "Bless the Lord, O my soul; and all that is within me, bless his holy name."

Or, "I will lift up mine eyes unto the hills, from whence cometh my help." The effect of articulating these passages in rhythm with walking is to activate blood circulation, toning up of the system and the mind. This practice, I assured her, would activate enthusiasm, shake down her worries and increase her capacity to exercise faith.

And I stressed that it would be through rejuvenated faith that the real cure of her worry would occur. "The whole effort is to open, enlarge and build up your shattered faith capacity. Then you will enter upon a normal, creative and even happy life."

I then told her of the "job" I had secured for her at the agency, and further informed her that I had promised she would go to work on the agreed schedule next day. This was rather a shock. She was a slow starter mornings, and to report to an office by nine o'clock would be a startling new departure. I gave her no comfort in this objection, merely remarking that a "startling new departure" was an integral part of the cure of a worry problem. Whether it was the stimulation of the vigorous walk or the prospect that a new life might open, or both, she did agree to undertake the agency work on the specified condition. She reported the next day on the stroke of nine.

The man in charge phoned me a couple of weeks later to say, "This lady is a rare find. She is mastering our system of work and entering into it enthusiastically. She has a warm, human sympathy for the unfortunate people we deal with. Her eagerness to help them as persons is of a kind we rarely see in professional social work."

I think I need not belabor this case further except to say that a strong and vital enthusiasm took over in this woman's mind. As this occurred prayer became meaningful and presently she said, "I'm on the way to getting that dependence upon God you spoke of."

FORMULA FOR HANDLING A WORRY PROBLEM

To sum up the suggested therapy for a worry problem:
1. Practice vigorous walking.
2. Engage in disciplined regular human service.
3. Develop an awakened concern, even love, for the unfortunate.
4. Find new meaning in prayer and the actual reality of God's presence.

These factors produced a curative enthusiasm that canceled out the festering worry which threatened this woman's future, and it has been effective in other cases as well.

ENTHUSIASM MAKES HARD DAYS GOOD DAYS

I was a guest in the home of my friend, Dr. Georg Heberlein, head of the great Heberlein textile company at Watwill, Switzerland. At dinner Georg asked the title of my new book. When I told him it was *Enthusiasm Makes the Difference,* he expressed approval of the theme as being extremely important to anyone who really wants to do something with himself. As a successful industrialist he knows that enthusiasm plays a vital role in success and failure. His son-in-law Mark Cappis, a dynamic young man whose enthusiastic participation in business and civic affairs marks him as a coming leader, at once affirmed that worry can have no control over an enthusiasm-conditioned person.

Mark told how he and his young wife Bridgett came to New York to make their way in a foreign country, to learn English, make friends and thus prepare themselves for their important international business. Day after day, during a down period in the economy, Mark tramped the streets of New York looking for a job which he insisted on getting on his own, without pull or influence. There are, thank God, still young men like him in the world. The couple lived in a tiny two-room apartment and used a packing box, covered with travel posters, as their dining table.

"Didn't you get discouraged during those hard days?" I asked.

"They were not hard days," Mark and Bridgett exclaimed together. "We had fun. It was exciting to be together with the future entrancingly before us. How could we worry?" Mark added. "You see, we were excited about life and about the United States. We loved the people there. We were overflowing with enthusiasm about everything, and so naturally worry just didn't have a chance with us."

And that is just about the truth of the matter. Keep enthusiastic and worry will never have a chance to get its grip on you.

I was driving one night with John Robison, from Columbus to Findlay, Ohio, where I was scheduled to make a speech. I noticed soft, yet efficient lights on poles near many of the farmhouses we passed. John, who is connected with the Columbus and Southern Ohio Electric Company, explained these were mercury-vapor lamps. They light up automatically at twilight, being triggered by the dark, and go off automatically at sunrise. The protecting light relieves the farmer from worry about possible night intruders.

It seemed a kind of parable. It is a fact that anyone who keeps the light of enthusiasm burning in his mind at all times dissipates that darkness of the mind in which worry grows. Remember, worry and enthusiasm simply cannot occupy the same mind at the same time. They are utterly incompatible.

It was summed up by the Honorable Dan Liu, Chief of Police of Honolulu, recently voted the most popular man in the Hawaiian Islands. The Chief said simply, "Due to Christ I never buckled under any anxiety and have always been sustained in the dangers of my profession." Spiritual enthusiasm does indeed cancel worry.

I have always liked that familiar and reassuring statement by Victor Hugo, "When you have accomplished all that you can, lie down and go to sleep. God is awake."

And a physician has a good idea. He tells his patients to say their prayers and then to say further, "Good night worries. See you in the morning."

And I may add, as you develop some real enthusiasm, worries won't be there to trouble you in the morning. Or if they are, you will be able to handle them. And never forget those tremendous words of Isaiah (35:4): "Say to them that are of a fearful heart, be strong, fear not."

FIVE

TRY ENTHUSIASM
ON YOUR JOB

One of the most exciting races in American sports history took place in the Dwyer Stakes at Aqueduct in July 1920 between two famous horses, Man o' War and John P. Grier. Man o' War was the outstanding racehorse in America, undisputed champion of his time, and one of the most notable of all time. There have been few horses to equal him. What a magnificent animal he was!

I saw him run only once but the race lives in my memory. The jockey and the horse seemed as one. Watching that magnificent animal in action was one of the greatest sports experiences of my life; an exalted, unique and unforgettable moment—comparable to the occasion when I saw Jackie Robinson at Ebbets Field steal three bases, including home plate, in one game. Man o' War had been the champion for a long time. Then another horse began seriously to challenge him. But that horse, as it later proved, did not have the heart of a real champion.

I am indebted for an account of this memorable race to my friend, W. Clement Stone, who with Napoleon Hill co-authored the inspiring book *Success Through a Positive Mental Attitude* * in which this story appears. The challenger, John P. Grier, looked real good and many people

* © 1960, Prentiss-Hall, Inc., Englewood Cliffs, N.J.

actually thought he might be the one to beat Man o' War who, the sports writers suggested, was slipping while John P. Grier was in his ascendancy. The coming runoff was the talk of the hour. Could the upstart put the old champion in the discard?

Finally the great day came and the two horses were poised and ready. At the starting bell they got away cleanly. They were even at the first quarter post; neck and neck at the second. Then the immense crowd leaped to its feet electrified. John P. Grier was edging ahead. Man o' War was facing the challenge of his career.

The experienced little jockey riding Man o' War did some quick thinking. He knew his horse to the depths of the great animal's being, knew the immense reserves of strength and spirit which it possessed. He had never touched Man o' War with a whip. The magnificent horse had always delivered sufficient power without its use. But evidently this time Man o' War was not coming through with enough power to win. As the jockey watched John P. Grier's nose edge slowly ahead, he knew the moment for summary action had come. Down went the whip against the flanks that had never before felt its prodding.

The whip worked instant results. The response to the stinging lash was immediate. From somewhere deep within Man o' War came an enormous surge of power, a new and tremendous motivation. The charging legs beat like pistons as every ounce of muscle, wind and spirit were drawn upon; and the new spirit carried him like a ball of fire past John P. Grier. To the roar of the crowd Man o' War crossed the finish line several lengths ahead. He was still champion. Men pounded each other's backs, shouted themselves hoarse; tears were in the eyes of many. It was the race of a lifetime.

This fascinating story from the history of American track has a significant point to be considered with profit. The question is what happened to John P. Grier? The race in which momentarily he passed the old champion was, it seems, his chief moment of glory, his one great opportunity. Apparently his defeat with victory so close had a devastating effect on the animal. I am no authority on the psychology of a horse but it would appear that deep down inside himself John P. Grier was too soft. He was no real competitor, for at a moment of crisis the spirit went out of him.

Had a horse the power to think, he might have reasoned: "O. K., I almost beat that old Man o' War. A little more practice and next time I will take him over for sure." He evidently did not have within him the true makings of a champion. But Man o' War was of a different breed. He possessed those qualities that keep horses and men, also, on top of life's competition. He almost lost that race but at the crucial moment he drew on the extra power which he possessed. Man o' War had a deep enthusiasm for victory. His job was to run and to win. And he won gloriously when in a crisis his basic enthusiasm for competition was reactivated.

There is, I believe, a profound relationship between sports competitions and the problems of life itself. You and I too have that extra built-in power. The Creator put it into men as well as horses; into men infinitely more than in horses, I am sure. Deeply built into human beings is the desire to excel. It is in the essence of nature for men to compete, if not with others, at least with themselves. And perhaps competing with oneself, ever trying to improve over present performance, is the highest form of competition. But unhappily many men live and die without ever drawing upon that extra power from which comes greater excellence and higher achievement. As a result some fall behind when actually they need not. The cure for such failure is to probe deeper into the spirit and to find new enthusiasm for the job one has to perform.

THE BOY WHO USED ENTHUSIASM AS A STEPPING STONE

It has been demonstrated that enthusiasm makes a considerable difference in any person's work performance. Expose your daily occupation to apathy, as many individuals tend to do, and your job can scarcely be anything but difficult and tiresome. It is hardly possible that a job will go well for the person who considers it just another dull chore that has to be done, that provides neither satisfaction nor interest. Let's face it, you may say, my job is dull. But could it be that you have a dull attitude toward it? Try enthusiasm on your work, whatever it may be, and watch it change. And, incidentally, see how you change with it. Enthusiasm changes the quality of a job because it changes people.

Never let the excuse that yours is a tedious job keep you from applying enthusiasm in an effort to enliven it. Many enthusiasts have had tremendous results with jobs that originally appeared devoid of interest. Take, for example, a job that very well might be considered dreary, that of a busboy in a big hotel. This work consists of picking up used dishes in the dining room and carrying them to the kitchen. In the rigid hierarchy of European restaurants, it is about the lowest job in the echelon of white coats at the bottom and white ties and tails at the top. Most busboys consider the job so lowly that they treat it with contempt and perform it in a perfunctory, even surly manner. As a result it becomes a dull, boring job performed by a dull uninterested person. It becomes self-defeating.

But I know one young man who used enthusiasm on that job with astonishing results. He gave it that extra-touch technique and what exciting creative results came about! His name was Hans and I met him one summer when we were staying for a month in a European hotel. I soon noticed this pleasant-faced, good-natured German boy in the dining room. He had an outgoing manner and was so interested and enthusiastic that he stood out among the other service personnel. He was alert to everyone's needs and eager to be helpful, not only to the guests, but to his fellow-workers as well.

He assisted the waiters with their work, doing whatever needed doing—unlike the men who refused to perform the slightest function outside their own specific jobs. One came to realize that this busboy was a distinctly different type. He liked responsibility and it showed in his manner. Enthusiasm was what he had in extraordinary measure and with it he was upgrading his job so it eventually became an opportunity.

"You seem to be enjoying yourself, Hans," I commented.

"Oh, yes, this is a wonderful hotel. I love the excitement of mealtime in a dining room where the service is the best and is done just right. This is dining at its best. And the guests—they are the finest in all Europe. And our chef—he is the greatest artist in the business." So ran his enthusiastic conversation. That he was the lowest on the totem pole in that dining room did not bother him in the least.

Talk about enthusiasm on a job! It was evident in his every move.

From our talks, I learned that Hans had a goal, a specific goal—not a fuzzy, hope-to-get-somewhere-someday one. His objective was precise and sharply defined. He wanted to become the director or general manager of a great European hotel. And being the best possible busboy was, his keen mind knew, the start of reaching his objective. He also knew that giving the best possible service in the most pleasant manner played a big part in achieving his goal. But he was not simulating happiness and enthusiasm for an ulterior purpose. He just happened to be cheerful and enthusiastic.

To reach his goal he knew it was necessary to go to London for essential training in the international restaurants there. "But," he added, "London seems a long way off and my pockets are empty."

"Empty pockets never held anyone back," I said. "It's only empty heads and empty hearts that do it. You are on the right track. You know exactly where you want to go. Meanwhile you are giving this job all you've got. Begin now believing that you are going to reach your goal. Hold this picture in your conscious mind until, by a process of mental and spiritual osmosis, the image of your goal sinks into your subconscious. At that point you will have it; for it will have you, all of you. Meanwhile, study and observe carefully the people who do every job the best. Continue to make friends. Practice loving people. Remember that some of the people in this dining room are unhappy, bearing heavy burdens of sorrow and discouragement and trouble. Just keep on loving them personally and they will love you in return. People who love people go far in this world, believe me."

I gave him a copy of the German edition of my book *The Power of Positive Thinking*. "You are already a positive thinker if I ever saw one," I told him, "but I want you to read this book and learn the principle of putting your life in God's hands, of being divinely guided, of thinking right and eliminating negatives." During his off hours I saw him poring over the book and he would occasionally come to our table to discuss certain points.

Well, we left the hotel at the end of our vacation period and gradually I forgot about Hans. Several years passed. One day we were in London having dinner in a well-known restaurant that was crowded to the doors. The headwaiter, immaculate in dark coat and striped trousers, came to our table. He described the various items on the menu in a manner that made everything sound so delicious. His whole attitude was exceptionally friendly and he made us feel very much at home.

Some of his German-English expressions made us take a closer look at him. Then with a smile he said, "I'm still practicing positive thinking, Dr. Peale."

"Hans!" I exclaimed. "It's Hans, our old busboy!"

"The same," he agreed.

"You're the same, yet not the same. You've grown. You've developed. So you made it to London! And you're still on your way."

"*Ja, ja,*" he replied, "I'm still going for that Director's job."

"And you're still helping people in the same kindly way, aren't you?"

"*Ja,* I'll always be doing that, I promise."

Will Hans attain his goal? How can he miss? In the story of Hans, who began as a busboy, there is vivid proof that dullness is not inherent in a job, but rather in the individual who does the job. When a person applies enthusiasm to his job, the job will itself become alive with exciting new possibilities. So if you long for a new job, try instead to apply enthusiasm on your present one. See what amazing things happen to it and to you.

HOW FRED HILL WENT ENTHUSIASTIC

Well, how does one go about applying enthusiasm to his present job? For answers to that question, let us return to the case of Fred Hill mentioned earlier in this book. This man was in line for an opening soon to occur, but the personnel executive felt he could not recommend advancement, despite Fred's recognized abilities, the main reason being that he lacked enthusiasm.

The company official stated, however, he might justifiably recommend Fred Hill for the promotion if within six months we could instill some enthusiasm in him. Could it be accomplished within the allotted time, and how? That was the problem.

I gave considerable thought to the matter since the future of Fred Hill and his family was definitely at stake. The executive gave me permission to discuss the problem freely with Fred, even to the extent of warning him that his future in the company was in jeopardy. A natural opening came when I ran into Fred at a luncheon.

After the amenities, I led into the situation by remarking, "Fred, you must have an exciting job down at your place."

"What makes you think it's exciting?" asked Fred a bit sourly. "It's pretty dull if you ask me."

"Why," I countered, "I should think that you, as one of the executives, would get a big kick out of making decisions and seeing your thinking turn into creative action."

Whereupon Fred proceeded to set me straight on how unimportant, to his mind, an executive actually was. "Don't think that a guy is necessarily a big shot because he is labeled an executive," he grumbled. He followed with a dissertation on the power structure in a big organization and how no one man makes decisions, not even the corporate president. Fred described the latter as a "highly paid errand boy who has to consult this or that committee before authorizing the purchase of a box of pencils." It was quite a bitter analysis of big business where, according to him, "the individual is an infinitesimal frog in a huge puddle packed full of other little frogs.

"I work," he continued, "in a building with nine thousand people who jostle one another in commuter trains, subways and elevators. No matter how important you are, or think you are, when you get pushed around in that daily mob you know you are nobody! So what do you mean 'exciting'?"

It was evident from these remarks that Fred's problem was not only apathy but also resentment, perhaps even the sort of contempt for his job that many humdrum employees experience. So I put it to him straight. I asked him what his reaction would be if he failed to go any further up the ladder in his organization. "I don't believe I would care too much," he said, to my surprise. "From what I observe, the higher you go, the duller it gets; and the more of a stuffed shirt you have to become." Subsequently though, I found that Fred did care, and very much.

Meanwhile, I realized at once that we had to be honest with Fred, and he agreed to an appointment for a talk. When we met, I proceeded to describe the situation in regard to himself in his business. He turned pale. "You mean they are going to hold me back just because I'm not the typical eager beaver? Why, those dirty double-crossers!" His anger came out in the open. Then getting quieter and more reasonable he asked what he could do "to improve his image." Now, having emptied himself of his spleen, his sincerity shone through and it was clear that he *did* care. He really wanted to correct his failure. He grew terribly concerned as the import of his problem sank in.

"What we must do," I suggested, "is to work on building up that required enthusiasm. But first, may I point out that griping does not go with an enthusiastic attitude. So let's get rid, of all gripes and resentments you came out with in our luncheon talk." He disclaimed these on the grounds that the day of our previous talk happened to be one of his bad days, but I persisted in asking him to empty himself of all anger and frustrations. He had managed to keep these feelings well out of sight of most people.

Under urging, he finally emptied himself of hatred for people and for the modern way of life in which he was trapped and for which he felt such contempt. This cleansing process was not accomplished easily. A number of interviews were required before he could rid himself of an accumulation of resentments and hatreds. In the organization he was regarded as a calm and quiet man—too quiet, perhaps. No one had any idea of the tempests that seethed behind his quiet exterior. I had the distinct feeling that the churning angers of this man included a deep dissatisfaction with himself. To this he presently admitted. So we were ready for the next step.

VITAL CENTER FOR CREATIVE LIVING

In dealing with personality problems it has frequently been my practice to get the people involved, whenever possible, to come to our own Marble Collegiate Church in New York. We have attempted over the years to make this church a vital center for creative living. An atmosphere of concerned understanding, victorious living, genuine joy, and personality healing is felt, I believe, by nearly all who enter its doors. It is a church composed of several thousand people, most of whom have worked through difficult problems by utilizing spiritual techniques, the kind that change attitudes and so change life itself. We believe, and long experience has validated this belief, that anyone who opens himself to the atmosphere of this church will in time acquire the power of faith, the kind of faith in depth that awakens enthusiasm and makes the difference in one's life.

Fred was a spiritual believer in an apathetic sort of way. But for the most part, he was a non-churchgoer. When I prescribed regular exposure to the dynamic atmosphere of Marble Church, Fred groaned, "You mean I've got to travel fifty miles every Sunday morning to go to church?"

"Yes, you said it. It is not merely your going to church that I am interested in, but rather that you expose yourself to a personality revamping. If we can accomplish this for you, it will be worth the fifty-mile trip and then some."

By now Fred realized that his future depended upon carrying out the mental and spiritual treatment recommended and he agreed to follow all directions. After a month of exposure to a dynamic spiritual atmosphere, he admitted it was taking hold. "Something is getting to me," he said. That it was indeed doing so was evident by his voluntarily expressed determination to stop hating people and to start loving them. The churchgoing had stimulated valid insight. He saw his irritation and hate as a definite impediment to the creative enthusiasm we were working to develop.

To implement further change, I suggested to Fred that he start practicing a constructive principle that I had known to work in similar cases. He was deliberately to send out kindly thoughts to people on commuter trains, subways and in elevators. He was to see them not as exasperating mobs but as individuals, each of whom was trying to live meaningfully. This practice at first struck him as rather absurd. But he did try it and actually got so he enjoyed it. As the irritations were siphoned off, he began to change, so much so, that he actually arrived at work feeling, as he put it, "Pretty good, in fact *very* good." He began to act really happy.

As a result he started conducting himself with a new vitality which amazed everyone. It was real too, not assumed. In fact, he changed to such an extent that the difference was evident to all who had known him before. Enthusiasm was generating within him.

I must point out that this change did not come easily. As a matter of fact, in a weaker man it would have been much longer in coming. But Fred basically was top-quality, the type for whom there is no weakening once the decision to change is made. He meant business. Of course, change in depth cannot be expected to happen overnight. But neither does the process have to be interminable.

Now, to conclude the case of Fred Hill, as an example of how one develops the capacity of trying enthusiasm creatively on the job, let us recapitulate.

(1) He had to learn enthusiasm or go no further in his work.

(2) He had to see himself objectively as he was—well equipped but lacking in motivational power.

(3) He had to rid himself of an accumulated mass of well-concealed but ill-controlled complaints, hate and resentment. These had been effectively blocking the enthusiasm he so greatly required.

(4) He needed to be exposed to a scientific and stimulating spiritual treatment.

COME ALIVE WITH ENTHUSIASM

As a result Fred's personality now began fully to come alive. His personality took on the characteristics defined by Dr. Rollo May, educational psychologist, who in an address to the New York Academy of Medicine said: "Your personality means the aspect of yourself which makes you effective in life. It is evident that there are two aspects of effectiveness of individuality. First, how do you affect or stimulate others? This is your stimulation value. Second, how do others affect you? How do you respond to others? That is your response aspect of value. Put these together, your effect upon others and others' effect upon you, and that is virtually your personality."

Well, Fred did exactly that. He put these two aspects of personality together and his rapport with people improved tremendously. Consequently, his personality took on remarkable new vitality and enthusiasm. The job situation, so my executive friend reported not without awe, was immeasurably upgraded. Fred could now have the promotion. But then there was an ironic switch. Fred did not want the promotion. Inspired by new-found enthusiasm, he decided to go into business for himself. The new enterprise was based on his recently achieved confidence. "This proposition is out of this world," he said, with elation, "and I know I'm going to put it over big. I am having the time of my life with it!" Fred did succeed, as anyone will, who really puts enthusiasm into his work.

Among other effective techniques for applying enthusiasm on your job which have been successfully used is one suggested by the late Dale Carnegie, a good friend of mine. Dale wrote one of the great best sellers of all time, *How to Win Friends and Influence People*. He also developed the Dale Carnegie speech courses. Through his books and programs he probably helped more men and women release personal talents and abilities than any man of our time. He came from a background of poverty and adversity. The hardships suffered in youth developed in him a positive obsession to help others move up, always up, to better lives. Thousands owe their success to the inspiration and guidance of this great man.

Like all men of accomplishment Dale Carnegie had a highly organized but sensitive nature and suffered moments of deep discouragement and depression. "But," he said brightly, "I figured out a mental trick for reinstating my usual enthusiasm for life and the job. I would deliberately imagine that I had lost everything: job, property, reputation, family, everything I valued. I would sit in the deepest possible gloom. Then I would start adding up what I had not lost, which included that entire list in reverse; and presto the old enthusiasm for the job was back and at a new high. Try that sometime. It really works," he said. I was impressed and did try it. He was right. It does work.

WHAT WOULD AN IMAGINATIVE PERSON DO WITH YOUR JOB?

Another effective technique may be tried on the job for which you have little enthusiasm, which you may even regard as obnoxious and deadly dull. Try asking yourself what someone else might see in this job. Let your imagination consider what he would do with it. Perhaps he is an individual who is doing exceedingly well in his own work. Try to imagine what such a man would do if suddenly he took over your job. How do you think he would react toward it? What fresh and imaginative action would he take to put new life and achievement into what you consider a dull job? Jot down on paper what you think that person might do if he had your position.

Then apply to your work those skills you think that man would use if he were in your shoes. Because you've had experience in the job, there are within you hidden qualities, both of knowledge and experience, which he lacks. There is always something new and imaginative that you can bring even to a familiar job. This fresh approach will inspire you with unexpected strength and enthusiasm for the task.

The sales manager for a wholesale grocery house once told me a story that illustrates our point—what a man with imagination can do with a job that has been branded as hopeless. This company sold its merchandise in four key cities. In City B, a section of the town had been designated by the salesman as an area where nothing could be sold. He had a fixed idea about it. He had accepted this notion from his predecessor, who wasn't a particularly competent salesman either, and it didn't add incentive to his already pessimistic frame of mind. So he dismissed this section as worthless, convinced that no selling could be done there.

In time, management transferred this pessimist elsewhere. They brought into City B a new man who had no idea there were designated arid spots in his territory. Since he was by nature friendly and energetic he approached customers with the idea of sales and service. Since he had no foreknowledge that "no one could sell in that particular section," he was not paralyzed by negative thinking. He began to call on potential customers in that neglected area and soon he was making impressive sales. He reported enthusiastically to the home office that there was virgin territory here and he was moving in on it. He couldn't understand why previous salesmen had neglected it.

There may be a lesson for all of us here. Is it perhaps possible that there is virgin territory in your job that can be turned similarly into a veritable gold mine? Enthusiasm for possibilities increases those possibilities and so in turn increases enthusiasm itself.

This kind of thinking is essential even to a calling like mine. At Marble Collegiate Church in New York City, where I have been minister for thirty-five years, we are constantly reexamining and requestioning our methods in order to develop more imaginative and creative means of reaching the greatest possible number of people.

An important factor in any job is timing. This is the art of doing the right thing at the right time in the right way. Those who approach a job in a negative way sacrifice the delicate sense of timing. No matter how well a task has been done previously, it can be improved by the application of imagination and enthusiasm and timing.

Unending search and the subsequent satisfaction of discovery put excitement into the structure of a job and compound its interest. No work need be dull or unproductive if you make up your mind to find the potentials in the job and develop them. You may fear there are no possibilities for those who are stuck at the lowest end of the job scale. But before you turn to the government for help, assert your sense of independence for the final attempt at improving your condition. Pray, think, work with enthusiasm, no matter how inconsequential the job. Often enthusiasm is the bridge between poverty and prosperity.

WHAT ENTHUSIASM DID FOR A PORTER

"I wrote you some time ago," a man wrote me recently, "about being laid off from a job I'd held seventeen years and the difficulty I had finding other work as an unskilled laborer. But I continued to have faith and confidence as you said, and finally I took a job as a porter. Months went by and I kept asking God, 'Is this the abundance Dr. Peale was talking about, above all that I could ask or think? God, I have two boys ready for college and a girl going into high school. How am I going to take care of their needs as a porter?' "

His faith sometimes slipped a bit. But he stuck doggedly to his dream and he ended each prayer with, "I believe everything is going to be all right, abundance more than I could ask for or think of." Finally after six months, there was an opening for a handyman. He took it and his pay went up to $78.00 a week. He said in his prayers to God, "It is a little better. At least we are moving."

Then he went to the library and borrowed books on boilers. Think of it, a porter studying about boilers. He asked God for guidance; he worked hard; he believed that hard work and cooperation were necessary. He finally took the test for No. 6 Oil Burner License and passed. Two weeks later, his boss asked him if he would run a school that needed a superintendent. He prayed for God's guidance.

"Well, God and I took the job," he continued in his letter. "Since He had put all the material down here so they could build the school, I knew that we together would not have too much trouble running it, so God and I are making $145.00 a week and I love my job.

"This is not the end because God and I will someday manage a whole group of buildings and manage them well. My son has a bank loan to go to college. My other son has a $4,000 scholarship to college and my daughter won an appointment to high school which carries a scholarship. You are wrong, Dr. Peale, when you say God gives in abundance. You should say God gives in super-abundance."

Here is a man, humble, poor, struggling, with little education. Yet he has learned one of the greatest truths in life, that a man who believes, who thinks confidently, who is full of faith in God, and who will work and study can accomplish amazing results.

The enthusiasm of the writer of that letter is as boundless as his faith. The result is that he reactivated remarkable blessings in the lives of his family and himself. He gives the lie to those dreary prophets of gloom, who usually blame the American way of life for their own personal failure.

It has been my experience that those who are fired with an enthusiastic idea and who allow it to take hold and dominate their thoughts find that new worlds open for them. As long as enthusiasm holds out, so will new opportunities.

HOW A PIECE OF PIE ACTIVATED ENTHUSIASM

I spoke one night in Indiana to a large crowd at dinner. Sitting beside me at the head table was the president of the organization that had staged the affair. He was a most interesting and enthusiastic man. We had a stimulating conversation about various matters and I was impressed by his lively manner and alert attention. This was a man who seemed to be enjoying life immensely. He told me he was in what he considered "the greatest business in the world." This statement interested me and I asked, "Just what is the greatest business in the world?"

"I make pies," he said with a smile, "and what this country needs is good pies, the kind I make."

I drew him out and discovered that formerly he had been a salesman. He did pretty well on his job but the results were scarcely spectacular. Then one day something happened that was to determine a new career for him. He ate a piece of pie. This epoch-making piece of pie was served to him in a plain little restaurant in a small town where he had stopped for lunch. Never had he tasted pie like this! It was a delicious work of art. On his rounds the following week, he stopped in again. The pie was just as delicious. This routine went on for some weeks. Then one day the pie turned out to be just another piece of pie: tasteless and commonplace. So he asked the restaurant owner what had happened. The man explained that the woman who baked the pies was taken ill and could no longer deliver.

To my dinner companion, this news came as a major disaster. No more of those delicious pies! On his way home, still shaken by the news, he remembered that his wife had culinary skills. As a matter of fact, she used to bake superbly, but recently she had fallen back on the bakeshops for desserts.

Whereupon, my enterprising friend persuaded his wife to bake a half-dozen assorted pies. He sampled one and it was great. He took them to a local restaurant and invited the proprietor to sample them. The restaurateur bought all six and ordered more. Pies in bakeshops were then selling for 39¢ but my friend thought his were worth 75¢ and asked for that sum. The restaurateur said the price was high, but not "if it kept customers coming back." The home baked pies were an instant success and the man's wife went into the venture full time. Business grew so rapidly that additional helpers soon were required. Ultimately the couple had a large pie plant that delivered fresh baked goods each morning to all the restaurants.

The man beamed. His voice vibrant with conviction, he assured me that the original homemade quality and the personal touch still distinguished his product. Being a born pie lover myself, to the distress of my waistline, I shared his enthusiasm. That night when I reached my room and made ready for bed, a knock came. There was a bellboy holding two hot pies that my friend had thoughtfully sent; one apple, the other cherry and every bit as delicious as I expected them to be.

Here was a man who really tried enthusiasm in his job and with an amazing result. I gathered from others that his enthusiasm, triggered by the excellent pies, extended to the community at large in which he took considerable leadership. He found that enthusiasm makes the difference, a real difference, whether for pies or whatever your commodity happens to be.

ENTHUSIASM BRINGS GOOD DAYS

Religion is designed to provide strength and enthusiasm for living in a difficult world. Not all so-called religious people are enthusiastic, indeed far from it. Some appear to have the curious notion that gloom and pessimism are the hallmark of Christianity. This is a distortion of the message of Jesus Christ who said, "These things have I spoken unto you, that my joy might remain in you, and that your joy might be full," and who also said, "Rejoice in the Lord always: and again I say, Rejoice." Christianity can put joy and enthusiasm into people's minds for the purpose of helping them to live creatively and victoriously in this trying world.

One man who holds to this faith happens to be one of the most efficient salesmen in American industry. He has marketed some of the most widely used items in the economy today. He is a keen-minded, brilliant activist whose service to church and community is outstanding. From humble beginnings he rose to influential leadership and his benefactions to all kinds of human service are notable. I asked what he thought about the future. He replied that he thought it would be very good. When pressed for his reasons for optimism and enthusiasm, he declared that "good days are ahead for the very good reason that we will make them good days."

He stated his belief that "God Himself gave us power and authority over every day to make it either good or bad. Every morning," he said, "we have the choice whether it shall be a good or bad day. As for me I decide every morning that with God's help I will make it a good day. I can tell you that as a result, my days while not always easy are still good." This man believed that a day called bad by some people could be transformed into a good day by taking charge of it to make it good.

He said he had a "foolproof" formula for making good days—a six-point technique that I've found will indeed help anyone who wants to use enthusiasm on his job.

FORMULA FOR MAKING ANY DAY GOOD

1. *Think a good day.* To make a day good, first see it good in consciousness. Do not allow any mental reservation that it will not be good. Events are largely governed by creative thought, so a positive concept of the day will strongly tend to condition it to be as imaged.

2. *Thank a good day.* Give thanks in advance for the good day ahead. Thank and affirm a good day. This helps make it so.

3. *Plan a good day.* Specifically and definitely know what you propose to do with the day. Plan your work and work your plan.

4. *Put good into the day.* Put bad thoughts, bad attitudes, bad actions into a day and it will take on bad characteristics. Put good thoughts, good attitudes, good actions into a day and they will make the day good.

5. *Pray a good day.* Begin each day with that powerful affirmation from Psalm 118:24: "This is the day which the Lord hath made; we will rejoice and be glad in it." Start the day with prayer and finish it the same way. Then it is bound to be good even if it brings tough experiences.

6. *Fill the day with enthusiasm.* Give the day all you've got and it will give you all it's got, which will be plenty. Enthusiasm will make a big difference in any day and in any job.

The top sales producer who gave me these rules said, with a chuckle: "Here's a quotation I picked up somewhere; a fellow named H. W. Arnold said it. I believe it's on the beam. 'The fellow who is fired with enthusiasm for the boss (that is to say the job) is seldom fired by the boss.' "

This reminded me of an employer who told me he was going to fire a man out of the business. I asked, "Why not fire him into the business? Get him to try enthusiasm on the job." He did, and the employee became presently a very important man in the concern. He was fired all right but it was not out. Enthusiasm fired him to new participation in his job. He became a new personality: successful, happy, creative. Try enthusiasm on your job. The result can be amazing.

SIX

TENSE? NERVOUS? LET ENTHUSIASM COME TO YOUR AID

We sat together at the speaker's table looking out on a crowd of ome fifteen hundred people that filled the large hotel bal oom. This man, master of ceremonies for a big dinner event, was the most nervous of toastmasters. He picked at his food and constantly moistened dry lips. His hand shook like an aspen leaf, and once when inadvertently it touched mine, it felt cold as an icicle.

"You seem a bit nervous," I commented sympathetically.

"Well, if you think I am nervous now, you should have seen me six months ago," was the surprising reply.

"Were you more nervous six months ago than you are now?" I asked.

"Sure was," he said, "and when I introduce you, you'll hear how I started improving."

Presently the toastmaster arose, knees shaking, voice trembling, and came out with the following: "Friends and fellow citizens, tonight I want to introduce our speaker, a man who has done me no end of good. Some time ago, tense and full of stress, I was on the edge of a nervous breakdown. I couldn't sleep nights and everything was upsetting to me. But just at that time a friend sent me a book by our speaker. I took the book to bed with me and believe it or not, I hadn't read three pages before I was sound asleep."

This well-intentioned remark rocked the crowd with laughter, a reaction that did not appreciably reduce the toastmaster's tension. Later he asked if we might talk privately. When we were alone I said, "Let's face the fact that you are by no means out of the woods on this tension problem, though you are making progress." I reminded him that there are two kinds of tension: (1) the good type, which puts directed drive into a person, and (2) the bad type, which shakes a man to pieces. To overcome the latter and gain the former, I urged him to become a practicer of enthusiasm. For enthusiasm has the power to take one out of himself and change his thinking from that acute state of self-reference and ultra-sensitivity in which tension thrives. The less conscious one is of himself, the weaker the hold of tension upon him is likely to be.

Whenever enthusiasm for any reason declines, tension seems to increase. That is the time for action. Personally when I feel a diminution of enthusiasm I carefully appraise my state of tension and if possible, even for a brief period, I try to get away to a place which has tension-reducing qualities. Usually this is my farm in Dutchess County, New York.

But after one particularly busy season, I needed to get far away, so I boarded a jet and seven hours later landed in Switzerland. I drove at once to a serene and peaceful place, the high Alpine Valley of the Engadine, often called the roof of Europe. Here three great mountain passes, the Julier, the Maloja and the Bernina shield the traveler from the outside world. Such a retreat from the tension of the job enables one to cope with problems upon return to the familiar routine. To find relief from tension does not require a trip abroad, of course. Often a walk down the street under the stars will do the trick, and much more cheaply.

St. Moritz is a lovely Alpine spa nestling in a magnificent mountain-encircled valley six thousand feet above sea level. The air is tonic, always fresh and crisp-cool. Golden sunshine warms you by day. Bright stars that seem very near indeed light the evening sky when the incredible afterglow has faded. Nights are cold and one snuggles contentedly under huge puffs that produce a gentle warmth in which deep slumber comes.

My friend Andrea Badrutt, one of Europe's delightful hosts, whose Palace Hotel is where I stay, says the air, sun and water of the upper Engadine have worked wonders in the lives of some of the world's busiest people. "Tension cannot remain in you," he declares, "in the soothing, relaxing atmosphere of a valley where people have come since ancient times to be healed."

With so much tension in modern life one must occasionally retreat *from* the world, in order to live effectively *in* the world. The governor of an American state told me that he joins a group of men in a yearly retreat where, in a religious atmosphere, strict silence is imposed for forty-eight hours.

"How," I asked, "can a politician keep quiet for two days? It seems incredible."

"That is part of the cure," he replied with a grin. "The tension-healing value of discipline is helpful, and in silence you may rediscover yourself and God. Deeper insights come as the fitful fever of life is eased."

He quoted Thomas Carlyle's wise remark, "Silence is the element in which great things fashion themselves." And I thought of Isaiah 30:15: "In quietness and in confidence shall be your strength." This text incidentally expresses an interesting progression. Silence leads to confidence, and confidence to strength. And silence, confidence and strength pay off by making you a more competent and certainly a happier, more enthusiastic person.

Well, the tension subsided for me on that visit to the wide sunbathed valley framed by massive peaks. Dark forests gird broad mountain flanks, and above, a deep blue sky suggests Italy just beyond the Bernina peaks. Here the air is lighter than in lowlands, and possesses a tonic quality which, with the powerful sunlight, seems actually to produce a kind of gentle massaging effect. Mineral waters and Alpine peat baths contribute to a sense of well-being.

Yet something more basic than sun, air and water is required, for the control of tension may be psychological and spiritual. The secret of overcoming tension is a controlled mental attitude and this often depends upon spiritual factors.

At St. Moritz a wealthy, balding playboy told me he had "nothing but time and money." He had taken the cure in every spa in Europe, but complained that still he "itched" constantly. "Must this miserable itching go on forever?" he asked pathetically.

I told him of a woman who had "itched" for several years. Her medical doctor sent her to me, explaining that for some reason she was "scratching herself on the inside." She was extremely tense. Our talk uncovered an old bitter anger for a sister over their father's will. This hatred, according to the physician, had no doubt caused the physical manifestation of itching. We persuaded her to give up the hate and gradually, as tension abated the itching ceased.

It is not necessary to settle for being tense, even in an age of anxiety. You can live without tension, and one way to do so is through the development of enthusiastic attitudes and techniques.

Your tension problem may be in part or entirely medical, in which case treatment will be handled by a physician. On the other hand, it may be a result of psychological or spiritual factors. If so, read on, for this chapter is intended for you. It may creatively aid you.

BUSINESSMAN HEALED OF TENSION

I was able to help bring about healing of tension through enthusiasm in the case of a well-known business leader, a longtime acquaintance. He was seriously troubled by tension and desperately wanted help. He was able to get help because he humbly followed a workable program. Any person can be helped if he really wants to be, and if he will study, believe in and practice techniques that have proved beneficial to others with similar problems.

This man, Joe K————, started coming to hear my sermons in the hope that he might get relief from an acute tension condition. Shortly thereafter he made an appointment to see me and described his highly nervous state, one manifestation of which was an inability to make decisions. Whenever called upon to make a decision he would "get into a cold sweat" and feel like he was "going to collapse." This state of mind was a serious problem for in his business he had to make important decisions each day.

Formerly, decision-making had not bothered him at all. Indeed he had been very intelligently decisive. Otherwise, he could not have arrived at his present executive position.

Doctors had diagnosed his trouble as acute hypertension, a decision phenomenon, so they explained, resulting from an old subconscious anxiety. Medication had been prescribed. When an important decision faced him, one that "had a lot of implications riding on it," he would take the medication and it would pull him through. "But," he said plaintively, "I can't grab a pill the rest of my life every time I have to make a decision. My only hope lies in some permanent easing of tension, else I guess I'll have to retire and then die."

He sat silently for a long moment, then in a most affecting manner he said, "I believe God can heal me. Yes, I believe He will heal me."

"Since you believe that, sincerely and in depth," I said, "healing is already taking place." I referred to the immense power inherent in faith and reminded him that the New Testament is filled with instances of healings—and how very important in each circumstance was the power of simple belief. For example, the sick woman who reached out timidly through the crowd and touched the hem of Jesus' garment. She did not even speak to the Lord, but simply believed that she would get well if she could just touch His garment. And she was right, for she was healed.

"Though you are an important man, Joe," I said, "you seem also to have the rare genius of childlike faith, and as a result I believe you can be healed of your tension." I quoted the words: " 'If ye have faith as a grain of mustard seed . . . nothing shall be impossible unto you.' "

"I believe that. I do for a fact," he exclaimed. "Now, what do I do?"

"Nothing at all," I said, "except to keep on believing, deeply and confidently. Just continue thanking God for His healing grace, and for giving it to you now. Don't ask for it as something to be granted later, but give thanks for it as a current fact. That is to say, affirm it with gratitude as having been received. Also underscore every statement in the New Testament about faith and commit as many to memory as you can, so that your mind may become deeply saturated with faith. Fifteen minutes a day devoted to this will work wonders. The chief purpose of this treatment is to deepen faith, for primarily it is faith, rather than any activity, that will heal you."

THE HEALING POWER OF ENTHUSIASTIC FAITH

The patient almost at once began to develop release and with release came enthusiasm—indeed in such a torrent that he would telephone me saying, "Listen to this. Isn't this terrific?" And he would quote a statement from the Bible about faith or healing or peace. "Sorry to bother you," he would then apologize, "but boy, isn't that one a honey? Goodbye, see you soon."

He was a rare breed; the all-out type. People of this sort enthusiastically take faith and go all-out with it. They are true believers—and this kind of believer always sweeps everything before him, including tension and nervousness, or whatever the problem may be.

Joe had been a go-getter all his life. So he was conditioned to the psychology of belief and, as pointed out, he also had the quality of humility. All-outness together with humility is a tremendous combination in personal power build-up. He had the quality of mind that was big enough to be simple and he possessed that superior faculty, the capacity to believe.

Perhaps Jesus Christ had big-minded men like Joe in mind when He said, ". . . whosoever shall not receive the kingdom of God as a little child, he shall not enter therein." If you have what it takes to become simple, humble and unaffected, with a childlike belief that nothing is too good to be true, it is possible for you to enter into the greatest blessings of this life. At any rate, Joe was able to develop an enthusiasm that really made a difference in him.

Another thing we taught Joe was to practice God's presence. It is said that "Jesus Christ [is] the same yesterday, and today, and forever." So we may assume that healings similar to those He performed in His physical lifetime are occurring today in His continuing spiritual lifetime. When the sense of Presence becomes strong, the individual who practices it finds himself in the flow of the same healing power as were those persons whose healings are recorded in the Scriptures, and with similar results.

Therefore the process of relieving tension in this man showed progress when he started strongly affirming belief. Since he accepted the idea that healing was in process, curative enthusiasm was stimulated to start coming through. As he continued to saturate his mind with faith and to practice "the Presence," the tension began to lessen; enthusiasm took hold. The procedure was so successful that in time Joe developed a boundless excitement and vitality, of which there has since been no lessening.

An associate of this man who confidentially knew the treatment being given commented, "I wouldn't have believed possible the amazing change in Joe." And he added feelingly, "Only God could have done it."

And that is a fact. Only God could have done it. And God did do it. Why not, for "in him was life; and the life was the light of men," meaning that you really live when God puts new life in you. Tolstoy expressed it conclusively, "To know God is to live."

This healing of tension was brought about by thinking, believing, practicing—the magic threesome. Since tension existed in the mind, it was ousted by mental displacement in which a more powerful thought pattern, built around the concept of God, was substituted. This powerful concept was strengthened by daily practice. We suggested that upon awakening Joe should "talk" to God, giving thanks for a good night's sleep, and adding all of his reasons for being grateful and joyous. Then, mentally he was to place the day in God's hands, believing that guidance regarding all his activity would be given to him. He was to say, "Lord, I have some important decisions to make today. Since You are going to guide me in every one, how can I possibly go wrong?"

Then he was to do some vigorous physical exercises, affirming meanwhile: " 'This is the day which the Lord hath made; we will rejoice and be glad in it.' "

At the office before starting work he was to say, "Lord, I must go to work now. Stay with me and help me." I told him of a framed statement that my friend the late Fulton Oursler, the famous writer, had by his door, where he could always see it upon leaving the house: "Lord, I shall be very busy today. I may forget thee but do not thou forget me." I never was aware of Fulton forgetting God, and he was assuredly one of the most enthusiastic of men.

Joe was also urged to repeat fragmentary prayers throughout the day. For example, he might have a telephone call of importance. He was to pray, "Lord, guide me in this conversation. Thanks." When about to dictate a letter, a quick similar prayer might be said. Such fragmentary "flash" prayers were designed to drive into consciousness the fact of God's presence, not as a dim figure off in the sky somewhere, but as a guiding friend. As he followed these procedures, which he did in a sincere and believing manner, decision-making gradually became easier for him, until one day he told me excitedly, "I've finally relearned how to make a decision and then having made it, to forget it. I'm no longer making myself tense through nervous post-mortems." His new-found enthusiasm lifted him above tension. As a result of this he found revitalized mental power and gained a firm grasp of each situation.

Finally, at night he was to say, "Thanks, Lord, for being with me all day long. We had a good day together. Now bless me with restful sleep. Goodnight, Lord." As the sense of Presence grew in this man's mind, the upthrust of enthusiasm drove tense and nervous thoughts from consciousness and he became finally a well man. Enthusiasm had once again worked its healing power.

I knew he was truly well when, forgetting himself, he began to say, "Lord, what can I do for You?" This latter emphasis is important too, for the cure of tension is never complete until the individual becomes enthusiastic enough to get outside himself. Seneca said, "The mind is never right except when it is at peace with itself." And the mind cannot be at peace when abnormally concerned with self. Indeed the more tied up one is, the more likely that tension will develop. Actually tension is not so much the problem of the busy person as of the acutely self-centered. Those disorganized, hectic and even frantic individuals— the mentally undisciplined—are tense, and naturally so. But people with organized outgoing minds, the mentally well-controlled, are able to live in an urbane manner and without tension.

FORGET YOURSELF AND TENSION FORGETS YOU

A man consulted me who complained desperately that "tension was driving him crazy." Indeed he was not far from a state of hysteria. It seemed that living in New York had all but driven him "nuts," and he just couldn't take the noise, stress and confusion much longer. If only he could get to the country, among hills, meadows and babbling brooks. . . .

"John, a move to the country wouldn't help you any," I said, breaking into his halcyon dream of peace. "You would find the same tension there. Your trouble isn't in the city: it's in your mind." I told him of the man I once met on a street in New York, who in answer to my routine inquiry regarding his health, began a long high-strung dissertation on how tense he was. He waved his hand as though to take in the entire city and exclaimed, "The very air of this town is filled with tension." I had to disabuse him, by replying, "If you took a sampling of this air into the laboratory for scientific analysis, no doubt there would be plenty of dirt. But not one speck of tension. Tension is not in the air but in the minds of people who breathe the air."

Having told him this story, I urged the troubled man to try putting enthusiasm in his thoughts in order to counteract the mass of self-concern which was building up nervous tension. "Enthusiasm," he snorted, "that's the last thing I've got."

"Maybe that is what is wrong," I replied. "So let's try getting some for you."

"All right," he growled, "you're the doctor. But just how?"

"If I'm the doctor, I'm going to prescribe something that will get healing enthusiasm to work in your seething mind."

Now be assured that I knew my man quite well. I was completely aware of his abnormal self-interest and his excessive concern for his own well-being and physical comfort. I knew that seldom, if ever, did he give money either to his church or social enterprises, and he never gave time either. He was inbound, ingrown—a tied-up person, although he did have many amiable and attractive qualities. His tension was actually a sickness brought on by self-emphasis as well as by pressure. To reduce it would require rather extreme measures; that is, extreme for him.

"John," I asked, "can you spare an hour to do something for me?" He was a bit surprised, but agreed that maybe he could. "All right then, I want you to call on a friend of mine who is having a lot of trouble. His son got mixed up with a hairy crowd. The boy considers himself a liberal and therefore is in rebellion against everything, from his father to the United States government. He got smart with his employer whom he called a fat capitalist and was fired. Since then he has steadily deteriorated. He is so obnoxious that nobody will have him around. He sponges off his father, who can ill afford it, since his business is not too prosperous.

"But recently an even harder blow struck the father. The doctor broke the news that his wife is desperately ill. No hope is given for her recovery. I've been trying to be supportive but the poor man is in real trouble."

"Boy, I feel sorry for the poor guy," John said, "but hasn't the man any faith? Faith is what he needs." Such a comment was the last reaction I expected to get from John.

He protested that he had nothing to give the stricken man, and reminded me that he himself was in trouble, that he had come for help. "And what could I possibly say or do to help this man?" he asked.

I told him that often I myself had the same problem, but that I simply sent up a little prayer asking for direction, then tried to say and do what seemed best. "Just try that method," I suggested. "Go and see this man for me, and let me know how it goes."

He went doubtfully and hesitantly. I did not hear from him for several days, and was beginning to think he had failed me. Then he telephoned to give the most amazing report. "I've really got this old boy on solid ground," he reported excitedly. "I told him that there was no trouble that faith can't handle. Believe it or not, I prayed with him. First time I ever prayed with anybody. And I had him out to dinner last night. You know that beatnik son? Well listen, that kid isn't too bad. He is just mixed up. Could be that some of his gripes about society have some basis in fact. Anyway, believe it or not, he is going to dinner tonight with me. But I insisted that he put on a jacket and a clean shirt. And do you know, he said he was fed up with looking like a bum. He actually seems glad that a friend told him to dress up a bit."

"You seem to be enjoying yourself with this case, John. How's that tension of yours?"

"My tension? Well, don't think I haven't still got it. But Dick's problems make mine look like kindergarten stuff. See you later." He did see me later, much later. Indeed he became so preoccupied with Dick and the son that he had no time for his personal problems.

I conducted Dick's wife's funeral some months later. And there was John, sitting by the husband and son. It was evident that he was the rock upon which they depended in that sad hour of bereavement. John has been back to see me, but not about his tension. His enthusiasm for people wiped it out. He has moved out of town now to a midwest city, and the last I heard he was creatively doing some real human service in a new kind of tension, racial tension. In an effort to heal that larger social problem, his own personal problem has eased up. Enthusiasm helped in his healing.

Medical men emphasize the danger of stress in physical illness. Any procedure that can cut down tension adds to well-being. And, sound, well-directed enthusiasm helps in many cases. Dr. Hans Seelye has for some years been saying that stress is a root cause of all disease, due to its imbalancing effect upon the function of the human organism. A prominent heart specialist showed me X-rays of the hearts of three people taken when each was sixty-five years of age. He pointed out certain evidences in the X-rays and said, "Actually, they should be dead. But as a matter of fact, they are now about seventy years old and living satisfactory lives." Asked the reason, he replied that each had mastered tension and stress. They had thrown off gloom and developed healthy enthusiasm. As a result, the prognosis in each case looked very good indeed.

ENTHUSIASM IS GOOD MEDICINE

Dr. Paul Tournier, a celebrated European psychiatrist, in his book *The Healing of Persons* * develops the thesis that wrong thinking can have physically devastating effects. He says, "Most illnesses do not, as is generally thought, come like a bolt out of the blue. The ground is prepared for years, through faulty diet, intemperance, overwork, and moral conflicts, slowly eroding the subject's vitality. When at last the illness suddenly shows itself, it would be a most superficial medicine which treated it without going back to its remote causes." Quoting a fellow doctor, Dr. Tournier adds: "Man does not die. He kills himself."

* *The Healing of Persons* by Paul Tournier, Harper & Row

A patient was sent to our clinic at Marble Collegiate Church by an upstate physician, who said, "This man is actually killing himself by abnormal depression. I know of no medication that can heal him. Give him some fresh enthusiasm for living or he may die." Fortunately we were able to help the man to take the "medicine" of enthusiasm, and he not only lived but overcame his depression.

Dr. Tournier points out that "every act of physical, psychological or moral disobedience of God's purpose is an act of wrong living and has its inevitable consequences." Many doctors whose technique is that of treating the patient, rather than the disease, and who are perhaps not so religiously oriented as is Dr. Tournier, nevertheless subscribe to this doctor's conclusions as to the effect of hate, evil, gloom, and depression on mankind.

One doctor, for example, who states that he never attends church services or uses any religious terms, told of one patient who died of "grudgitis." He defined this as "a deep sickening hatred so virulent in nature that toward the end his breath became unbelievably foul, the body organs seeming to deteriorate at once." Then he added, using a quotation with which I was surprised to know he was familiar, " 'The wages of sin is death.' "

Wrong thinking does not always result in illnesses as dramatic as the foregoing. But it is an authenticated fact that any procedure that upgrades and freshens the mind as do hope, optimism and enthusiasm is on the side of health and well-being. Therefore, if you are tense and nervous, enthusiasm can help you as it has helped so many others.

WORRY BEADS, FIDGET STONES AND TWISTED PAPER CLIPS

This age of tension seemingly has affected people everywhere. Having made many journeys to the Middle East, an area far removed from the materialistic climate of Western civilization, I have observed even there a tendency toward nervousness. Devout Moslems usually carry a string of beads behind their backs as they walk, fingers restlessly moving from one to another of the thirty beads, each bead representing the name of some deity. Used as "worry beads," they are supposed to be efficacious in reducing tensions and anxiety.

If you are inclined to write off this practice as "superstition," may I tell you about my visit to a Fifth Avenue shop where the owner showed me his outstanding inventory of jade? Among other objects, he exhibited a flat piece of jade, perhaps two or three inches long and a couple of inches wide, with an indentation to fit the contour of the thumb. This he called a "Fidget stone." He generously presented one to me and said he was selling them in large numbers to New York City and Westchester residents.

The stone came in a chamois cover with a small folder conveying the following message to the purchaser: "Relaxation is at your finger tips. Pressure and tensions vanish as your fingers move over the soothing surface of the Fidget stone. It is of jade, beautifully handcarved as though fitted to your personality and you will be proud to show it. For centuries orientals have attributed their tranquility and impassiveness to the effect of fingering pieces of jade. Everything good was attributed to jade and everything evil was prevented by it."

So now it appears that sophisticated Americans, like the supposedly "superstitious," are clinging to the hope that fingering jade has some mysterious, magical soothing effect. Possibly a restless fidgeting and doodling may momentarily arrest anxiety. Thousands of paper clips are twisted daily into all kinds of shapes by tense businessmen. Thus it seems that worry beads, Fidget stones and twisted paper clips are symptoms of an unconscious desire for release from tension. But the futility of such procedures is obvious, for the real cure is not in agitated use of the fingers, but in controlled, cultivatable mental attitudes. Only in deeper levels of the mind can peacefulness be found.

TO STOP BEING TENSE, STOP

The current style in dealing with emotional problems is usually analysis in depth with supportive psychiatric assistance. This is both proper and valid. But it is also a fact that much tension can be conquered once a patient makes a commitment deep within his consciousness that he is resolved to overcome tension. Of course, insight is required into its causes, and insight can be achieved by counseling. But there must come a moment when one actually decides to substitute controlled emotional reactions for those of an undisciplined nature. Perhaps not everyone is strong enough to employ this disciplinary method, but some are, perhaps more than they realize. No matter how much psychiatric counseling one receives, and regardless of the quality of such guidance, the ultimate fact is that every person, on his own, by himself, with God's help, must take that final decisive step that activates the cure of unhealthy mental patterns.

For example, a few years ago I dined with friends one evening in the open-air terrace restaurant of the Royal Danielli Hotel in Venice. The night was balmy. A full moon was overhead and the romantic songs of the gondoliers came across the silvery waters of the Grand Canal. The conversation turned on the beauty and peacefulness of the evening and how beneficial such environment was for tense and hard-driving people such as those gathered about the table—a New York business executive, a Hollywood producer, a metropolitan stock broker, and their wives.

The movie producer aired his opinion that current ways of dealing with emotional problems should attach more curative value to what he called "disciplined decisiveness." He emphasized his point by a story concerning his father. "My father," he said, "was the most controlled man I ever knew. He was completely in control of every emotional reaction. However, he was not a cold personality as might be expected from this description. On the contrary, he was a man of vast enthusiasm and warm deep feeling. But emotional control was his middle name."

He told how his father, before age forty, had had a wild and ungovernable temper. He would fly into fearful rage, then fall into deep black depression. "This fiery and undisciplined conduct was repeated often in my youth. But about the time my father was forty years old he suddenly took hold of himself. He changed, absolutely, and I never again knew him to go into a rage or a depression. Instead, he became a controlled person of tremendous enthusiasm and happiness. Emotionally he was completely normal—all abnormalities disappeared.

"Years later," continued the Hollywood producer, "I asked my father how he managed to effect so dramatic and complete a change. His answer was classic: 'Son, I simply got tired of being the way I was. I believed in prayer and in God. So I told God I was fed up with the kind of person I was and asked Him to change me. I believed God would do that and, of course, He did. My prayer was answered; that's all there is to it. I asked God to change me and He did.' My father apparently never doubted his prayer would be answered.

"I asked Dad if he ever felt the old anger coming up again. He replied, 'When I do, son, instead of flying into a great rage, I fly into a great calm.'

"My father always said that God, decision, guts and enthusiasm saved him from a crack-up. That may be a crudely expressed formula, but if you ask me, it proved a pretty effective combination."

Whenever I encounter people who insist hysterically that they cannot overcome tension, my mind goes back to that conversation in Venice. The important fact is that you can do more in a disciplinary way with yourself than you think possible. There is a certain sardonic humor in the story of the New York business executive who had a nervous breakdown. Turning the business over to a staff of young subordinates, he went off to a famous spa for treatment. This executive believed he had overworked himself into a nervous breakdown, but it would be more accurate to say he had wished himself into it. But having plenty of money, he could afford the nervous breakdown.

While he was having his breakdown, his young staff got into trouble. He was implored to return to the firm to "get it out of a hole." He became keenly interested in the problems which had accumulated, and as a result began to feel much better. Knowing that his stay in his office was only temporary until the situation improved, he did not feel as much pressure as formerly. Indeed, he had quite the time of his life for six months until the problems were straightened out. Then, there being nothing further for him to do, he said, "I'm no longer needed here, so I will return to the hospital and resume my nervous breakdown."

This case reminds me of the poor woman who had experienced one trouble after another, but still preserved her quiet composure. Asked the secret of her imperturbability, she replied, "Well, I just handle each trouble as it comes, and if two troubles come I handle both of them. I have to, you see. There is no other way. Of course, if I were a rich woman I would just have me a nervous breakdown."

I do not mean to minimize the actuality and misery of

tension. I know full well its dangers. Nor do I present enthusiasm as merely a buoyant spirit, a rosy glow, and ebullient effervescence. In its deeper meaning, enthusiasm is a calm and practiced attitude of mind that exercises quiet control.

For years I have known a man with an impressive ability to maintain calm in the midst of commotion and stress. Always in full control of himself, he is a particularly enthusiastic person. Formerly he had been very tense, but he had "practiced his way out of that miserable condition." This emphasis makes sense, for practice is indeed important in the cure of tension. This man made use of a four-word program described as follows: 1. Enthusiastically. 2. Gratefully. 3. Phlegmatically. 4. Philosophically.

He said, "I live enthusiastically. I receive gratefully. I face failures phlegmatically and I take whatever comes philosophically." That four-word formula must have value. It worked for him. Tension ceased to be a problem; enthusiasm and quiet control took over.

DAILY ANTI-TENSION TECHNIQUE

There is another helpful technique which I once wrote out as a "prescription" for a man who had long suffered from tension, and it proved to be effective in his eventual healing. It consists of "healing" statements to voice and to meditate upon daily throughout the week.

MONDAY—
Peace I give unto you . . . Let not your heart be troubled.

TUESDAY—
Thou wilt keep him in perfect peace, whose mind is stayed on thee.

WEDNESDAY—
My presence shall go with thee, and I will give thee rest.

THURSDAY—
Rest in the Lord, and wait patiently for him: fret not thyself.

FRIDAY—
Come unto me, all ye that labour and are heavy laden, and I will give you rest.

SATURDAY—

> *Let the peace of God rule in your heart.*

SUNDAY—

> *He maketh me to lie down in green pastures: he leadeth me beside the still waters. He restoreth my soul.*

The man to whom I gave this suggestion carried the quotations in his wallet until, by repeated use, the Bible verses became imbedded in his consciousness. Presently they induced a peace so satisfying that tension gradually gave way and a fresh zest for life developed. Faith and enthusiasm in depth revamped his thinking and brought about a quiet control that changed his life.

JUST A FINAL WORD

I do not mean to imply that tension is altogether undesirable. It has a proper use as a motivating force. Tension is also designed to key you up to a creative level which is vital to above-average accomplishment. Steel without tension is lacking in quality. Similarly a person without tension is innocuous and flabby. The most important thing is to make tension work for you rather than against you.

Batten and Hudson in their book *Dare to Live Passionately* * quote Dr. James G. Bilkey as saying, "You will never be the person you can be if pressure, tension and discipline are taken out of your life."

Still one can have plenty of relaxed drive without abnormal tension. To attain relaxed power is an important secret of successful living. One man who learned this skill is my old friend John M. Fox, president of the United Fruit Company. Years ago I heard Mr. Fox, who was then merchandising frozen orange juice, tell of his struggle with tension. In a speech before the Rotary Club of New York, John Fox said that enthusiasm had made a great difference in life though he, like many, had to conquer tension to attain it.

"I should like to tell you of an experience I had during the early days of the company," he said. "It happened in

* *Dare to Live Passionately* by J. Batten and L. Hudson, Parker Publishing Co., Inc., 1967.

the winter of 1947. Our problems were seemingly insurmountable. The new 'mousetrap' we had brought to the world had laid a giant egg—nobody was beating a path to our doorstep. Working capital had fallen to a zero level, sales were nonexistent, the frozen food industry generally was on the verge of going broke. As the saying goes, 'When the tide goes out, the rocks begin to show.' Everywhere I looked there were rocks!

"At this point I decided to attend the canners' convention in Atlantic City," John Fox continued. "This was a mistake. My gloom was merely an echo of the gloom I found on all sides. Misery loves company and I found a crowd that year on the boardwalk.

"My stomach began to ache. I worried about the stock we had sold to the public. I worried about the employees we had wheedled away from secure, well-paying jobs. I went to sleep—eventually—at night worrying. I even worried about the sleep I was losing.

"My family lived in Atlantic City so I was staying with them. Besides, it saved hotel expense we could ill afford. One day near the end of the convention, my father asked me if I would like to accompany him to a Rotary Club lunch. I had little stomach for it but I knew he'd feel hurt if I refused.

"My unhappiness deepened when I learned that the guest speaker was a minister of the gospel. I was in no mood for a sermon. The minister was Dr. Norman Vincent Peale. He announced that his subject would be, 'Tension—the Disease That is Destroying the American Businessman.'

"From the first words he uttered I felt as though he were talking only to me. I knew I was the tensest man in the audience. It was a great speech, one that he has given again and again all over this country. His formula for relaxing and putting aside worry I would like to repeat:

"First, you relax physically. This is done by stretching out in bed or in a comfortable chair. Then you methodically and carefully concentrate on relaxing each part of your body. Start with your scalp, then your face, your neck, your shoulders and so on down until you are as loose as a pan of ashes.

"Second, you relax your mind. You recall a pleasant incident in your life—a vacation, your honeymoon, a play, a book, anything that brings back into your mind's eye a pleasant scene.

"Finally, you relax your soul. This for most of us businessmen is a little tougher. But it can be done by renewing your faith in the Lord. You get right with God. You check your fears and worries with Him. He can handle them much better than you can. You do this in prayer. If you know no other prayer, the age-old children's one will do quite well. 'Now I lay me down to sleep. I pray the Lord my soul to keep.'

"The first thing you know you'll be fast asleep. I know because in desperation I tried it out that very night after hearing Dr. Peale tell about it. It worked, for I awoke the next morning refreshed and renewed and convinced we would get out of our jam some way. We did."

Such is the testimony of a very successful businessman who tried my suggested techniques and found that they work.

SEVEN

ENTHUSIASM WORKS MIRACLES IN PROBLEMS

Eleven words can make an amazing difference in your life. Here they are: *Every problem contains within itself the seeds of its own solution.*

This eleven-word formula, a masterpiece of insight and fact, is by Stanley Arnold who is considered by the many business leaders who have employed his problem-solving talents as America's idea man number one.

In fact, Stanley Arnold has built the business of problem-solving into a million-dollar enterprise. Where others see nothing but discouragement and defeat, he finds amazing opportunity that leads to achievement. He discovered and utilizes the fact, unrealized by so many, that every problem has buried within itself an inherent good. But his own classic phrase says it best. *Every problem contains within itself the seeds of its own solution.*

Stanley Arnold has dedicated his entire life to solving problems, his own and others. He does his job by thinking and reflecting. And he learned this skill early in life. In the book *The Executive Breakthrough* * Auren Uris describes Arnold's early beginnings.

"Stanley Arnold, thirteen years old, leaned against a

---

* *The Executive Breakthrough* by Auren Uris, Doubleday & Co., Inc., 1967.

backyard tree and brooded about the fact that he was probably the worst broad jumper in the entire Cleveland school system. 'If I'm so bad at jumping forward,' he thought, 'maybe I could learn to jump backward.' Stanley stood up, hopped back, and tumbled down on the lawn. He tried it again, and this time, didn't stumble. Before long, he was able to jump backward several feet, with even a measure of grace.

"When he told the gym teacher about it, and suggested that the class might have a backward-jumping contest, the man looked at his spindly pupil and said, 'Perhaps; it might be fun.' At the next gym class, the coach announced, 'Now we'll try a standing back jump.' The teacher explained that it was like a regular broad jump, except that the contestants would be measured on the basis of how far back they could go.

"One by one, the class's top athletes took their positions, flung themselves backward, and landed a few inches away, flat on their rumps. When Stan's turn came, the others leaned forward, expecting the usual clownish performance. He bent low, and then unwinding like a coiled spring, flew gracefully in reverse, landing neatly on his feet. Unquestionably, the school had not only a new and exciting event, but the world's first champion backward broad jumper.

"Since that time, Stanley Arnold has jumped on to considerably greater things, invariably creating the same sort of excitement for his clients that he created as a youngster for his schoolmates. Today, he is president of Stanley Arnold & Associates, Inc., an organization whose sole function is to contrive novel ways for companies to increase the sales of their products."

So, always remember Stanley Arnold's great statement: "Every problem contains within itself the seeds of its own solution." And you will have the enthusiasm that works miracles in your problems.

ENTHUSIASM EQUAL TO THE TOUGHEST PROBLEMS

Enthusiasm is no Pollyannish, sweetness and light, bright and fortuitous concept. It is a strong, rugged mental attitude that is hard to achieve, difficult to maintain but powerful—so powerful!

The word enthusiasm from the Greek *entheos* means

God in you, or full of God. So when we claim for enthusiasm the power to work miracles in solving problems we are actually saying that God Himself in you supplies the wisdom, courage, strategy and faith necessary to deal successfully with all difficulties. We need only to discover how to apply efficiency, enthusiasm and right thinking to our problems. And let's start with a really tough one.

I have dealt with several cases, all somewhat similar in nature, of which that of a West Coast woman is an example. While I was on a speaking engagement in that area, a woman telephoned me; she was sorely distressed, for her husband had left her for a twenty-three-year-old woman who ran an expensive cosmetic shop. It seems he had told his wife he was infatuated with this female. As I delved into the problem, it seemed to me that the predatory young woman, who obviously was not uninterested in his money, knew how to get around the fellow. She had asked sweetly for his advice about her affairs. It seemed that the cosmetic business wasn't going too well. The fatherly advisor status had taken on a more romantic nature. So the husband had advised his wife that although he loved her, he just had to follow the insistent call of romance and take himself off with the young beauty. And the wife, like an indulgent mamma, had allowed him to go, telling him tearfully that she would be patiently waiting for his return. "But now what shall I do?" she asked me poignantly. "That sacrificing spirit doesn't seem to work, and I just don't like it at all."

Despite her rather naïve attitude, I became aware that I was dealing with a woman of potential strength and insight, who, for all her efforts to be "modern," was profoundly shaken. "Well, now," I said, "let's apply the technique of creative enthusiasm to this problem."

"Enthusiasm!" she echoed unbelievingly. "How in the world can this possibly be a time and place for enthusiasm?"

"Enthusiasm can release powerful forces and get them working for you. They can rehabilitate your shattered marriage," I replied.

I described the curious wife-mother-lover relationship sometimes existing between a husband and wife; how a man can for a fact actually love his wife and at the same time fall into an infatuation. That he had told her the situation so frankly indicated also that he regarded her less as a wife than as an indulgent mamma who would give him anything he cried for. And when he did not want it any more he could come home to mamma (the wife-mamma) whom he loved. Home to him was understanding affection plus a nice, indulgent forgiveness. In this manner would he find peace of mind and freedom from guilt. But this curious mental mechanism does not take into account the fact that the wife-mamma may also turn out to be a real woman, who wants not a child, but a man. The fact that he could desert his true love for a physical infatuation was considered by her a violation of herself as woman-wife.

"Let's understand the situation," I said to her, "men your husband's age often become infatuated with younger women. It has to do with their fear of getting old. And it is just possible that you are not as aware and as understanding of the physical factors in your own relationship with your husband as you ought to be."

Then I advised the wife to change her attitude. Her husband felt too secure about her. This old security should be shattered. "Give him a big surprise," I advised. "Go off some place where he cannot possibly find you. If he cannot locate his always present, loving mamma, he may become desperate. Stop being the tender forgiving wife, waiting for the wanderer to return. Disappear. Become a wife dropout. Let him find you if he can."

She was loathe to follow this suggestion but finally agreed to the strategy. In fact she said she would hie herself to Japan. "Well," I said, "Japan is a super-way of carrying out this prescription. But if absence makes the heart grow fonder, maybe distance will do the same. And distance often produces perspective. Besides Japan is about the last place he would look for you, isn't it?"

"Maybe," she replied shrewdly. "We have always said if our romance ever declined, we would go back to Japan in cherry blossom time. You see, that is where we met. Our parents were missionaries over there."

Smart girl, I thought. I warned her that we were taking a gamble, but I had a sneaking feeling that it might just work. So I said, "Get going to Japan and settle down there. It may be quite some time before bad little boy wants his mamma."

I urged her meanwhile to reflect upon her own responsibility for her wandering husband's romantic proclivities. Had she grown indifferent after that basic biological function of marriage—the production of children? Was she disinterested in the art of lovemaking? Did she think it silly for two middle-aged people still to be interested in sex? Did she feel their relationship now should be just a lovely companionship? Had she in any sense driven him away?

She admitted this was not the first time he had strayed. "But even though he does these things, he just cannot seem to leave me," she said in bewilderment.

"And you made it tough for him when he did return?" I asked.

"I sure did. I gave him a terrible going over."

"And then," I continued, "in sex relations, he was rather, if not completely, impotent—was he not?"

"Why, yes. But how do you know that?"

"That's easy. In his deep unconscious he was attempting sex relations with a berating, punishing mother figure."

"But," she demanded, "do you mean that I should let him come home from some other girl, and just gush over him in a honey sort of way?"

"Not at all. But for goodness sake, use what God gave you: your femininity. Get yourself up so attractively that you can outsmart any other female. Really pretty yourself up. Get a hair-do at the swankiest shop in town. Deck yourself out in the smartest clothes you can buy. Charge them to him."

OUTSMARTING A GOLD DIGGER

"Look what is on your side," I continued: "love in youth, ties of family, honest-to-goodness marriage and devotion to God. Balance that with what is on the girl's side: clandestine practice, danger of disease perhaps, the fear of disgrace. You've a powerful lot going for you; a lot more than the other woman.

"So take a trip. Do some soul-searching and some real changing. Try to restore the qualities he first fell in love with. You've got what it takes to outsmart that character he has momentarily fallen for. I believe he will come running home to mamma wiser, though certainly poorer. But on his return, don't let him find a mamma whom he doesn't need, but a fascinating woman whom he *does* want. Then bring some spiritual know-how into your lives.

Put some dynamic positive enthusiasm into this project, and I'll wager that you'll be in."

So off to Japan she went. Several months passed. Spring had come round when a man called me on the telephone from California. "Dr. Peale, do you possibly know where my wife has gone? I've just got to find her. I've thought of putting the Missing Persons Bureau on her trail but I found a note saying she is O.K. but is gone for good—that as I left her, so she was leaving me. Someone told me she talked with you. Do you have any idea where she is?" He was truly upset.

"How are you doing with the sweet young thing?"

"Oh, I'm so fed up with her that I've told her to go to hell."

"That's what it always comes back to, isn't it—hell?" I mused.

"It sure does," he said contritely.

"Do you really want a wife or do you want a mamma?" I asked.

"I only want my wife." He really sobbed this time.

"O.K.," I said. "Cherry blossoms is the answer."

"Cherry blossoms?" he repeated mystified. "Oh, cherry blossoms! I believe I get you."

"I advised her to meditate in the Stone Garden of Kyoto, that ancient peaceful Shinto shrine and to try to figure how to become a better wife."

"Good bye," he shouted, "and thanks. Oh, thanks a lot!"

HE GOT HIMSELF A NEW WIFE

Much later I had a long distance call from San Francisco. "A lot you know about women," a man's voice said. "You don't think I found her meditating in the Stone Garden of Kyoto, do you? Do you know where I found her? Well, I'll tell you. I found her, looking ten years younger —a dream of a gal, dancing with some Englishman at the Miyako Hotel. She didn't seem what you call thrilled to see me, but I convinced her that there is nobody in the world for me but her."

"Great," I replied. "You sure know women."

I never did tell him that I cabled her that he was on his way to Japan. There is more than one way to solve a problem. But one day I "remarried" them at the altar of the church in a symbolic renewal of vows. There was now genuine dedication and love between those two.

Enthusiasm, prayer, strategy will solve any problem, however tough. In fact, they just don't make problems tough enough for that powerful combination. Enthusiasm can work miracles in problems.

THE PHILOSOPHY OF ENTHUSIASM

Enthusiasm to perform such miracles presupposes a sound and workable philosophy. It is a fact, I believe, that a problem is widely considered rather a bad thing, something to be avoided if at all possible. It would seem that most persons take a dim view of a problem. But actually is a problem a bad thing, or on the contrary, might it not be a very good thing?

Let me answer that question by telling of an incident. On Fifth Avenue in New York City I saw approaching me a friend by the name of George. From George's disconsolate and melancholy demeanor it was evident to me that he was not filled to overflowing with the ecstasy and exuberance of human existence. His obvious depression aroused my sympathy and so I asked, "How are you, George?"

This was only a routine inquiry but it represented an error on my part. George took it seriously. For fifteen minutes he enlightened me in detail on how badly he felt. And the more he talked, the worse I felt. "But, George," I finally asked, "what seems to be the trouble? I would like to help you if I can."

"Oh," he replied, "it's problems. Life is nothing but problems. I've had it. I'm fed up with problems." George became so exercised about the matter that he quite forgot to whom he was talking and began to castigate his problems, using in the vitriolic process a great many theological terms. I knew what he meant. He had the power to communicate.

"What is it that I can do for you, George?" I asked.

"Get me free of these problems, that's what I want. Tell you what. Get me free and I will give you a thousand dollar donation for your work."

Well, I am never one to turn down such an offer. I

meditated and cogitated and came up with a solution which I thought possessed merit. But apparently George did not go for it. I have yet to receive the aforementioned one thousand dollars.

"So, you want to be completely free of problems, do you, George?" I asked.

"You said it!" he fervently replied.

"All right, here is how it can be done. The other day I was in a certain place on professional business, if I may thus characterize it, and was told that there were in that place over one hundred thousand people, and not a single one had a problem."

The first indication of enthusiasm lighted up his eyes and suffused his countenance. "Boy, that's for me. Lead me to this place."

"O.K., you asked for it," I replied, "but I doubt you will like it. It's Woodlawn Cemetery."

And of course no one in that or any other cemetery has a problem. For them "life's fitful fever" is over; "they rest from their labors." They have no problems.

Problems constitute a sign of life. Perhaps the more problems you have, the more alive you are. The man who, let us say, has ten good man-sized problems is twice as alive as the apathetic character who has only five problems. And if you have no problems at all, I warn you, you are in great jeopardy. You are on the way out. The best procedure might be to pray to the Lord saying, "Don't you trust me any more, Lord? Please give me some problems."

A new in-depth philosophy of the good values inherent in problems should be accentuated. Problems are treated these days as inherently evil. In the social services, a genial idea has gained currency that human well-being can be served only by relieving people of all problems. Overcoming injustice, relieving poverty, the promoting of better housing—these are extremely valid and important, but so also is the basic American concept that people grow strong and create better conditions by facing problems and solving them.

I was walking on Nob Hill in San Francisco when I met an intellectual. Now how did I know he was an intellectual? He told me so. Had he not done so, I would not have suspected. For the valid intellectual I have the profoundest respect, but the fake intellectual is something else again. This character was definitely in the latter category.

One clearly evident characteristic of the pseudo-intellectual was his so-called "profoundly concerned" look. But, being a simple soul, I appraised it as a sour look. Nowadays this sour look is an inevitable concomitant of a sobersides type upon whom there seems to rest a heavily weighted "concern" for the whole world. One is not really "in" unless he goes about mouthing traditional sociological jargon and wearing upon his face the concerned-sour look.

What a switch from the old days! Formerly this sour look was on the visages of those who wished to give the impression of piety. They, like their modern intellectual counterparts, were the pretentious pious of those earlier times.

How well I recall as a boy sitting in church beside my mother. Nearby sat old "Brother Jones," a leading deacon and ostensibly a pillar of the church. This character always had a sad expression on his face. I used to whisper to my mother, "Why does Brother Jones have that sour look?"

"That is not sour. It's a pious look," my mother replied. My mother seemed to equate a pious look with saintliness. This did not impress me, for I and the kids around town knew a few things about Brother Jones that my mother did not. We boys had him realistically sized up.

But nowadays the genuine exponent of bona fide Christianity wears a happy look. And why not? He has been released from conflicts and misery. He has experienced victories. Having discovered that they possess within themselves the power to handle problems, creative Christians long ago abandoned the sour look which has become currently the hallmark of the modern pretentious intellectual.

A second characteristic of this curious fellow on Nob Hill was the outlandish manner in which he was dressed. It is odd that not a few beatniks seem to equate individuality with alienation from the bathtub.

In Geneva, Switzerland, my wife and I were sitting in the lobby of a hotel when a young crowd arrived for a fashion show. Personally I couldn't care less for such a show, but my wife insisted on watching. However, it didn't take long for her to be as revolted as I by the utterly unattractive dresses worn by the models and by the crowd in attendance. I could have endured it, however, had there been just one pretty girl. But all had successfully eliminated every whit of charm and beauty so as to equate with the ugliness of the costumes. And the boys were even less attractive. "I've had it," I said to my wife. "Let's get out and breathe some fresh air." And this, dear friends, was in the most luxurious hotel of an international city in Europe.

NOT A HAIR ON HIS CHEST AND NOT A POSITIVE THOUGHT IN HIS HEAD

Well, to return to our friend on the street in San Francisco, he wore a black shirt of good quality, obviously costly. His shirt was open to the third button—no jacket or necktie, naturally, and no undershirt, the effect intending to reveal a manly chest. But the chest looked rather peaked to me; there wasn't a hair on it. The slacks revealed no familiarity with a pressing iron, and the white shoes, also of good quality, had been deliberately beat up, from which I concluded he was a beatnik who probably lived in a garage and spouted existentialist glumness, taking a dim view of the world in general.

Well this fellow fixed his sour-concerned look on me and said, "I'm glad to meet you." I asked the Lord to forgive me and told him I too was glad to meet him. He said, "You're that bright, happy Pollyannish individual who runs around the country prattling about Positive Thinking, aren't you?"

"Well," I replied, "since you have propounded this inquiry in your urbane, academic and scholarly manner, let us carefully consider the implications you have so meticulously raised." I can throw the jargon around also when necessary. Continuing, I said, "I do run around the country, and I do talk about Positive Thinking, which is not bright-happy nor Pollyannish, as you indicate. Perhaps a definition of a positive thinker might provide you with some enlightenment. A positive thinker is a tough, rugged person who sees every difficulty and faces all facts realistically. But he is not licked by what he sees. He practices the philosophy of optimism which holds that the good in life outbalances the evil thereof, and he believes that in every difficulty there is inherent good which he intends to find." I added, perhaps more maliciously than proper, "A person must be somewhat of a man to be a positive thinker, which makes it difficult for some people I might mention."

But then, thinking he really had me, he asked, "But don't you know that the world is full of trouble and problems?"

"You don't say so!" I exclaimed. "Do you think I was born yesterday? Why, son, in my business we know more about troubles and problems in five minutes than you will know in five years. And there is a further basic difference between us. Despite all the difficulty of this world, we aren't licked by it—as you are. For we know that difficulty contains all kinds of creative possibilities."

I came up with a comeback. Most of my comebacks come to my mind long after they are needed. But this one emerged right out of the subconscious, and I said, "Certainly the world is full of trouble and problems, but the world is also full of the overcoming of trouble and the solving of problems." This baffled him; he went down the street shaking his head. I could hear it rattle all the way down the block.

STRUGGLE IS PART OF NATURE

Of course the world is full of trouble, deep, dark, grievous trouble. The world is full of problems, too, hard knotty problems. It always will be so. If any politician or preacher tells you that all problems are going to be eliminated from this world through some panacea, do not fall for it. The constitution of the universe does not support it. The world is made on the basis of struggle; and struggle is inevitably attended by difficulty, often by pain plus hardship.

The Bible, the writers of which had seen a lot of life and evolved an in-depth philosophy of human existence, says, "Man is born unto trouble, as the sparks fly upward." (Job 5:7) And again, "In the world ye shall have tribulation." (St. John 16:33) But the Bible also says, "Be of good cheer; I have overcome the world" (St. John 16:33), meaning through faith in Christ we, too, can overcome all that the world throws at us. Religion does not blithely promise some sort of no-trouble, no-problem, no-poverty world; but rather a spirit, a power, an enthusiasm that endows every one with the ability to overcome any and all of it. Out of struggle we produce better conditions.

But as to trouble and problems you can count on them all your life.

A psychiatrist has said, "The chief duty of a human being is to endure life." That is a fact. There are certain things in life that must be endured. There are inevitabilities from which there is no escape and for which there are no alternatives. But if the psychiatrist's appraisal was the whole story, life would be grim and bleak indeed. A better statement of the matter is, I believe, that the chief duty of a human being is not merely to endure life, but to master it. So, a sound philosophy is important in order to deal effectively with problems.

Enthusiasm helps to work miracles in problems by helping us master them in thought and practice. Enthusiasm is an attitude of mind, and mental attitude in a difficult situation is the important factor in its solution. In a public speech, I made the statement that attitudes are more important than facts. A man who heard this remark had it made up on a laminated board suitable for hanging on an office wall. He sent one to me. This man said it had made him aware that he was being defeated not by hard facts, but by taking a defeated and negative attitude toward those facts. Enthusiasm changes the mental outlook of fearing facts to the solid belief that there is an answer.

One man looking at a tough problem says glumly, "There are the facts. There is nothing I can do but accept them." So the facts have him defeated. Another man, blessed with enthusiasm, looks at the same facts. "Sure, those are the facts all right, and they are indeed tough. But I never yet saw a set of facts to which there was not a solution. Perhaps some facts cannot be changed, but maybe I can by-pass or weave them into a new pattern or readjust my strategy. If necessary I can live with them and ultimately use them to advantage." That man's attitude brings the magic of creative believing into play. That in turn stimulates hitherto unused and unsuspected ingenuity.

If you question the practicality of this principle, let me tell you of a man I met at a convention at which I was a speaker. He remarked, "Wish I could get hold of that magic of believing you were talking about at the convention session this morning."

"Figure out a method of your own for practicing the magic of believing," I suggested. "You will find that it works."

He really did figure out a method, one that worked very well indeed.

THE MAGIC OF BELIEVING

Like many executives, he had on his desk a receptacle for incoming mail and other papers, and a second container for outgoing mail and papers. Here is what he did. He added a third receptacle labeled, "With God All Things Are Possible." (Matthew 19:26) In it he placed and let rest all matters for which he did not yet have answers; and problems for which no solution had been determined. To use his own phrase, he held these matters in "prayerful thinking. I surround the matters in that box with the magic of believing and the results are amazing." So reported a highly respected executive who tested out in actual practice the principle that faith and enthusiasm work miracles.

This man's experience demonstrates still another principle, one that first came to my attention in a book by a friend, the late Albert E. Cliffe, an outstanding Canadian food chemist. His book called *Let Go and Let God* * is a simple, direct-style chemist's formula type of book, one which makes sense and is full of workable ideas. "As a chemist," Cliffe writes, "I have faith in science and I can prove it every day. I am no theologian and have no desire to study theology in any university. I simply believe that God is my Father, and I am His son, and that my mind is part of His divine mind—and by this magic of believing I can be in tune with that tremendous mind of His at any time I choose, and by so doing and by so believing I can gain the answer to any problem which I have to face."

Dr. Cliffe early in his career faced an acute health problem, indeed was given up to die. In his hospital bed he read the Bible text, "All things are possible to him that believeth." (Mark 9:23) Sick as he was, he felt this was his message of hope. So he reached out mentally for healing, believing implicitly in this promise. "I let go and let God; and God healed me," he said simply. This he believed to be the explanation of his restoration to health. He said further, "What you get out of religion is entirely up to

* *Let Go and Let God* by Albert E. Cliffe, Prentice-Hall, Inc., 1951.

you. You can make your faith a super-atomic dynamo, or a routine affair without progress. You can be healed and your healing can start at any time, regardless of how serious your condition may appear to be, if you will let go your fears and give God His rightful place in your life."

Al Cliffe had an enormous and undiluted enthusiasm for faith and to my personal knowledge stimulated many healings. He told me that in his moment of deepest sickness when the life force was at lowest ebb, he felt a warm glow of assurance and with it a steady inflow of healing power.

As a result, this scientist spent his subsequent life enthusiastically urging people to let go and let God. Actually, the Bible—textbook for believing—is a book of power techniques and power formulas. Jesus said, "Ye shall receive power . . ." (Acts 1:8) It is a power promise and a power delivery to those who believe and practice, who let go and let God. Such believers discover to their amazement that enthusiasm can indeed work miracles in problems.

I have observed that, generally speaking, men who enjoy problems do better in solving them. I gave a talk at the twenty-fifth anniversary of a prominent industrialist. About two thousand people attended the dinner honoring him on a quarter-century of leadership during which his company achieved remarkable growth. Seated together on the dais, I asked him, "What has been your greatest satisfaction in your quarter-century as head of this organization?" I was certain that he would refer to the company's growth and development. Instead he answered, "It's the fun I've had with problems. And believe me, some have been plenty tough. When you have no more problems, that is the time to watch out, for enthusiasm will go next and then you will go. That's why I'm suspicious of a big dinner like this. It could give the impression we've licked all our problems, and when that happens I'll be through. And I don't want to be through. Not me. I like working with problems too well."

SELF-MOTIVATORS AS PROBLEM SOLVERS

My friend, W. Clement Stone, president of the Combined Insurance Company of America, with whom I am proud to be associated at the American Foundation of Religion & Psychiatry, has more real, genuine enthusiasm than any man I know. Furthermore, it is of the kind that never takes defeat for an answer. I once asked him: "What is the secret of your enthusiasm, as it applies to problems, either business or personal?" And this is what he told me:

"As you know, the emotions are not always immediately subject to reason, but they are always immediately subject to action (mental or physical). Furthermore, repetition of the same thought or physical action develops into a habit which, repeated frequently enough, becomes an automatic reflex.

"And that's why I use self-motivators. A self-motivator is an affirmation . . . self-command . . . platitude . . . or any symbol that you deliberately use as self-suggestion to move yourself to desirable action. You merely repeat a verbal self-motivator fifty times in the morning . . . fifty times at night . . . for a week or ten days, to imprint the words indelibly in your memory. But you do so with the *deliberate purpose of getting into action* when the self-motivator flashes from your subconscious to your conscious in time of need.

"When I have a problem, because I have prepared myself, one or more self-motivators will automatically flash from my subconscious to my conscious mind, such as:

(Serious personal problem) *God is always a good God!*

(Business problem) *You have a problem . . . that's good!*

Within every adversity there is a seed of an equivalent or greater benefit.

What the mind can conceive and believe, the mind can achieve.

Find one good idea that will work and . . . work that one good idea!

Do it now!

To be enthusiastic . . . ACT . . . enthusiastically!

"There is very little difference in how I meet business or personal problems. But, there *is* a difference. If a personal problem involves deep emotions, I always use man's greatest power *immediately* . . . the power of prayer. In solving business problems, I will also pray for guidance, but not necessarily immediately."

HE COULD TAKE ANY PROBLEM APART AND PUT
IT TOGETHER RIGHT

As a young man, I had close association with a remarkable human being. His name was Harlowe B. Andrews of Syracuse, New York. Andrews Brothers, wholesale grocers, was a famous upstate concern. Harlowe Andrews is credited with operating the first "supermarket" in the United States, bringing in perishable goods from California by fast, refrigerated express and having them on sale in his Salina Street store within four days. Some say he invented the first dishwasher, perfecting a workable machine that was later sold to a big company. He was very religious, and having made a fortune, retired to go into full-time religious work—leaving the conduct of the business to a brother who promptly lost the fortune. Brother Andrews, as he was called, returned to the business, made another fortune, this time retiring the brother and keeping that fortune.

A Syracuse banker told me he had never known any man with such a remarkable faculty for making money. To use the banker's graphic description, "All Brother Andrews needs do is to extend his fingers and by some special magnetism money springs to him." I was impressed. I hung around with Brother Andrews for a long time, but never acquired the gift.

Despite his religious characteristics, Brother Andrews had sporty tendencies. Long before the advent of motor cars, he raced a team of horses down James Street in summer and over frozen Onondaga Lake in winter. When motor cars came in, he was rated a local speed demon.

He had a remarkable sense of humor coupled with sharp, keen insight. Before Ruth and I announced our engagement—indeed, before we were quite aware of the possibility—I took her to visit Brother Andrews at his farm. Walking in his garden he picked a pea pod, opened it and pointing at two peas snuggled inside, remarked not too subtly, "You see, everything is designed in pairs." Whereupon he chuckled to his great enjoyment, my embarrassment, and Ruth's amusement.

The old man had so much downright native wisdom, penetrating insight and sharp intuition, plus the ability to think creatively, that he became a constant source of guidance for me. And I never knew a man who enjoyed problems as he did. He actually became excited by them; the knottier the problem, the more it interested him. He even thought that the big social problems were positively wonderful. His explanation of enthusiasm for problems troubling the world was a stimulating one. "Always be glad when there is trouble on the earth," Brother Andrews explained, "for it means there is movement in heaven; and this indicates great things are about to happen." Taken literally, that could mean things are really looking up for mankind.

Well, I had a problem that had me stumped. It seemed overwhelming and I wrestled with it for days. Finally I took it to Brother Andrews. "I've really got a problem, a terribly tough one," I announced glumly.

"Congratulations," he cried. "That's great. Always be glad when you've got a big, tough problem. That means things are happening, that you're on the move." This reaction astonished me, for I'm frank to say that I had not even thought of viewing the matter in the manner he indicated.

"Don't you know," he said with a chuckle, "that God has a sense of humor? God likes to play hiding games. When He wants to give you some big wonderful value, do you know what He does? He hides it in a big tough problem. Then He hands you that problem and says, 'Let me see you find that value I've hidden there.' And He watches with interest, pulling for you all the time. When finally you find that wonderful value, is He happy? He sure is.

"Tell me about it, son," he said. "Let's get this problem of yours right out here on the table and take a good look at it."

Thus urged, I really poured it out, enumerating one tough, hard situation after another, followed by a marshaling of negatives such as you never heard. Finally I ran down. "Well, that's about it, I guess. Some problem, isn't it?"

He got up from his chair and walked around the table making motions with his hands like heaping up an imaginary pile. "I'm heaping up this big problem of yours, and boy, it's a beauty." His eyes shone.

"Now, look, son," (he was always calling me son, and that suited me all right for he was like a father) "the first thing is to pray about it. What do our little minds know about it anyway? So let's ask God's guidance." After a few minutes, he said, "Thanks, Lord. Amen."

"Now, son," he said, "God is working with us, so let's start thinking. Get that sad look off your face. Get enthusiastic, for something big and wonderful is about to happen."

Once again he started walking around the table, poking his right forefinger at that heaped up problem. Brother Andrews had arthritis in his fingers, and a knob on the first joint made his index finger crooked. But he could point straighter with that crooked finger than anybody I've known with a perfectly straight finger.

He stopped and acted as if he had his finger in a hole in the problem. He worried it like a dog with a bone. He started to chuckle, "Ha, ha, son, come around here. What did I tell you? Every problem has a soft spot." Then he began to take the problem apart and reconstruct it with a skill and an understanding the like of which I never saw before or since. "Boy, what an opportunity you've got. The only question is whether you can handle it. But you can, because God will help you. And I will too if you need me."

With God and Brother Andrews, how could I miss?

I drove home through a starlit, moon-drenched night thrilled to my fingertips, having learned one of the greatest lessons of life, that enthusiasm works miracles with problems. Try eight sure-fire guidelines and see for yourself:

First: Don't panic. Keep calm. Use your head. You'll need all your wits.

Second: Don't be overwhelmed by your problem. Don't get dramatic about it. Just tell yourself confidently, "God and I can handle it."

Third: Practice de-confusion. A problem generally becomes surrounded by confusion. So de-confuse it. Take a paper and pencil and write down every element of the problem.

Fourth: Skip the post-mortems. Don't say, "Why did I

do that? Why didn't I do this?" Take the problem from where you now are.

Fifth: Look for a solution, not for the whole problem but for the next step. One step leads to another and so on to the complete solution. So be content with tackling the next step.

Sixth: Practice creative listening.

A friend of mine, the president of a big company, when faced with a tough problem would call his dog and go into the woods. He said his dog had more understanding than a lot of people. He would sit on a stump, the dog at his feet looking up at him. Then he would describe the problem out loud to the dog. Of a sudden he would hear—not by the outer ear but by the deep inner ear—the answer. He and the dog would then go home. You don't have to have a dog or go into the woods to practice creative listening.

Seventh: Always ask yourself what is the right thing to do in a given situation. If what you do isn't the right thing, then it is the wrong thing. Nothing wrong ever turned out right. So do the right thing and you'll come out right.

Eighth: Keep praying. Keep thinking. Keep believing. And keep enthusiasm going, for it works miracles in problems.

EIGHT

ENTHUSIASM—POWERFUL MOTIVATION THAT MAKES THINGS HAPPEN

This chapter is filled with exciting human stories about people whose dynamic enthusiasm acted with such powerful thrust that the most amazing events happened to them. The more I meet such individuals or am told of them, the more excited I become. For there is an amazing potential in human beings to grow taller and bigger than they are and to do much more with life than they ever believed possible. It was this tremendous realization that activated me to write *Enthusiasm Makes the Difference* for enthusiasm has made such an astonishing difference in the lives of so many people that I simply had to tell about as many of them as could be crammed into a book of reasonable size.

To begin with, here is one of the great human stories that I have encountered in a lifetime of collecting narratives of people who have done tremendous jobs with their lives. This is another thrilling American story, one of those deeply human episodes that warms your heart and fires your mind with wonder at life's limitless possibilities.

Mary B. Crowe was one of nine children. Her father worked in a steel mill in Ohio and never earned more than fifty dollars a week. But on this meager income he raised a large family.

It was Mary's job to wash her father's grimy overalls every day, and were they dirty! In those days, there were none of those magic detergents you see demonstrated on television. She really had to toil to get them clean. Then an amazing thing happened, and it took place in her thoughts, the place where all great things originate. Something that she had never heard of got to working in her mind. It was positive thinking and the motivation of the positive follow-through. It was the magic of the inspired mental image. As she sloshed overalls in that sudsy water, a breathtaking image flashed up in her mind. College! She saw herself in a cap and gown coming to the platform before a large crowd of people to accept her diploma, together with a handshake from the college president. Mary Crowe with a college degree? But how silly can you get? No money, no help, no pull, no chance at all. No member of her family had ever gone to college. It was inconceivable. Forget it! But she couldn't forget, for a creative image had come; enthusiasm had been born, and with it the kind of motivation that makes things happen.

So she kept on washing overalls, and meanwhile, she went to high school. Came commencement day and Mary graduated with honors. The parish priest called her into his office and pulled out an envelope from his desk, one which he had held there for four years. It contained a scholarship to St. Mary's of the Springs College. He had been waiting for someone to earn this coveted scholarship. He had been watching Mary's progress. The image was working—a scholarship for a girl who had never heard of St. Mary's of the Springs College, but who had imaged, dreamed, worked, and practiced positive thinking and studied diligently, while washing the inevitable overalls.

Enthusiastically she went to college; she worked as a waitress in the country club, as a housemaid, as a cook, anything to get the funds to prepare for the life to which her faith and enthusiasm were motivating her. But things got very rough. In her senior year, it seemed as though she would have to quit college. But a member of the country club was so impressed by the spirit and ability of this girl that he lent her $300 on a $1,000 policy with a cash value of $20, and that pulled her through to graduation, again with honors.

That loan did something more; it interested Mary

Crowe in life insurance. Her career had been saved by life insurance. Could it not do miracles for others also? She took a course in insurance. She went to an insurance office and asked for work as an agent. But the manager snorted, "What do you know about life insurance, or about selling? You don't know anyone. Besides," and this was the clincher, "you're a woman. The answer is no!" This man turned her down time after time as she continued to ask for a chance. But she sat in his office daily until finally in desperation and to rid himself of her, he snapped, "O.K., here's a rate book and a desk, but no drawing account and no help. Starve yourself to death if you want to." She failed to oblige, and a few days later came in with her first policy sale. As the years passed she made the Million Dollar Round Table. Twenty-five years after she was grudgingly hired, her associates gathered at a dinner honoring her as a distinguished insurance saleswoman. Her formula of success? Well, it was a process of imaging, praying, having faith and positive thinking, plus enthusiasm and motivation. Taken together, the power-packed formula made things happen. Mary Crowe demonstrated that enthusiasm is a powerful force, backed by prayer and faith, that motivates top job performance, overcomes every potential defeat and makes big things happen. Since it was not in her plan to take defeat, she became a winner.

"You *can* change your thinking and thereby change your life," says Mary Crowe. "You can do this by deliberately imaging into your subconscious good ideas, positive images, instead of negative ones. You are constantly in a state of *becoming*. And *you do become what you think!* This philosophy does not mean, of course," says Mary, "that your life will be without problems. What it means is that feeling the presence of God within you and about you, you will be able to meet any problem that life presents, full of confidence that God will give you the courage and the strength to face it, and that He is standing ready to help you solve it. You need only ask—and believe!"

Mary Crowe's stimulating story proves once again that enthusiasm is the powerful motivation that makes things happen. And, of course, if this can happen to one person, it can happen to others; it can even happen to you.

GOOD LOSERS BECOME STEADY LOSERS

The process of creative imaging is also part of the successful philosophy of one of our great athletes.

"How do you become a successful quarterback in professional football?" was asked of Fran Tarkenton, star quarterback of the New York Giants.

"Carry the image of victory in your heart," Fran quickly replied. "In our society of today," the famous football star says, "we seem to go to extremes. For a while there was an overwhelming emphasis on the importance of winning. It went all the way down to the kiddie leagues. Then a reaction set in. 'We're not being realistic,' intelligent parents would say. 'Our children must learn how to lose, for isn't defeat a part of life?' Quite true," says Fran Tarkenton. "Winning can be overstressed. We need to know how to lose gracefully. But then the extreme comes. Kids who think too much about being good losers forget that the purpose of sports, and life too, is to succeed at what they are doing. You show me a good loser, and I will show you a steady loser."

The famous quarterback tells how he went into a playing slump, one so discouraging that he considered quitting the game altogether. But "still down in the deep reaches of my heart I carried the image of the first big victory I'd had. And I did not give up on the idea that I could recapture that success. Many games later I did. But without this image of victory to sustain me over so many defeats, I could well have quit on myself."

This demonstration of steady, deep-rooted enthusiasm as a powerful motivation that makes things happen, and happen well, brings to mind a significant point by Bernard Haldane, the success motivation teacher. "Learn from your successes, rather than from your failures," he counsels. This is, of course, a switch from the usual advice. A failure can show how not to do something. But who wants to know how not to do it, when it is more important to know how to do it right and good? So when you do it right, and succeed at what you are doing, it is smart to success-educate yourself. Ask yourself, "Now just how did I do that so well?" Then try to repeat the next time. Let us say you make a terrific golf shot. Don't blithely move on, thinking, "Boy, what a shot!" Ask yourself meticulously just how you executed that shot. Then deliberately try to repeat it.

You can learn from your failures. Edison is said to have remarked after many failures to make an incandescent bulb, "Well, that adds up to over five thousand ways how not to do it." But finally when he succeeded, he made other bulbs on the basis of what he learned from that success. So be a good loser, but not so good that you work losing into a virtue. Get enthusiasm for winning so deeply imbedded in your consciousness that it becomes a powerful urge for making things happen right.

In his fascinating book, *The American Diamond,* a classic on the great American game, Branch Rickey selects his own list of baseball immortals, the two outstanding being Ty Cobb and Honus Wagner. Rickey calls Cobb "the choice of that one player for the one game that had to be won," meaning, of course, that Ty Cobb was first, last and always a competitor. He had only one object—to win. "He had an uncontrollable urge to excel. His genius removed him from all courtesies of sportsmanship when in strife or contest. In physical struggle, he was a competitive paranoiac. In rivalry on or off the field his genius was a do-or-die personal effort to beat someone or something. Cobb would have been the only Greek necessary at Thermopylae."

Rickey declares that Cobb's competitive spirit, his unbounded enthusiasm for winning made him one of the most scientific players the game ever produced. "Cobb did not have a great arm, but accuracy and elevation of the throw and right rotation of the ball were his habitual possessions. He never took a double step on his throw from the outfield. He threw now, right now, when he caught the ball. 'The runner is moving at full speed and will run fifteen feet while I am stepping five feet.' He was precisely scientific in every move. No one ever heard of a base runner taking chances on Cobb's arm—no one.

"He practiced almost by the clock," continued Rickey. "In throwing from the outfield, his objective was to have the ball skip when it hit the ground on its first contact— not bounce with retarded speed. That meant definite control of the spin and proper trajectory. Did anyone ever hear of a baseball player who voluntarily and alone would impose upon himself arduous practice of this sort? I never did."

Of course, Cobb had vast enthusiasm and a restless, ceaseless motivation to make the greatest possible things happen in baseball, which was his life. That attitude made him the one and only Ty Cobb, the "Georgia peach," the greatest of them all.

Rickey himself said, "The game of baseball has given me a life of joy. I would not have exchanged it for any other." But Branch Rickey did not become the greatest baseball man of all time without a burning enthusiasm. This was his motivation that made great things occur in his life.

I once asked, "Branch, what is the greatest experience you have had in your fifty years of baseball?"

He pulled down those big beetle brows. "I don't know," he snapped. "I haven't had it yet." Enthusiasm—that's what makes great men who make great things happen.

PUT UP A REAL FIGHT—ENTHUSIASM WILL GO FOR YOU

Get the good old tough competitive spirit going. Rugged enthusiasm will motivate you to put up a real fight in life. Human beings have in them by nature the creative instinct, the desire to excel. To deny this is actual suicide of personality. One of the basic statements made in American history, one that will forever hold a high spot in Americana, was made by the sweet but tough-minded mother of Abraham Lincoln. In the poverty and hardship of the western wilderness, she said to the gangling boy in whom she instinctively sensed a strange greatness, "Abe, be somebody."

But how times have changed. "Be nobody" seems to be the concept of the far-out-left-wing of our time. But the be-nobody concept won't last since it is a false notion running counter to human nature. Even as a seed put in the ground naturally grows up toward the sun, so does a human being in the essence of his nature want to move up —always up. So this book is definitely, deliberately, unashamedly designed to cater to people who want to get somewhere, and to stimulate and motivate people to be winners, not losers; in other words, to be somebody and stop deluding themselves that it's so nice to be nothing.

Life is a struggle, a fight, no matter how much emphasis is put on reducing the harsh, hard elements. To lift burdens off the backs of humans, or at least to ease them; to improve the lot of all mankind; to wipe out ghettos and slums; to overcome injustice; and to improve race relations —these are important objectives. But even when all these are accomplished, life will still not be one grand, sweet song, one continual happy party.

Therefore, whoever wants to be somebody and have good things happen had better figure on the element of struggle in his life program. And if he has enthusiasm, he will possess the powerful motivation that will help him "fight the good fight" in order to make those things happen.

It would be highly unfortunate if the youth of our affluent society were ever to forget the plain downright courage that went into the making of this country. This nation was created by a breed of people who practiced what I call the five Gs—grit, gumption, guts, grace and God. It can be maintained only by the same kind of people.

Donna Reed, writing in *Guideposts,* gives a heart-moving vignette of people whose enthusiasm and fight against every difficulty helped to shape the prosperous land we have today.

"Sitting in the comfort of our lovely Beverly Hills home, I began to talk about how I was one of four children and how we lived on a farm near Denison, Iowa.

"My family on both sides had pioneered in that state before I was born. As children all of us had chores to perform. I could and did milk the cows and drive the tractor, bring in water from the pump and coal and wood for the stove; to this day I can bake my own bread. The most obvious difference between my childhood and our children's is not that I lived on a farm, but that back in Iowa during the terrible pressure of the Depression years we were quite poor.

"I doubt that any people in America suffered more than some of the Midwestern farmers of the early 30's. These people, our friends and neighbors, were struck with a series of Job-like afflictions. Times were bad everywhere, of course, and there was little money, but on top of this came the drought that withered crops and parched the earth only to be followed by the wind that swept the dry topsoil into great, dark choking dust storms. Family after family loaded their belongings into rickety automobiles and left. . . .

"Poverty, need, these are awful things to have happen to you, but worse, I think, to watch in others. I remember the sounds of our animals crying for food and water. I remember how a little girl from a nearby farm came to say that she would not be playing with me any more because her family was going away. She didn't know where they were going; they were simply leaving, giving up.

"When I think back to those harsh days, I think mainly in terms of my parents, and the anguish I felt inside as I saw them up early and late to bed, day after day, laboring hard with no returns. As children we had few toys and I always yearned for a bicycle which I never got, but I can't recall these things as having been very important to me when I knew so well the inescapable realities of our situation. We might have left the farm, too, if it had not been for Dad.

"His name is William Mullenger and he is a stubborn man. He would not give up. One by one we had to sell our livestock. One by one our neighbors deserted their farms and each time my father would say to us calmly but with undeniable vigor shored up by his faith:

" 'It will not always be this way.'

"I used to wonder how Dad could be so sure when so many others were not. And then, on Sundays, I'd get a glimpse of the answer. On Sundays, Dad would pile Mom and the four kids into that old car we drove for 15 years and we'd rattle to the Methodist Church in Denison. You could get strength just from sitting next to Dad in church. When the minister would read from the Bible, Dad would lean forward a little, as though this especially he had to hear. Watching his face, we children could see that the ancient words were food to his spirit, strength to get him through one more week.

"Our minister used to read a lot from those books of the Bible that rang with hope. Only recently, I searched through the Bible to see if I couldn't find some of the familiar passages and there, in Isaiah, I came across some verses which brought back the whole experience of parched farms and poverty as clearly as though I were there again, sitting in the pew next to Dad. Just listen to these words:　·

" 'When the poor and needy seek water, and there is

none, and their tongue faileth for thirst, I the Lord will hear them . . . I will make the wilderness a pool of water, and the dry land springs of water.' (Isaiah 41:17-18)

"Dad was a family man, a real family man. 'If there is family strength,' he used to say, 'that old Depression's not going to get us.' And the Depression did pass and it did not get us."

This father had the faith and determination that made things happen. He made good things happen because he had in-depth enthusiasm for something basic, and he possessed motivation, incentive to action, and perseverance. And moreover, he had those good old five Gs going for him—grit, gumption, guts, grace, and God. It's pretty hard to turn out a loser if you stay with that combination.

What a tremendous theme, the dynamic fact that enthusiasm, when lodged deeply in the human mind, becomes a powerful activating factor that makes great events take place, causes amazing things to happen. Believers, positive thinkers, enthusiasts—these people do big things.

ONE OF THE WORLD'S
GREATEST POSITIVE THINKERS

Let us take, for example, one of the world's greatest positive thinkers and practitioners of enthusiasm. It was not in America, traditional home of positive thinkers and enthusiasts, that I met this man, but rather in the wilderness of Judea, where long ago John the Baptist preached. His name was Musa Alami, and he made the desert to blossom as the rose—a desert which in all the history of the world had never blossomed heretofore. He succeeded because he believed that he could, and kept at it until he did, which, of course, is the way you succeed at anything.

Musa, a young Arab, was educated at Cambridge and came back to Palestine where he became a well-to-do man; that is, by Middle Eastern standards. Then in the political turmoil he lost everything, including his home.

He went beyond Jordan to the edge of Jericho. Stretching away on either side was the great, bleak, arid desert of the Jordan Valley, the lowest spot on earth—1,290 feet below sea level. In the far distance to the left, shimmering in the hot haze, loomed the mountains of Judea, and to the right, the Mountains of Moab.

With the exception of a few oases, nothing had ever been cultivated in this hot and weary land and all the experts said that no crop could be raised, for how could you bring in water? To dam the Jordan River for irrigation was too expensive and besides, there was no friendly power to finance such a project.

"What about underground water?" asked Musa Alami. Long and loud they laughed. Who ever heard of such a thing? There was no water under that hot, dry desert. That sandy waste of parched earth had lain there since the beginning of time. And having been covered ages ago by Dead Sea water, the sand was full of salt, which further added to its aridity.

Musa, meditating, saw the shimmering surface of the Dead Sea nearby and agreed that the saltiness of the earth was indeed a problem. But what were problems for but to be solved? God, so he reasoned, had made it a good earth even here and all that was necessary was to bring life-giving water to it.

He had heard of the amazing rehabilitation of the California desert through subsurface water. He decided that he could find water here also. So sure was he that he went ahead and mapped out roads for a ranch where he intended to establish a school for refugee boys. All the old-time Bedouin sheiks said it couldn't be done, government officials agreed, and so did solemn scientists from abroad. There was absolutely no water there.

But Musa was unimpressed. He thought there was. A few poverty-stricken refugees from the nearby Jericho Refugee Camp helped him as he started to dig. With well-drilling equipment? Not on your life. With plain old picks and shovels. Everybody laughed as this dauntless man and his ragged friends dug away day after day, week after week, month after month. Slowly they went down deep into the sand where no man since creation had plumbed for water.

For six months they dug. Then one day the sand became moist, and finally water gushed forth. Life-giving water had been found in the ancient desert! And they who had known the burning sands for centuries could not speak, so great was their wonder and gratitude. They did not laugh or cheer. They wept.

A very old man, sheik of a nearby village, heard the amazing news. He came to see for himself. "Musa," he asked, "have you really found water? Let me see it and feel it and taste it."

The old man put his hand in the stream, splashed it over his face, put it on his tongue. "It is sweet and cool," he said. "It is good water." Then placing his aged hands on the shoulder of Musa Alami he said, "Thank God. Now, Musa, you can die." This was the simple tribute of a desert man to a positive thinker who did what everyone said could not be done.

Now, several years later, Musa Alami has many wells supplying a ranch three miles long and two miles wide. He raises vegetables, bananas, figs, citrus fruit and boys. In his school, he is cultivating citizens of the future, farmers and technicians, experts in the trades. Produce is flown to Kuwait, Bahrein, Beirut, as well as to nearby Jerusalem. Imitating Musa, others have also dug until now many thousands of acres are under cultivation and green growth is spreading over the ancient sands of the onetime desert.

I asked this amazing man what kept him going, kept him believing when everyone said it couldn't be done. "There was no alternative. It had to be done," he said and added, "God helped me."

As twilight turned the Mountain of Moab and the Judean Hills to red and gold, I sat watching a huge stream of water gush from the heart of the desert. And as it splashed into a deep, wide pool, it seemed to say, "It can be done, it can be done." So don't let your difficulties get you down and do not believe those malcontents who say you cannot do it. Remember Musa Alami, positive thinker of the wilderness of Judea. And remember that enthusiasm is the powerful drive that makes things happen. Enthusiasm makes a difference in the wilderness of Judea, just as it can make a difference in the wilderness of many people's lives.

The thrilling fact is that there are people who have a sound, solid, irrepressible enthusiasm for real values and are willing to give all of themselves to attain the goal they're enthusiastic about.

ENTHUSIASM AND THE FIRST MOTOR

Henry Ford had a burning enthusiasm for the motor car. People said he was "touched." He was; he was touched by enthusiasm and the object of his enthusiasm took shape. Edison was enthusiastic about electric light and the talking machine and a lot of other inventions, and due to his insatiable motivation they all happened. The Wright brothers were enthusiastic about a machine that would fly. It flew. Kettering was enthusiastic about a self-starter and about paint that could be sprayed on automobiles, which of course "they" said could not be done—but both were done. Continue with the list right up to the present day, for the principle still withstands the acid test —what you are enthusiastic about can happen.

But invariably someone comes up with the pious reproof that it is wrong to encourage people to hope for something they cannot attain, that only the gifted, the well-favored can attain the goals. But such individuals are wrong, as usual, the plain fact being that any person, however seemingly impossible his circumstances, who develops enthusiasm for something and the fortitude to carry it out can make the most utterly astonishing things happen.

NOBODY COULD DO IT, BUT HE DID

For example, if you entertain the foolish notion there is something you cannot accomplish because of vast odds and obstacles, consider the following story by an African boy, Legson Kayira, from our magazine *Guideposts*. His amazing story is called *Barefoot to America*.

"My mother did not know where America was. I said to her, 'Mother, I want to go to America to go to college. Will you give me your permission?'

" 'Very well,' she said. 'You may go. When will you leave?'

"I did not want to give her time to discover from others in our village how far away America was, for fear that she would change her mind.

" 'Tomorrow,' I said.

" 'Very well,' she said, 'I will prepare some maize for you to eat along the way.'

"Next day, October 14, 1958, I left my home in the village of Mpale, in northern Nyasaland, East Africa. I had only the clothes I wore, a khaki shirt and shorts. I carried the two treasures I owned: a Bible and a copy of *Pilgrim's Progress*. I carried, too, the maize my mother had given me, wrapped in banana leaves, and a small ax for protection.

"My goal was a continent and an ocean away, but I did not doubt that I would reach it.

"I had no idea how old I was. Such things mean little in a land where time is always the same. I suppose I was 16 or 18.

"My father died when I was very young. In 1952 my mother listened to the words of the missionaries of the Church of Scotland (Presbyterian), with the result that our family became Christian. From the missionaries, I learned not only to love God, but also that if I was ever to be of value to my village, my people, my country, it would be necessary for me to have an education.

"At Wenya, eight miles away, was a mission primary school. One day when I felt I was ready to study, I walked there.

"I learned many things. I learned I was not, as most Africans believed, the victim of my circumstances but the master of them. I learned that, as a Christian, I had an obligation to use the talents God had given me to make life better for others.

"Later, in high school, I learned about America. I read the life of Abraham Lincoln and grew to love this man who suffered so much to help the enslaved Africans in his country. I read, too, the autobiography of Booker T. Washington, himself born in slavery in America, who had risen in dignity and honor to become a benefactor of his people and his country.

"I gradually realized that it would be only in America that I would receive the training and opportunities to prepare myself to emulate these men in my own land, to be, like them, a leader, perhaps even the president of my country.

"My intention was to make my way to Cairo, where I hoped to get passage on a ship to America. Cairo was over 3,000 miles away, a distance I could not comprehend, and I foolishly thought I could walk it in four or five days. In four or five days, I was about 25 miles from home, my food was gone, I had no money, and I did not know what to do, except that I must keep going.

"I developed a pattern of travel that became my life for more than a year. Villages were usually five or six miles apart, on forest paths. I would arrive at one in the afternoon and ask if I could work to earn food, water and a place to sleep. When this was possible, I would spend the night there, then move on to the next village in the morning.

"It was not always possible. Tribal languages change every few miles in Africa; often I was among people with whom I could not communicate. This clearly made me a stranger to them, perhaps an enemy; they would not let me into the villages, and I had to sleep in the forests, eating herbs and wild fruit.

"I soon discovered that my ax sometimes gave people the impression I had come to fight or to steal, so I bartered the ax for a knife I could carry unseen. I was actually defenseless against the forest animals I dreaded, but although I heard them at night none of them approached me. Malaria mosquitoes, however, were constant companions, and I often was sick.

"But two comforts sustained me: my Bible and my *Pilgrim's Progress*. Over and over again I read my Bible, particularly finding confidence in the promise 'Trust in the Lord with all thine heart, and lean not unto thine own understanding. . . . Then shalt thou walk in thy way.' (Proverbs 3:5, 23)

"By the end of 1959, I had walked 1,000 miles to Uganda, where a family took me in and I found a job making bricks for government buildings. I remained there six months and I sent most of my earnings to my mother.

"In *Pilgrim's Progress,* I read many times of the tribulations of the Christian who wandered through the wilderness seeking God, and I compared this to my own wanderings toward the goal I believed God had put into my heart. I could not give up, any more than the Christian had given up.

"One afternoon at the USIS library in Kampala, I unexpectedly came upon a directory of American colleges. Opening it at random, I saw the name of Skagit Valley College, Mount Vernon, Washington. I had heard that American colleges sometimes gave scholarships to deserving Africans, so I wrote Dean George Hodson and applied for one. I realized that I might be refused but I was not discouraged. I would write to one school after another in the directory until I found one that would help me.

"Three weeks later, Dean Hodson replied: I was granted a scholarship and the school would help me find a job. Overjoyed, I went to the American authorities, only to be told that this was not enough. I would need a passport and the round-trip fare in order to obtain a visa.

"I wrote to the Nyasaland goverment for a passport but it was refused because I could not tell them when I was born. I then wrote to the missionaries who had taught me in my childhood, and it was through their efforts that I was granted a passport. But I still could not get the visa at Kampala because I did not have the fare.

"Still determined, I left Kampala and resumed my trip northward. So strong was my faith that I used my last money to buy my first pair of shoes. I knew I could not walk into Skagit Valley College in my bare feet. I carried the shoes to save them.

"Across Uganda and into the Sudan, the villages were farther apart and the people were less friendly to me. Sometimes I had to walk 20 or 30 miles in a day to find a place to sleep or to work to earn some food. At last I reached Khartoum, where I learned that there was an American consulate and I went there to try my luck.

"Once again I heard about the entrance requirements, this time from Vice-Consul Emmett M. Coxson, but Mr. Coxson wrote the college about my plight. Back came a cable.

"The students hearing about me and my problems, had raised the fare of $1,700 through benefit parties.

"I was thrilled and deeply grateful; overjoyed that I had judged Americans correctly for their friendship and brotherhood. I was thankful to God for His guidance and I pledged my future to His service.

"News that I had walked for over two years and 2,500 miles circulated in Khartoum. The Communists came to me and offered to send me to school in Yugoslavia, all expenses paid, including travel, and a subsistence during my studies.

" 'I am a Christian,' I told them, 'and I could not be educated into the kind of man I want to be in your godless schools.'

"They warned me that, as an African, I would have racial difficulties in the United States, but I had read enough in American newspapers to feel this was a diminishing factor. My religion had taught me that men are not perfect, but as long as they strive to be they will be pleasing to

God. The American effort, I felt, was why the land was so blessed.

"In December, 1960, carrying my two books and wearing my first suit, I arrived at Skagit Valley College.

"In my speech of gratitude to the student body, I disclosed my desire to become prime minister or president of my country, and I noticed some smiles. I wondered if I had said something naïve. I do not think so.

"When God has put an impossible dream in your heart, He means to help you fulfill it. I believed this to be true when, as an African bush boy, I felt compelled to become an American college graduate. This became true when I graduated from the University of Washington. And if God has given me the dream of becoming president of Nyasaland, this too, will become true.

"It is when we resist God that we remain nothing. When we submit to Him, whatever the sacrifice or hardship, we can become far more than we dare dream."

This remarkable story, this "utterly impossible" experience, demonstrates how enthusiasm acted as the powerful motivation to make something tremendous take place. I wonder why everyone does not realize and predicate his actions on the fact that enthusiasm does activate the greatest possible achievements. So many could be spared the dullness of mediocrity, the frustration of failure, the loss of hope, if only they would cultivate the amazing power of enthusiasm.

Some people not in the know regard the job of a minister as lacking in color, romance and dramatic achievement, but believe me, the principle of enthusiasm as the motivating factor that makes things happen operates in this field as elsewhere.

Take, for example, the case of Dr. Robert H. Schuller, who was sent by the Reformed Church in America, the oldest Protestant denomination in the United States, the religious body to which I myself belong, into Orange County, California, to establish a church. In this county, said to be the fastest-growing in the nation, our denomination had not one single member. Schuller was given a modest salary and $500 for promotion and told to start a church. But Dr. Schuller was as long on enthusiasm as he was short on money, and he had a powerful motivation. He wanted to build a great, modern church in the midst of a teeming population explosion.

So he leased a drive-in movie theater for Sunday morning services and by attractive advertising began to build a congregation out of the people that were flocking into Southern California. He gave them friendship and the inspiration of the Gospel. A year after he began from scratch, I spoke at his invitation to thousands of people seated in their cars. He told with conviction about the "great" church that was to be. I knew then it would be in fact, for it already existed in his mind, and he had the energy, ingenuity and the faith to bring it to pass.

Ten years later, Dr. Schuller invited me to return to speak, this time in a shining modern structure of steel and glass set in twenty acres which were planted with grass and flowers and dotted wth splashing fountains falling musically into pools of water. Now he had over 3,000 members, an average attendance Sunday mornings of more than 4,000 persons who packed the church and adjoining gardens, still other hundreds listening in cars that overflowed the huge parking area. I helped turn the earth for the "Tower of Hope," a graceful soaring ten-story structure where trained counselors will help the troubled find peace and a constructive way of life.

As I looked at that vast congregation both inside and outside the glorious church and its lovely gardens, I realized once again the tremendous fact that enthusiasm is indeed the powerful motivation to make things happen.

NINE

ENTHUSIASM BUILDS POWER UNDER YOUR DIFFICULTIES

Suppose you must face extra hard difficulties and problems. Are you then expected to practice enthusiasm? If so, how can you? Well, that is just the kind of situation in which enthusiasm comes into its own, when it really goes to work and produces big results. For enthusiasm builds power under difficulties—under all difficulties.

Let's get down to cases. Let me tell you about a friend who had enough enthusiasm and faith and courage to lick two extra-sized difficulties—alcoholism and cancer.

His name is J. Arch Avary, Jr., and he is one of the best known and most highly regarded citizens of a large southern city. His story, for sheer courage, faith in the Lord and enthusiasm, can scarcely be matched. His difficulties were overcome by the power of enthusiasm, and it was an enthusiasm for something specific, namely, his faith in Jesus Christ and God. He is an example of the astonishing power that can be built under any difficulty.

Incidentally, I wrote to one of those professors who teach the "God is dead" theory and asked how he would explain the rehabilitation of Arch Avary on the basis of God being dead. He replied to the effect that God had nothing to do with this amazing comeback: Avary was rehabilitated by what this theological babe in the woods called "the caring community." This was a grim joke. The

153

community couldn't have cared less. In fact, the "caring community" kicked the poor fellow in the teeth.

Mr. Avary granted me permission to use his dramatic personal story, saying: "Your other books helped me, and I should certainly want my experience to help others."

Arch Avary, at twenty, was elected secretary of the Central Florida Institute of Banking and at twenty-one became its president—which I believe is still a record in United States banking circles. From then on his rise in banking was meteoric. At twenty-seven, he became an officer of the First National Bank of his city. In the Air Force during World War II, he rose quickly to rank of colonel. Back at First National again, regardless of his knowledge of banking and wide acquaintance in the industry, he was fired in 1956 for excessive drinking.

HE HIT BOTTOM WITH A BANG

His decline was as rapid as his rise had been. He really hit bottom. His wife filed for divorce. He was broke. Each job, poorer than the last, had the same result. He was fired for being a drunk.

Arch describes his skid to the bottom thus: "Drawing blanks brought on my greatest fear. Spending much of my time at two social clubs and at their bars, I saw many influential people each day. When they would see me in the bank the day following a big night, and would mention a subject we had discussed, and about which I could not recall one thing, I would suffer a cold chill along with a great wave of fear. I didn't know what I had said and what might result from it.

"As this experience repeated itself, and my nerves began to show strain, I required more liquor in order to calm down, and that produced more dire results. This went on for nearly ten years when I was in a senior position, very close personally and officially to the president of the then largest bank in the Southeast. The president was 'retired' early and in about a year he put a pistol in his mouth and ended his life. This should have sobered me, but it didn't. About two years later I was 'retired' for the same reason."

Those who knew the facts tell me that Avary, but for this weakness, would have become president of one of the greatest banks in the country. Instead, he was forced to walk the streets panhandling from friends and former associates; anyone who could spare a handout.

He knew he had to take himself in hand so he committed himself to a state institution for alcoholics and soon was wearing the uniform of an inmate. He was set to washing dishes, but apparently he was a failure at this too. After he had finished the first dishwashing chore, the woman in charge told him that her father was a trackworker on the same railroad of which he had been a director. She said, "Arch Avary, you have been a big banker, and a railroad director who went to West Point on the front of a locomotive with a special train. Fire sirens blew and flags were waving to celebrate the centennial of the Atlanta and West Point Railroad. But today you are a plain inmate of this institution and an ordinary drunkard like the rest. So get your hands back into that dishwater and get those dishes clean that you left in such awful condition."

A HOBO WHO KNEW HIS STUFF

Arch was rocked by this experience, which had a therapeutic effect upon him. A few days later while the ex-banker and ex-railroad director was raking leaves on the institution grounds (another job which made him do some more basic thinking), he began talking with a fellow inmate, a hobo who confessed he had often "ridden the rods" on Avary's railroad without benefit of ticket. The hobo, a thoughtful fellow, commented on Arch's membership on the official board of the First Methodist Church. "Avary," he said, "I like you a lot but I have been wondering. I have no religion. Don't want any, and know very little about it. But I would like to know what kind of religion you have that would let you wind up in a place like this, same as I?"

"I didn't sleep that night," Avary declares, "and it dawned on me that if a professional tramp in a state institution for alcoholics believed my religion needed to be reexamined, it was high time I was doing the same thing. I saw that my so-called religion was only part of a pattern —like belonging to the Piedmont Driving Club, the Capital City and Breakfast Club, like wearing the gray flannel suit, the mark of a successful banker. Mine was no religion at all; it was a sham and it broke down, so I landed in a state institution for alcoholics."

Avary resolved to find some real religion and he went all out to get it. "As I walked through those iron gates at Briarcliff, something walked out of there with me, stronger than man, because I have never since had the slightest desire to touch a drop of alcohol. And for a man who consumed over a fifth a day for over ten years, I submit that I do have a faith that has been made real and rewarding.

"When I walked under that iron arch over those massive gates," Arch continues his story, "I stopped and looked back and asked the good Lord to give me strength and courage to straighten out my life. If he would do that, I would do my part in working at it and begin to pay off my debt by constructive service in the vineyard of the Master. I have been at it ever since. I asked the Lord for an opportunity to get my chaotic life straightened out. I had to take over the running of my life like I knew it should be run.

"When I left Briarcliff," he continues, "I returned to my old hometown. I was broke, had very few friends, and didn't deserve any. My wife was suing me for divorce. For the next six months, I stayed with my father and mother. I didn't go anyplace except to church which was located next door to my home. I had a circuit that I walked every day which was about twelve miles. I would stop at the foot of Pine Mountain and sit in the old spring house from which I drank as a boy. I got me some cedar and white pine that I would whittle. As I sat there in the spring house whittling, I could hear the train whistles blow and I would think about that old hobo back at Briarcliff when he asked: 'What sort of religion do you have?' "

HE STOPPED RUNNING FROM HIMSELF

"For the past twenty-five years I had been running from something, mostly from myself. You can't run from anything, particularly yourself. As I sat there the first two or three days I was nervous and jittery, until all of a sudden a Bible verse came to my mind, 'Be still and know that I am God.' My nervousness left me and I haven't had it since. During those days of whittling at Pine Mountain, I made the greatest discovery of my life. I discovered a man named Arch Avary from whom I had been running for many years. When I really got to know him, I found out that basically he was a fairly decent person who had been on the wrong track for a long time.

"I did a lot of thinking and walking in those six months. Every day at Pine Mountain I conferred with myself for at least an hour. While I was wrestling with my chances to make a comeback and reestablish myself, I was indulging in a lot of soul-searching. I didn't have much courage, but one day this verse from the Bible came to my mind, 'If God be for us, who can be against us?' This gave me a lot of encouragement. The more I thought about it, the more I thought that with the help of the good Lord I could do anything I made up my mind to do. Another verse came to me, 'Commit thy way unto the Lord; trust also in Him; and He shall bring it to pass,' and this gave me a lot of encouragement.

"About ten years before this, my mother had given me two of Dr. Norman Vincent Peale's books hoping these might bring me to my senses. I had never cracked them. But now I began to read *Faith Is the Answer** and *The Power of Positive Thinking*. One day the thought occurred to me that if I really believe faith is the answer, I could take this philosophy and combine it with the power of positive thinking and make a package deal out of it. I tried it. It won!"

Well, one thing is sure, Arch Avary found faith; not a vague faith but a powerful life-changing faith in Jesus Christ. As he himself eloquently expresses it: "First and foremost my soul has been saved. I am blissfully happy." I have known many enthusiastic Christians in my experience but no one more so than this man.

But this new-found faith, this happiness and life change which came to Mr. Avary were in for a formidable test. He moved back up the business ladder and in due course was once again one of the leading bankers of his city. Quite a feat when he had been told that the chances of his returning to the business life of his community was in the ratio of ten thousand to one, so badly had he wrecked his career. But now he was sober, keen, competent, once again outstanding in business and religious influence. He

* *Faith Is the Answer* by Norman Vincent Peale and Smiley Blanton, Prentice-Hall, Inc., 1950.

was asked to speak before all kinds of groups, telling them
how God can change lives and free men from any defeat.
His enthusiasm was boundless.

FIRST ALCOHOLISM THEN CANCER

And then the blow came. He had cancer of the colon.
Years before a friend of his had had a colostomy. Arch
was so moved that he vowed if ever he came to this state,
he would end his misery with a pistol. So this tragic news
was expected to unnerve him; would he reach for the bottle again? That was an erroneous assumption, for now he
had faith and spiritual power to hold him steady. He had
a new enthusiasm that made a big difference. In fact, after
being told of his cancer, he went to Sea Island to speak to
a group of a thousand women bankers. At the convention,
he attended several cocktail parties and was urged by
some unthinking people to take something to "steady the
shock" but he did not need anything beyond the new
power within him.

"The fact that I had no desire for a drink under these
circumstances convinced me that I was pretty well cured,"
he observed. Indeed the astonishing thing is that he had so
licked his problem, the problem being himself, that not
only was he without fear, but he was also in firm control
of his new tragedy as well. In fact, he turned his colostomy, which he defines as a "hole in the stomach" into an
asset. He uses the daily irrigation time of an hour and a
half for reading, study, prayer and meditation.

"When they removed the bandage from my stomach and
put a plastic receptacle on it, I couldn't look at it," he
said. "My doctor suggested that I change this receptacle
instead of letting the nurses do it, because the sooner I got
used to doing so the better off I would be. I balked for
four or five days, but finally made up my mind that I had
to live with this thing.

"When I made the decision to face my problem and
look at that hole in my side and not let it scare me, I won
one of the greatest victories of my life. Changing that receptacle one time changed me, and gave me confidence
that opened a new vista of sunshine to an otherwise dark
outlook—the courage to face unpleasant things.

"I decided I was going to live with this hole in my

stomach and make it a blessing instead of a curse. I recalled preachers talking about Paul and his infirmities. I figured if the greatest man in Christendom next to Jesus Christ could use his infirmities and do what he did, that I could make mine an inspiration also and try to use it to the best advantage. I never had any idea that I was a Paul, but I did agree with what he wrote to the Philippians, 'I can do all things through Christ which strengtheneth me.'

"I had read many times Norman Vincent Peale's book *The Power of Positive Thinking.* It was so helpful in my troubles with alcohol, I read it again and renewed my inspiration and determination to face again and master a difficult problem."

Well, for several years now Arch Avary, ex-alcoholic, ex-panhandler, ex-cancer victim—now cancer victor—has been president of the state cancer society. He is an enthusiastic and compelling speaker and has saved hundreds of lives by persuading people to have examinations.

THE WORST TROUBLE COMES TO THE BEST MEN

Eugene Patterson, editor of the *Atlanta Constitution,* says of Mr. Avary: "A man like that just might defeat anything. Maybe the worst trouble comes to the best men because they can handle it."

What is your difficulty or problem? Whatever it is, you can handle it. Do as Avary did and get yourself some real faith. Go far beyond formal belief in God; really go into faith in depth. Out of it will come dynamic enthusiasm and you will have the same kind of strength, and gain the same fabulous victory. Never settle for any defeat. Stand up to your difficulty courageously with lots of faith, and let enthusiasm put power under it. With God's help you can lick your difficulties and problems.

Put this one great fact in mind: God himself is on the side of the enthusiastic believer. That being true, how can you lose?

Consider, for example, the case of a man named Ed Furgol who became one of the greatest golfers in the history of this popular sport. When Ed was ten years old, he fell from a swing onto a concrete pavement, landing hard on his left elbow, which was driven up through the skin, projecting out of the arm. He was rushed to the hospital, where everything was done that could have been for the little boy. But he found himself with a left arm nearly ten inches shorter than the other. The traumatic effects of such an accident on a normal, vigorous ten-year-old boy might have been great indeed. But these were overcome by a vital power that had captured his mind: enthusiasm. His enthusiasm was for golf. He actually had a burning and consuming ambition to become U.S. Open Champion. But how pathetic, how utterly unrealistic can one get? Someone must gently remove such ideas from the mind of this poor kid with a hopelessly withered shortened arm. Thus people must have talked sadly. And, of course, the average, negative person would have folded completely in the presence of such a handicap.

But Ed Furgol was of a different breed. He had some immense assets working for him. When he added them up, they outbalanced in his mind that withered arm. And what were those assets? One was a goal, not a fuzzy vague sort of goal, which of course is not a goal at all; but a specific, clearly defined objective, to be a golf champion. Crippled arm or not, that was what he wanted, what he expected for sure. He believed in himself. He was convinced that with God's help and his own efforts, painful though they surely would be, he could manage to put the golf ball where it was supposed to go. And he knew that anyone who could do that could become champion. Difficulties or no difficulties, he intended to be champion.

DON'T BE AN IF THINKER—BE A HOW THINKER

Ed had another asset, an important one. He was not an *if* thinker. He was a *how* thinker. The *if* thinker says: "If I hadn't done that . . . If it had not happened to me . . . If only I'd had a better break"—one hopeless *if* after another. Well, this so-called handicapped boy bypassed all the *ifs* and emphasized the *hows*. He asked himself, *How* do I compensate for this short arm? *How* do I get my whole body into the shot? Yes, *how* do I become champion? All of which underscores the fact that Ed Furgol had the quality of enthusiasm which generates power under difficulty. Difficulty was what he had for fair, but his enthusiasm canceled out difficulty.

He had to compensate for his short arm by using his

whole body in a golf shot. He had a kind of hacking motion as he went at the ball. But he brought the whole body into a flow so that its full weight hit the ball. Observers say that until one got used to it, Ed did look a bit pathetic playing alongside some of the most magnificent physical specimens in the United States. Here was this boy with a ten-inch differential in one arm trying to play big-time golf.

Before the big competition, he was awakened in the night, he tells us, by a voice which seemed to whisper in his ear, "Ed, tomorrow you will be the Open Golf champion." The next day the *how* thinker, the handicapped lad with the enthusiasm that makes the difference, did become champion.

Reporters asked Ed to predict future champions, suggesting names. "No, he'll never make it," Ed said of the first person they suggested.

"Why will he never make it?"

"Because he hasn't suffered enough."

A second name was mentioned. Again, he shook his head, "No, he'll never make it either."

"Why not?" they asked.

"Because he's never been hungry enough."

Of a third, he said, "He won't be champion ever, because he has never been defeated enough."

It seemed that none of these golfers had enough trouble or experience or the enthusiasm that makes the difference. It takes struggle, a goal, and enthusiasm to make a champion.

Well what is *your* ten-inch-short arm? Maybe it is not a physical handicap but a weakness of mental attitude or a defect in your arm of faith. Most of us do not appreciate the power of faith in helping people be what God meant them to be, and what they want to be. By the power of God, anybody can be free from any weakness; anyone can be released to creative living, no matter what obstacle stands in his way.

To believe this is an essential qualification of the person who desires to move forward in this life. It is a fact that difficulty does help to make strong people, and happy ones, because in the long run no one can be either strong or happy or efficient who has not had rough spots knocked off by the refining process of living.

ENTHUSIASM AND THE TUMBLING BARREL

Ever hear of a tumbling barrel? Well, I had not either,
until Andrew van der Lyn, a friend in the manufacturing
business, told me about it. Some ideas he got from tumbling barrels helped him to overcome difficulties so successfully that I became interested in his philosophy of re-
lating difficulty to enthusiasm. A tumbling barrel is an industrial device for smoothing newly made pieces of metal.
It is a cask or drum equipped to revolve at a predeter-
mined speed. In it are put steel castings or manufactured
metal pieces. An abrasive such as powdered alumina or
Carborundum, is put into the barrel; or maybe sand, rub-
ber pellets or steel balls, depending upon the character and
hardness of the metal parts. In some cases water is added.

The tumbling barrel is then rotated. With each revolution the metal pieces are carried part way up the side of
the drum; then they fall free and drop back down. As they
tumble and spill against each other and are rubbed by the
abrasive, the burrs disappear and the rough edges are
smoothed. They are then in shape to function properly.

This ingenious process strongly suggests the way men
are tumbled about in life. We come into the world with
burrs and edges characteristic of raw newness. But as we
go along, we tumble against each other and also rub
against hardships and difficulties. This affects us much as
the abrasives in tumbling barrels affect new pieces of
metal. Such friction and attrition make for a rounding and
maturing of personalities.

There are well-meaning people who believe that life is
too harsh. They are the ones who would like to plan and
arrange the world so that no one need suffer. But without
struggle, how could the end product of personality be
achieved? How could a person become rounded and mature and strong?

When you realize that not only are trouble and suffering
inevitable, but serve a definite creative purpose as well,
you are upgrading your philosophy of human existence.
You no longer waste time complaining or pitying yourself,
getting resentful or giving in to discouragement. You gradually learn to take difficulties as part of the maturing
process. So when the going gets tough, take the attitude

that rough spots are being knocked off, that you are being shaped for the real purpose of your life.

This shaping process makes men. As tough and unpleasant as difficulty may be, it is the source of potential development. Surround every difficulty with prayer, with faith and with straight thinking. Then let enthusiasm build power under it. On this basis, you can handle any situation that can ever develop.

AIRLINE HOSTESS FACES DEATH—BUT—

Let me tell you about a young woman who certainly did get shaken about in the tumbling barrel. But a long acquaintance with God developed such a sense of inner victory in her mind that even a terrifying experience could not overwhelm her.

Jackie Myers, airline hostess, did not foresee on that beautiful morning when she walked out to a huge jet on the runway that within moments she would face the greatest crisis of her life. For shortly after takeoff, Jackie suddenly found herself face-to-face with death. At what seemed certain to be her last moment a remarkable realization came to her; that she had such faith and enthusiasm for God that she could even meet death without fear.

"Eleven minutes after takeoff," Miss Myers says, "our beautiful, huge, shiny jet went into a nosedive. We were 249,000 pounds of weight hurtling through space. We went into a dive at 19,000 feet and it wasn't until 40 seconds later that the captain pulled us out of it at 5,000 feet —just 8 seconds before we would have crashed!

"As we pulled out of the dive, the No. 3 engine tore out of the wing and dropped to earth. No. 4 was hanging by a few bolts. We lost most of our hydraulic fluid and a lot of electrical power. Several other mechanical failures developed.

"But our captain landed that powerful plane at an Air Force field as gently as one would handle a newborn baby. Had eggs lined the runway, they would hardly have been damaged. It was truly the greatest miracle I shall ever experience."

Jackie Myers tells of her feelings and thoughts in those agonizing forty seconds during which the plane was in a nosedive. It is said that a person can relive a large part of his life in a few seconds. Here is an instance of it.

"When we started to encounter turbulence, I ran to my jump seat in the tail of the plane. I was thrown off balance and grabbed onto a shelf when we nosed over. At first I just couldn't believe it was happening. I knew our pilots were superbly skillful. I felt certain they would be able to pull us out of it.

"But the fact was unmistakable—we were smoothly and quietly plunging through space. I became very close to God when I accepted this. I felt no fear. I thought of a beloved aunt who always says a little prayer for me every night. I thought how happy I was to have been a small part of our church. I thought how strongly I had endorsed the power of positive thinking and the Golden Rule. At no time did I experience fear. I was so happy about my life including religion. I did tell God there were so many things I wanted to do yet. I wanted to stay just a little while longer. I said, 'Lord, I never got my happy marriage and my happy family.'

"But we were still hurtling downward and I reluctantly terminated my conversation with God. I accepted the fact that we would be blown to bits upon impact. I added a little P.S. to God: 'If this is the way You want it, Lord, I guess this is the way it's going to be.' Then suddenly the plane righted! I could hardly believe my senses but it was real. We were flying merrily along on a level."

Later she said, "I found in this terrible experience that by positive thinking and right thinking from day to day, you can develop an inner condition that will sustain you through life's worst ordeals and roughest moments."

And that inner condition needed by everyone is a spiritually dynamic faith, and with it enthusiasm that builds power under difficulties. These change people so much that changed people change situations.

A businessman was having a hard time of it, and, in a dark mood, he told a friend that he was thinking of blowing his brains out.

"Why not blow your brains *up* rather than out?"

Startled, the depressed man asked, "What do you mean?"

"Get your brains blown up, full of enthusiasm," the other replied.

He got the discouraged fellow to attend Marble Collegiate Church where he became reactivated spiritually. Result: this man now has power, the kind that comes from spiritualized enthusiasm. When he started blowing his brains *up* rather than out, he made the amazing discovery that there was real potential in his brain. With so many new constructive ideas, he has gone on to become an executive in his company. When in his case spiritualized enthusiasm took over, it drove out the depression that had nearly taken his life. But instead of losing his life, he found it. Difficulties no longer bothered him for he had the enthusiasm that built power under them.

The real secret of dealing with difficulties is a proper conditioning of the mind. Anyone can make his mind perform as desired by conditioning it to thoughts of faith, courage, enthusiasm and joy. I do not minimize the harsh, cruel, and extremely difficult experiences that people have. But if while depending on the help of God you really try to build a dynamic spirit of victory under your problems, you will gain a new power over them. Let me tell you of two people whose lives demonstrated this truth.

A woman, a brilliant individual, suffered a sudden stroke. She recovered about fifty percent of the use of her members. She was deeply depressed. But ultimately she returned to her job as school principal. During her illness, she asked, "Give me a few words to say that will help me to have courage." I told her about Dr. Paul DuBois, the great Viennese psychotherapist who taught the therapy of words. He himself used to repeat the word *indomitable*. I also told her about the famous doctor who used the word *acquiescence*. I said that the word I like is *imperturbable* and that I repeat it often to myself. She wrote me, "I have a better word than any of those. It is the word *rugged*." She said, "I say it over to myself, rugged, rugged. Nothing can defeat me."

But the greatest words of all to put into your mind are those of the Scriptures such as (1) "Who shall separate us from the love of Christ?" (2) "I can do all things through Christ who strengtheneth me." (3) "If God be for us, who can be against us." (4) "In all these things we are more than conquerors through Him that loved us."

Next time you are faced with a difficulty, open the Great Book, pick out words like these, commit them to memory, repeat them until they take possession of your mind. Your mind will give you back exactly what you put into it. If over a long period, you put defeat into your mind, your mind will give you back defeat. If over a long period you put into your mind great words of faith, your mind will give them back to you.

A friend was in a hospital. He had had one leg amputated some years ago and recently the second leg was taken off. This man told me that he had the phantom foot. Though his foot was off he could still feel it and still wanted to move his toes. This could have produced a nervous and tense reaction. But this man was so happy, so enthusiastic that nothing defeated him. He was the life of the hospital.

I said to him, "Everyone tells me you are the happiest person in this hospital. You are not putting it on, are you?"

"No, no, I am as happy as can be."

"Let me in on your secret," I asked.

"Do you see that little book lying over there on the table?"

It was the Bible. He said, "There is where I get my medicine. When I feel a little low, I just read the Book and after I have read some of these great words I am happy again."

A drunken man came into the hospital looking for a friend and staggered around the ward with a bunch of flowers. Finally he said, "I cannot find my friend, but if I find a happy man in this hospital, I am going to give him my flowers."

The nurses were anxious to be rid of this unwelcome visitor, but they were afraid of him. They allowed him to go around peering into every room. He looked at each patient with a searching scrutiny and said, "I never saw such a gloomy bunch of people." Then he came to this man with no legs, and he put his face up close to his and looked at him for a long while. Then his brain seemed to grow sober and he said, "You have sure got something my friend. You have got what I am looking for. You are a happy man and I am going to give you my flowers."

TEN

THE CONTAGION OF ENTHUSIASM

"Enthusiasm, like measles, mumps and the common cold, is highly contagious," says Emory Ward.

But unlike measles and mumps and colds, enthusiasm is good for you. Hope you catch it, and good.

Recently, while writing this book, I happened to encounter Henry S., an old friend. He was favorably taken with the title. "Boy, do I go for that one," he exclaimed in his usual ebullient manner, "and you know why?" Of course I did know why, for in a small way I had a part in the change that saved Henry's life. "But don't water down what should really be said," he warned me. "It's not just enthusiasm in general that is important, but enthusiasm in particular—enthusiasm for God, for life, for people. So tell your readers for me that you're not kidding when you say that enthusiasm makes the difference. I believe there is a terrific contagion in enthusiasm."

There was reason for Henry's positive emphasis, for he had nearly become a victim to the American disease of overpressing, a malady which may be defined as anxiety-tension raised to the nth degree. The first result of his trouble was a decline in efficiency. For people work well only when there is harmony in the flow of power mentally, spiritually and physically.

To illustrate, take the case of a famous baseball pitcher

who some years ago went into a lengthy slump. Normally a pitcher of excellent control, he started walking batters and was "hit all over the lot" freely. Slow-motion movies had been made of him at the peak of his performance. Now similar pictures were taken of him in the slump. They revealed that when he pitched, his right foot was about three inches advanced, and his delivery was less smooth, even jerky and tense. Psychiatric and pastoral counseling brought to light family problems of a serious nature which were worrying him, one being the necessity for more income, for greater financial resources. The pitcher's mind developed such nervous anxiety about his performance that he wasn't functioning effectively. He was tied up in the effort to make good and to justify an increase in pay which he so desperately needed. The results backfired. He was pressing too hard and he went into a slump. Pastoral and psychiatric counseling helped to reduce the problem and a satisfactory solution was brought about. The anxiety tension relaxed. The foot was drawn back, the delivery became normal, and pitching efficiency returned.

In similar manner, Henry S. had been overpressing for a good while. He had grown tense and unhappy. His natural buoyant enthusiasm had given way to a grim, hard-driving, punishing pace, though he continued to mouth the jaunty jargon of the old happy, successful days that had made him a leader in the real-estate business.

Then something happened, the end result of which justified his forceful admonition to me to "lay enthusiasm on the line."

Henry S. was one of the most successful realtors in the rapidly developing section where he was "making a killing," which incidentally nearly killed him. In fact, he had a mild heart attack, a "warning," so he was told. That shook him up, but he was "a big strong guy and that stuff wasn't for him." So he passed it off as trivial and proceeded at the same fast pace, the hard sell by day and entertaining customers by night.

Result: another heart attack. This one laid him flat on his back in a darkened hospital room for several weeks. There he had opportunity to think. "I'm a damned fool," was the straightforward result of his cogitations, "and I've got to get on the common-sense beam, or the only real estate I'll be concerned with is six feet in a local cemetery."

But he wasn't as big a fool as he declaimed. He knew the score, and furthermore had a lot of basic faith, though he had not been exercising it. This parenthetically brings to mind a sign my brother, Leonard Peale, saw in a railroad station, "God isn't dead—only unemployed." So Henry came around to see me when a speaking tour brought me to his city. "What shall I do?" he asked. "I don't want to die or quit work. I want to live, and I mean live. That is to say, I don't want to be an invalid. How can I really live? Give it to me straight and I'll love you for it."

I liked his forthright spirit, and I knew God loved him too. God always loves real men like him, for He is a real God—a man-sized one, not a nicey-nice, as He is sometimes made out to be.

"O.K.," I said. "I'll give it to you straight. You better get right with God. Cut out the rough stuff in your life. Clean it up. You are better than you've been living. Surrender your life to Christ, or is that too pious for you?"

"I said I wanted it straight, and if you didn't give it to me that way, boy, would I be disappointed in you! So don't mince any words. I've asked for a real Christian treatment, and that's what I expect you to hand out," he declared resolutely.

So he opened up and spilled out all the dirt and then he asked the Lord to forgive him and "clean him up and help him go straight. I'm full of fear and tension and rot," was his plain statement to God in a simple, honest sort of prayer.

SPIRITUAL HEART TREATMENT

"But what about that old heart of mine?" he asked plaintively.

"Look, Henry," I said. "Do you recall those words of Jesus? 'Let not your heart be troubled; ye believe in God, believe also in me.'" He nodded. "Well, then," I continued, "here is what I suggest that you do. Every morning and every night, and maybe other times in between, put your hand on your heart and imagine it's the healing hand of Jesus, and say, personalizing the Scripture, 'Let not *my* heart be troubled, neither let *my* heart be afraid.' Do that and live this faith straight and joyfully, and I'll bank you for the long pull."

He looked at me wistfully and blew his nose. He didn't fool me, for I saw the tears. Anyway, he followed the suggested treatment. His tensions subsided along with his fears. His prayer was answered and peace came to him, and with it healing. It must have been a proper treatment, for it has been seven years and he is still going strong. He appears to be a healthy man, and very much alive. He has become master of the relaxed drive. He no longer overpresses. He is in that harmonious flow of body, mind and soul that was created in us, but which all too often we lose. And is he enthusiastic? Why shouldn't he be?

The contagion of his enthusiasm acts as a tonic on everyone who comes in contact with him. Few are aware of the cause, but they realize that obviously it comes from the deeper levels of spirit. This remarkable thing called the contagion of enthusiasm, this enormous fullness of joy, shows up in people who have undergone basic changes as Henry did.

CONTAGION OF ENTHUSIASM MAKES GREAT SALESMEN

For example, there is Charles Kennard, whose story of release from alcoholism many years ago I described in one of my books, though not by name. Charles Kennard is one of the most successful salesmen I have ever known, and I have spoken to scores of sales gatherings and know a host of sales people. Enthusiasm has made an enormous difference in his work and life.

Charles has sold an inspirational, interfaith magazine called *Guideposts* to a list of industrial organizations that could well be the envy of salesmen of any product or service. He has persuaded scores of hardheaded businessmen, who have a sense of responsibility and regard for people, to subscribe in enormous quantities to this inspirational publication for their employees. Charles Kennard believes that the deeply moving human interest and personal stories which *Guideposts* brings each month into some two million American homes will make better people, who will make better products, hence better business and a better country, and more important than all, a better life for everyone.

Because of his dedication, he is deeply convincing and the contagion of his enthusiasm transmits itself not merely into sales, but into the stimulation of a similar dedication in hundreds of people. As a result of his enthusiasm he has played a large part in one of the most dramatic successes in American publishing history, the development of *Guideposts*, from a small beginning to one of the most widely read and influential periodicals in the United States today. The story of Charles Kennard is an example of what the contagion of enthusiasm can do.

One of the most enthusiastic men I have ever known is Elmer G. Leterman, author of two fine books, *The Sale Begins When the Customer Says No* and *How Showmanship Sells.* Elmer is one of the great salesmen in America, and one of the most interesting personalities as well. He has boundless zest and self-reliance and a powerful lot of common sense. His contagious spirit is expressed in the following statement from his book, *How Showmanship Sells:*

"I can't fathom clock-watchers, people who regard their jobs only as a means of getting money for the things they want to do. Each working day must become a Chinese torture to them, a steady drip, drip, drip of monotony which, over the years, de-humanizes them.

"What a shame that these people do not learn that business is fun, that it combines the ingredients of all the better games and sports. And the ground rules change too often for it to become boring . . .

"When I look back over my career, I consider it one grand lark. I still go to work each day with relish. I enjoy setting new sales records—more in a day, more in a month, more in a year. I welcome the challenge of new men who appear on the scene, threatening my old records and keeping me from becoming complacent. To me, material success without enjoyment would be no success at all."

Newspapers recently carried an account of the continuing heavy program of public service of former Governor Averell Harriman of New York. Now over seventy-five years of age, he covers the world on assignments for the President, and seems constantly imbued with zest and energy. In reply to an interviewer's question, Governor Harriman said that the secret of an active and enthusiastic life at his age was to "pick your ancestors wisely, then keep up your enthusiasm." Well, there is little we can do about our ancestors, but there is much we can do to cultivate the contagion of enthusiasm. There is no doubt it will help to keep you going strong, for in my experience the people who, like Mr. Harriman, continue to be effective despite increasing years, are those who have indeed kept up their enthusiasm.

BRANCH RICKEY'S ENTHUSIASM LEADS TO HALL OF FAME

When I get to thinking of such people, one man always comes to mind. Branch Rickey, who died at the age of eighty-three and who was recently voted into Baseball's Hall of Fame, possessed such heartening enthusiasm as few people I have ever known. Branch Rickey, onetime head of the St. Louis Cardinals, the old Brooklyn Dodgers, and the Pittsburgh Pirates, was a big, rugged, lovable man. His last words, spoken to a large audience gathered to honor him and to hear one of his marvelously unique speeches, were these: "Now I am going to tell you a story about spiritual courage . . ." Then he slumped into unconsciousness from which he did not recover.

Those final words were entirely characteristic of Branch Rickey. Spiritual conviction was what he himself had to a high degree. He was just as enthusiastic about his religion as he was about baseball, which is saying a great deal. He had his share of courage, too. For example, once when he was head of the Brooklyn Dodgers, he was at a meeting negotiating a contract for pro football at Ebbetts Field. The deal involved many thousands of dollars. But suddenly Rickey threw down his pencil, pushed back his chair and growled, "The deal's off."

Surprised, the other men asked, "But why? We are coming along well in our negotiations. There's real money for all of us in this. How come this sudden break-off?"

"Because," said Branch Rickey, staring hard under his beetle brows at one of the football men, "you've been talking about a friend of mine, and I don't like it."

"But what friend do you mean? I haven't been talking about anyone, let alone a friend of yours."

"Oh, yes, you have," replied Rickey, "you've mentioned him in almost every sentence." Thus he referred to the other's constant profane use of the name of Jesus Christ.

"I get you," said the other man slowly, "I get you. I

won't do it again. You can depend upon it." To have broken off this negotiation would have cost Rickey a lot of money, but his contagious enthusiasm was not for money, but for conviction.

Later, when Branch was ill, I called on him, and the same man happened to be present also. I said a prayer. Then Branch asked his wife, this man and myself to join hands. "Now let me pray," he said. I shall never forget that prayer by the old master of baseball. It brought us all close to God. The football executive whom Rickey had rebuked could not hide the tears in his eyes. "He is the greatest human being I've ever known," he said to me afterward. He knew a man, this fellow did, when he saw one. That's the kind of spiritual courage Branch Rickey had, which helped to make him a beloved leader of men. Perhaps even more than courage made an indelible impression; it was also the contagion of spiritual enthusiasm.

I often sat in with him at the old Ebbets Field in Brooklyn. To be Branch Rickey's guest at a game was a rare experience. His knowledge of every player was encyclopedic. He knew their characters, their families, their histories; indeed, everything about them. His conversation was an exciting blend of baseball, psychology, philosophy and religion. And Rickey was a profoundly religious man, a sturdy Christian, truly dedicated. He deserves to be one of the immortals in Baseball's Hall of Fame.

BALL PLAYER LEARNS SOME SPIRITUAL KNOW-HOW

Rickey often told me that his greatest purpose in sports was not to win games, tough competitor though he was, but to make men. He had boundless interest in his young men and was always concerned about them. Once he had a player who after every inning would rush in and telephone his wife to make sure she was at home. Rickey said to me, "Maybe he should see one of the psychiatrists at your clinic."

I asked what kind of girl the wife was. "The very best," Branch replied. "Sweet, clean, good in every sense. Completely trustworthy and loyal." If she weren't, you could be sure Branch would have known, for he knew people.

I suggested maybe the player himself was off the reservation, two-timing his wife and projecting his own disloyalty upon her. So I suggested calling the player in and delicately sounding him out. Well, Rickey did call him in, but he wasn't what could be called delicate. He said bluntly, "O.K., son, let's level. Who you running around with?"

The player had his back to the wall and knew it. "Well, Mr. Rickey, you see, it's this way. You know how it is when you're on the road with the boys. There is a lot of pressure on you. . . ."

"Sure," said Rickey, "but where are your inner braces? If you had some, they would make a man of you instead of a cheat on that fine girl you married. Well, here's the way it is. I won't tolerate that kind of character on my team, so you'd better straighten out. Or else."

But Branch Rickey also had a creative answer for the wretched young man. He said, "Now look, son, if you really want to go straight, there's someone who can help you, and you know who he is, as you were brought up a good Christian boy by godly parents." And Branch actually prayed for that player.

I had heard Mr. Rickey pray in times of personal crisis, and I never knew any man who communicated with the Lord better than he. He was a two-fisted man and his spiritual enthusiasm was a contagious thing. He brought something real into that young player's life and saved a marriage and a player too. The boy stayed on the reservation thereafter and played good ball.

I used to get many a sermon illustration from Branch, and he knew it, for he often came to my church. Once, in a game in Brooklyn a batter was thrown out at first. Rickey exploded, "The boy could have made it if he'd really tried. But," he added, "there's a sermon illustration in that for you."

"What's the illustration?" I asked.

"Why, it's obvious," said Branch. "That runner just didn't try hard enough; he didn't run that baseline with all he had. And I can give you a Bible passage to go with it, too; 'This one thing I do.' You see, that player was chewing tobacco, and enroute to first he actually expectorated."

"Yes, but what's the illustration?" I persisted.

"This one thing I do: get to first base, then spit!" grinned Branch.

Here was a rare and unforgettable man who loved life, baseball, his country and God. The contagion of his enthusiasm inspired not a few of our greatest athletes and others over the years, and the fire he ignited is still burning in many men, including the writer of this book.

The attitude of a person toward himself, that is to say, his self-image, is vitally important in the quality of performance, and in the outcome of his whole life. It is a fact, at least so I have observed, that many people hold an unreasonably low opinion of themselves. They tend to underrate themselves and to minimize their abilities. Of course, there are some who seem to have an exalted and often unwarranted high appraisal of themselves. But these are in the minority, and actually in not a few such cases, it has been my experience that what appeared to be unjustifiable egotism was, in fact, bravado to cover up an inward conviction of inferiority.

In all such cases a proper infusion of enthusiasm can make a great difference. To gain a sense of enthusiasm for one's job and a good wholesome and healthy knowledge of one's self has often made a profound change in a defeated and self-minimizing person. Expose such an individual to true self-knowledge and the contagion of enthusiasm will take hold.

THE IMPORTANCE OF ENTHUSIASM TO THE SELF-IMAGE

A rather classic example which shows the importance of a positive self-image is told by John Murphy in his book *The Secrets of Successful Selling.*

"Elmer Wheeler had been called in as a sales consultant to a certain firm . . . A certain salesman always managed to make almost exactly $5,000 per year, regardless of the territory they assigned to him or the commission he was paid.

"Because this salesman had done well in a rather small territory, he had been given a larger and much better one. But the next year his commission amounted to almost the same amount as that he had made in the smaller one—$5,000. The following year the company increased the commission paid to all salesmen, but this salesman still managed to make only $5,000. He was then assigned one of the company's poorest territories—and again made the usual $5,000.

"Wheeler had a talk with this salesman and found that

the trouble was not in the territory, but in the salesman's own valuation of himself. He thought of himself as a $5,000 per year man, and as long as he held that concept of himself, outside conditions didn't seem to matter much.

"When he was assigned a poor territory, he worked hard to make that $5,000. When he was assigned a good territory, he found all sorts of excuses to coast when the $5,000 was in sight. Once, when the goal had been reached, he got sick and was unable to work any more that year, although doctors could find nothing wrong with him, and he miraculously recovered by the first of the next year."

When the salesman faced up to the fact that it was his attitude, not his salesmanship, which was holding him back, he quickly improved his record. It wasn't too long before he had doubled his yearly earnings.

Many of us are subtly bound by the same chains that held this man back. Often our low status in life is not because our abilities are inferior, but because our opinion of ourselves is inferior. Reevaluate yourself. Maybe you're a superior type who has settled for being a lesser personality. If so, make up your mind today, right now, to *re-gear* your thinking, *revise* your strategy and *rebound* from where you are to where you should be. Let the contagion of enthusiasm grip your mind. It can make all the difference.

ELEVENTH COMMANDMENT SUGGESTED

I am reminded of a stimulating observation by Amos Parrish, one of America's leaders in the merchandising field, who is a philosophical thinker as well. He says there should perhaps be eleven instead of ten commandments and suggests as the eleventh, "Thou shalt use all thy talents to the uttermost." It certainly fits the teachings of Jesus Christ, Who said He came to "preach deliverance to the captives." What captives? People behind bars in prisons? Well, maybe, but definitely, He wants to set free those who are incarcerated within their own fears, their inferiority feelings and self-doubts, who are imprisoned in their own depreciative states of mind.

And when contagious enthusiastic faith in God and in yourself releases you from the self-built prison of your mind, then you begin to change, and as you change, your whole life changes also. Buddha said, "The mind is everything. What you think you become."

Harold Robles, a successful businessman, found this to be true. "Approximately ten years ago," he said, "I was building skyscraper-sized obstacles in my mind. Nervous tension had me confused. Then a fortunate turn of events occurred which was to change my life. I will never forget the day I came to Marble Collegiate Church. It thrilled and stimulated my negative and dormant mind. I returned home exalted and free of all depressing and unhealthy thinking. My mind became alert; healthily composed, strongly directed. In time a positive concept developed within me." Harold Robles became a dynamic, spiritually reenergized man with a powerful source of enthusiasm motivating him.

The power of contagious conviction in making men, or in remaking men who have failed in their goals, is another reason that enthusiasm makes the difference. Defeat in due course comes in one way or another to everyone. So the question isn't whether or not you experience defeat, but how you handle it.

What are you going to do with defeat? Let it destroy you, or turn it into a positive, creative experience from which you can extract much know-how and wisdom; and thus gain strength to stage a comeback? The individual who has at the center of his thinking the affirmation "I can do all things through Christ" can recover from any defeat and creditably handle any situation.

At a convention in St. Louis, I got into conversation with a man who had been awarded an honor that year as the leading producer in his industry. This man was a complete extrovert. He said, "I want to tell you something. I'm really on the ball if I say so myself. I've read all those books about how to get ahead. And, believe me, I've gotten ahead. How about that? I'm now the biggest producer in the industry. And I'm on my way to realizing my big ambition."

"What is your big ambition?" I asked.

"To make ten million. Yes, sir, that is what my life is set up to accomplish. Ten million bucks."

"Fred," I ventured to remark, "it's all right to make money, even lots of it, but don't set that up as the big ambition of your life."

"Now don't give me any of that religious stuff," he retorted. "I'm going places. I'm for the money."

It didn't seem to me that he was making the most of Amos Parrish's idea.

But there was something engaging about this man, even though his ideas and values were mixed up. After that day, we became good friends and I would hear from him from time to time. And in grandiose manner he would write me, "I've done this or that. I've sold this. I've accomplished that." Then I noticed that the effervescence was missing in his letters. Finally he wrote me, "I don't know what's wrong with me. I've messed everything up. I've made one mistake after another. I've lost a lot of money. I'm a long way from that ten million." And in an access of self-pity and self-blame he went on, "I'm no-account. I don't amount to anything. I'm stupid. I'm a fool."

I decided this called for strong talk on my part, so I got him on the telephone. "Fred, when you let disappointment and setbacks get you down, you're just making it much worse for yourself. Let's start a creative comeback program. What do you say?" I suggested a series of steps for him to follow.

SEVEN STEPS TO A COMEBACK

1. Stop running yourself down. There's a lot that's right in you. You have the same capacity you had before. Empty your mind of your failures and mistakes and start respecting yourself.

2. Eliminate self-pity. Start thinking of what you have left instead of dwelling on what you have lost. List your assets on a piece of paper.

3. Quit thinking of yourself. Think of helping others. Actually go out and find someone who needs the kind of help you can give and give it. For you will never have a continuing flow of abundance if your thought is only for yourself.

4. Remember Goethe: "He who has a firm will molds the world to himself." Almighty God put a tough thing into human beings called the will. Use it.

5. Have a goal and put a timetable on it.

6. Stop wasting your mental energy on gripes and postmortems, and start thinking about what you do now.

Think, think, think, as my friend, W. Clement Stone, says so impressively, "Think, think, think. Amazing things will happen when you think constructively."

7. Last, but not least: Every morning and every night of your life articulate these words: "I can do all things through Christ which strengtheneth me."

Quite a while later, Fred telephoned me, "I want to tell you that something really special has happened to me," he said. "I now realize that I never really lived until I started going with those ideas you gave me. New insights have shown me how to turn defeats into victories. I've turned the corner."

Well, Fred got the message. And once he did, the contagion of enthusiasm began to take hold. Now to get ten million dollars and quickly was not his big goal. He still wanted to do well financially; but he had a bigger goal; to upgrade his life into a creative category that involved doing something for his church, his city and for people having a hard time making a go of life. And he developed an amazing outgoing enthusiasm for Jesus Christ. In fact, the Lord's program for this world became his consuming interest. "I'm on His team with all I've got, money included, but principally myself."

You can figure it as you will but Fred started moving in life and is still going with the power of enthusiasm. And it is opening for him a vision of life he never dreamed possible.

Let me conclude this chapter with another tremendous illustration of the contagious quality of enthusiasm. This is again one of those thrilling success stories that has made the American dream the wonder of the world.

GUIDANCE THROUGH ENTHUSIASTIC FAITH

One Sunday, Mrs. Peale and I were invited by our friends and church members, Mr. and Mrs. Frank L. Small, to a luncheon at one of the big hotels in New York. Their cosmetic company salesmen, about a thousand, were assembled, representatives of one of the most prosperous Negro controlled businesses in the country.

A large group of our church members are among the dynamic individuals who make up this great sales organization. I was given the honor of extending greetings and

then had the privilege of listening to one of the greatest
platform speakers I have heard since as a boy I was
thrilled by the incomparable William Jennings Bryan. And
indeed, this marvelous speaker, S. B. Fuller, had many of
the qualities of Bryan's—eloquence, humor, down-to-earth
salty wisdom, religious emphasis and inspiration of an unusually high order. Mr. Fuller's speech and the manner of
his delivery, were a memorable experience. I was tremendously moved by this remarkable man, a great business
leader and vital Christian.

His story is told in part in a fascinating book entitled
Success Through A Positive Mental Attitude by W. Clement Stone and Napoleon Hill. The contagion of enthusiasm transmitted by Mr. Fuller at the luncheon in New
York; how he used it to build a successful business enterprise is explained in the story of his life.

S. B. Fuller's parents were Negro tenant farmers in
Louisiana—the family was poverty-stricken. The boy went
to work at the age of five. By the time he was nine he had
become a mule driver. That was about as far as anybody
would have expected him to go.

But S. B. Fuller had one great blessing, an intelligent,
wonderful mother. Everybody in the community maintained that poverty is an act of God; people were poor because God wanted them to be poor. But young Fuller's
mother said to him, "Don't you ever believe that poverty
is of God. If that is true, then why did the Lord fill this
beautiful world so full to overflowing of plenty and joy?
God meant us to feast upon plenty. I'll tell you why we're
poor; because your father always thought he was meant to
be poor. Your father is a wonderful, kind man. But he has
the idea that we are God's poor." And she tried to get her
son to realize what great possibilities he had in him.

Can't you just see this intelligent little boy listening with
wide-open eyes and a wide-open mind and a wide-open
heart? And he came to believe in the potential greatness of
himself under God. He decided to get better work and
started selling soap in Chicago. He sold soap for twelve
years, earned good money—and saved it. Then he heard
that the company which supplied him was going on the
auction block and that the price for the company was one
hundred and fifty thousand dollars. He had saved out of
his earnings twenty-five thousand dollars. So he went and
put down all he had saved as a deposit. That left him a

hundred and twenty-five thousand to pay and they gave him ten days to raise it. The contract also specified that if he didn't produce this money he would forfeit the twenty-five thousand dollars he had paid down—all his savings.

He had built up his opinion of himself to the point where he had that glorious quality called courage which comes through faith. He also had made many friends. He went to see them. By the night before the final deadline, he had raised a hundred and fifteen thousand dollars. But after exhausting every resource, he was still lacking ten thousand dollars. So on his knees he prayed, "Lord, You came to me when I was a little boy and through my saintly mother You told me that I could do something in the world. And now, Lord, I'm in a difficulty. I can lose everything and this big opportunity unless You guide me now."

Do you believe in guidance? I do. And perhaps if you believed in it more intensely, you would have miracles taking place in your life.

For this is how it happened to S. B. Fuller. Within his being, he heard words of guidance and he truly believes they were directed by the Lord. "You drive down Sixty-first Street in Chicago until you see a light in a building." It was then about midnight. "And you go in there and talk to a man."

Now S. B. Fuller had such an uncomplicated, childlike faith that he went out, got in his car and started down Sixty-first Street. And after he'd gone a few blocks he saw a light in a building. He went in. He recognized a contractor whom he knew slightly and he said to him, "Would you like to make a thousand dollars?"

The contractor, who was worn out from trying to solve his own business problems, said, "I sure would."

S. B. Fuller said, "If you will loan me ten thousand dollars, I will bring you back eleven thousand dollars." And he explained the entire venture. The contractor looked at him and saw something in him, and loaned him the ten thousand dollars. The next day S. B. Fuller bought the company. He now owns that company and six other companies. Yet he might have lived all his life as a mule driver, if not for an upthrust in him, put there by God and released by God. And he became a victorious child of God.

What is your trouble, what is your problem, what is

your weakness, what is your difficulty? Bring up against these obstacles the glorious fact that the Kingdom of God is within you. Submit yourself to the higher power, for the only power is of God. God can release you so that you can go on to whatever heights in life you believe you can attain. Keep yourself always humbly obedient to His guidance and will, and you can release the God-power that is within you. You really can. Get aboard with the contagion of enthusiasm and you can make your life whatever you hope for, dream of and work toward.

ELEVEN

ENTHUSIASM
AND OUR FUTURE

Some young people seem to have no real happiness in living today. To them, enthusiasm is puerile and outdated. In their search for new values, they experiment in drugs, drinking, sex. But such excesses don't bring about new healthy values; instead, they send the searchers deeper into the vacuum of nothingness. "Let's live it up," they cry, but it sounds like a deathwatch and there is nothing more tragic than spiritual death in the young.

Some who are aware of the deep trouble in the young are shocked and worried. Others condemn them. But all too few look for a creative solution. This is odd, considering that there is a solution both creative and high in potential. That solution is simply the application of spiritual enthusiasm that puts genuine honest-to-God excitement back into life. I use the name of God advisedly, for as previously pointed out, *entheos,* God within, is a source of enthusiasm not only in semantics but in fact.

So I feel it is important to talk about the problem of youth, of youth in relation to the older generation, and certainly in relation to the new confusing problems that beset our country.

IS THE PLAYBOY SYNDROME LOSING ITS MOMENTUM?

People began to lose faith in our country's future as they watched on TV or read in the newspapers about the riots on the campus at Berkeley, the crudities and insulting behavior of rebellious youth and the cynical exploitation of sex in moneymaking books and films.

But those sordid disheartening days, it would seem, are on the way out. Perhaps American youth is finally disillusioned, for droves of them have started once again going for God, country and ideals.

It could just be that the playboy stuff and the pretentious cynicism are on the way out. For the new knowledgeable generation finds it hard to accept such infantile nonsense. All of which demonstrates that young Americans are not as dumb as the New Left presumes them to be. Sure, Americans are big for fads. They may be taken in for a while. But presently they grow wise and give cults and dubious characters their walking papers. So maintain your enthusiasm and faith in the young of our country.

America is due for a terrific rejuvenation. Actually, it has already started rolling. Those who have long been awed or cowed by the cynical weird ones, who were shamed out of their happy, enthusiastic idealism, are getting started on their own counter-rebellion. And it is gaining momentum fast. The trend is getting into reverse and maybe it won't be long before the oddballs will have struck out. They just didn't come up with what young Americans really wanted. Already lots of the young are making the turn and discovering that spiritual enthusiasm adds up to real vitality in living.

An important reason for the new excitement sweeping the nation is that we are getting into a real revolution; one that is bound to bring vast benefits of freedom, hope and well-being to millions who unhappily thought the best they would ever know is the disappointing world to which they have been accustomed for so long. This revolution is likely to be the biggest setback in history to the New Left, the new immorality, the sex exploiters, and to a shabby, depleted communism.

NEW DYNAMIC LEADERSHIP ON THE WAY

This world is longing for new dynamic leadership based on the ideology of the greatest revolutionary of all time. His revolutionary principles of love, integrity, honesty and brotherhood are ripe for the takeover. One reason the time is ripe may be that Communist world leadership seems tired, old and possibly all but passé. Look at its chief exponent today: Ho Chi Minh, a dried-up old man, dreaming the weary dreams of the aged.

Cannot communism come up with something better, some alert, modern leader drawn from youth, or is the movement itself so worn out and sick that it can no longer spawn vital, young leadership? And the same may be said for that creaking, old man, Mao Tse-tung, who seemingly is having a tough time trying to hold his decaying communism together. It is possible that communism has reached its peak and is on the way down. The wave of the future didn't have what it takes to wave. It just couldn't deliver and so it could be starting down the long road to oblivion that is littered with so many other highly touted ideologies.

So currently we do have a vacuum in leadership. The New Left with its new impudent morality seemingly cannot make it; which is not unnatural, since it is constructed only on protest and cynicism. Without a constructive program, it is doomed to extinction. Leadership in this great crisis in history demands healthy and vigorous action. That is why the new spiritual freedom movement may be the answer. It is vital, alive and youthful.

One of the creative spiritual leaders of our time was an Englishman, Peter Howard, a cynic, wielder of a bitter pen, a brilliant writer for the Beaverbrook press in England. Moral Re-Armament was becoming popular. This movement was based on the premise that we must develop a modern man equal to modern times: We must have not only scientific giants, but moral giants as well. It began to attract a lot of attention, so Beaverbrook told Howard to see what it was all about and expose it.

Howard went to scoff, but remained to pray. For the first time he saw that the real Jesus Christ is not at all the kind of Jesus Christ that he had thought Him to be. He saw that Jesus is the greatest brain with the best blueprint for human beings in the history of mankind.

Howard became in many ways the greatest spiritual leader of his time. A friend of Aldous Huxley, he said, "In my day the apostle of the new morality was Aldous Huxley. Later in life Huxley got honest."

In his great book *Ends and Means,* Huxley said, "I had motives for not wanting the world to have a meaning, consequently I assumed that it had none, and was able without any difficulty to find satisfactory reasons for this assumption—for myself, as no doubt, for most of my contemporaries, the philosophy of meaninglessness was essentially an instrument of liberation. The liberation we desired was simultaneously liberation from a certain political and economic system and liberation from a certain system of morality. We objected to the morality because it interfered with our sexual freedom."

What about that? To satisfy their own lust without sense of guilt these men actually led thousands of mixed-up youth down the path to emotional and moral destruction. And since it is a fact that a nation deteriorates in its thinking before it deteriorates in its institutions, this negative leadership laid the ax to the tree of Western civilization, but it is likely that we will recover from the blow.

Professor J. D. Unwin of the University of Cambridge in his book, *Sex and Culture,* a work of highest importance according to Huxley, says (in discussing the trends of society and the tides of civilization through centuries of time): "Sometimes a man has been heard to declare that he wishes both to enjoy the advantages of high culture and to abolish continence. Any human society is free to choose either to display great energy or to enjoy sexual freedom; the evidence is that no nation can do both for more than one generation."

So the great question is—shall this country deteriorate due to weakening from within; through sexual license as advocated by the New Left, New Morality? Or shall it be strengthened once again through the take-over by stronger, wiser men?

New, fresh, dynamic leadership is required. And we have that leader awaiting the signal to go if we are smart enough to follow Him. But youth has got to make the decision, for half of the population of the world is under 25 years of age. In Japan, it is under 20 years of age. In

Russia, fifty percent are under 26 years of age. In Red China, there are more children under 12 years of age than the entire population of the United States, that is to say, there are over 190 million human beings in China younger than 12. Leadership must come from youth, for the world is composed of youth. That is the problem. Will they go for Jesus? Mounting evidence is that they will.

I know what you will say in bewilderment, that we have the greatest universities, the highest-paid faculties in history, and the most complete laboratories ever devised. We have the greatest store of knowledge and know-how in the history of the world. Yet how come these universities turn out weird youth who growl about no meaning in life, who snarl that civilization is a flop, uncritical sycophants of the loud-mouthed minority, most of whom are not students at all, but professional exploiters on college campuses.

Vermont Royster writing in the *Wall Street Journal* said: "One way to revive your faith in the future of the species is to spend a few days among some of the young who do not conform to the stereotype. Even at Berkeley there are thousands of students who do not think they have lost their souls if they bathe their bodies, and who are quietly preparing themselves to better the world instead of just lamenting it."

ALL YOUNG PEOPLE NEED IS SOMETHING REAL TO GO FOR

I certainly don't mean to depreciate young people as a group. I think they are generally great. I went to Boston recently to make a speech and intended to fly back, but a blizzard grounded all planes, so I came back by railroad; five hours in a coach packed to capacity. People were standing in the aisle. Some were sitting in the aisle. Most were young boys coming from schools for Easter vacations. Of course, many of them wore the badges of the New Left—New Morality—ragged coats, unpressed trousers, dirty shoes. But do you know something? Five hours spent with them was enlightening. Some of the boys had swarthy faces, others light complexions, dark eyes, blue eyes, but all had lustrous eyes and wonderful faces. All that remained was to put a dream in those eyes, a light on those faces, to get them to follow a real leader.

DON'T BE DISCOURAGED—THE PAYOFF IS IN SIGHT

Will they pass up sex-conditioned cynicism for something beyond satisfying the biological urge? Well, let's see. Take Vietnam for example. I am told that a dozen students came to Premier Ky and said, "Turn over a province to us, let us administer it." He was startled at their audacity, but found they had dreams and practical plans to go with it. Whether they realized it or not, they were talking the language of the real leader, Jesus Christ.

"All right, boys," he said, "I'll give you a province."

So Ky gave them a province. University students in the Far East are never supposed to dirty their hands. They are in a class above that. Ky saw them digging in the mud and operating bulldozers. He saw a law student helping farmers with livestock. He saw a medical student with red mud oozing into his sandals. They drained the swamps. They cleaned up inadequate sewer systems. They built 600 homes. They erected a hospital and 17 health centers. This was a depraved section of 30,000 population, a hotbed for running Communist information in and out of Saigon. Inside of a year, they had closed up that leak altogether. They had cleaned up the entire surroundings; they had made it a place of health—so much so that Ky said, "I would that I could do with the whole country what you young people have done with one province."

Think what youth with a sense of meaning and purpose and who know the score can do for this world, following the most practical, has-what-it-takes leader of all time. Jesus Christ is no mystic figure in a stained-glass window. He is alive—fully alive, a tough man mentally and spiritually. And he has the answers that really answer. Will youth go for this? They will indeed. In fact, they are going for it in ever-increasing numbers, as will be pointed out later in this chapter.

And those who are going for it are not the oddballs, but the cream of the crop. Into this movement for an invigorating, revitalized world come strong, attractive, intelligent youth, best product of a land that is perpetually young and dynamic.

The dedicated, tough breed of real American men has not run out. Their enthusiasm for a renewed, reborn country will make the difference between a faded worn-out civilization and a healthy one with a promise of hope and opportunity for all.

HUNDREDS NOW LIVING NEVER HAD A THRILL

There are hundreds of thousands of young people living today who have never known a genuine thrill. Lacking it, they fall back on synthetic substitutes—narcotics and violence.

But they are entitled to know in their time what former generations knew in theirs: what it is to be part of something truly great—something that endows living with fascination and excitement. They simply cannot understand how spiritual commitment can supply this quality but when they really find it, they do go for it.

Now we come to the vital news of our time which promises real hope for the future. It is the amazing story of Christianity on the beaches—the surging power of the sing-out, up-with-people Youth Movement. This is the modern upbeat message to the youth of the world; indeed to everyone.

That the belief in spiritual enthusiasm can dent the cynicism of the so-called beat generation is demonstrated in the following story written for *Guideposts* by Van Varner. It shows that a new conviction is on the move, something thousands never heard of before. It's a new enthusiasm that will make a substantial difference in our country's way of life, and much for the better.

"Every spring vacation a modern phenomenon occurs," writes Van Varner. "College students pour out of dormitories and fraternities and by plane, train, car, or thumb they head for beach resorts in Florida and California.

"These are the places 'where the boys are' and 'where the action is' and each year tens of thousands of students are drawn together for a week of frenzied communion with nature and with each other.

"They bring with them only the barest necessities; surfboard, guitar and the inevitable six-pack. They preen themselves in the sun, shout their way through thronged thoroughfares, dance the latest fad-gyration into the night. Sleep is a minor concern—finding a *place* to sleep is often

major—but nothing matters so long as one has fun, fun,
FUN.

"The search for fun, however, often ends in either boredom or trouble.

"In the past few years a new trend has started. Into
these same resorts move thousands of students with a different objective. Picture, for instance, an encounter like
this one:

"A tow-headed sophomore from Pomona College is sitting alone on the beach. He is bored. Along comes a strap-
ping football player from Redlands U; and the two start
talking.

" 'Having much fun?' asks the Redlands man.

" 'No. Not really. Actually I'm a bit hung over.'

" 'What are you looking for?'

"The boy from Pomona laughs.

" 'Are you kidding? What is everyone looking for?'

" 'Not the same things. I'm quite sure of that.'

" 'What do you mean?'

"The boy from Redlands sifts sand through his toes,
reflecting: 'Two years ago I came down here looking for
some kind of blast and ended up finding something quite
different and wonderful.'

" 'Like what?'

" 'Jesus Christ.'

"Ordinarily the Pomona boy would have been startled
and pulled away. But there is something so natural in the
way this stranger speaks that he isn't repelled. In fact, he's
intrigued that there could be any compatibility between
Christ and a beach blast.

"And so the Redlands football player tells how two
years ago he met several young people from an organization called Campus Crusade for Christ. They were full of
fun and joy, but it obviously did not come from a bottle.
Their questions to him had been on target: 'Where was
real happiness and fulfillment? What was the main point
of life?' Soon he is shown that the answers lie in Jesus
Christ.

"The students from Redlands and Pomona talk at
length. Before his vacation ends, the Pomona boy has a
new direction to his life.

"A skylarking convention of vacation youth on the
prowl hardly seems the place for a serious approach to religion. Yet two years ago on the beaches of Balboa, a

thousand college students made personal decisions for Christ. Last year 2,000 made the same choice.

"These beach conversions don't just happen out of thin air. They are all part of a carefully planned campaign involving hundreds of rigidly trained Campus Crusaders. The remarkable thing about these Crusaders is that they are all such good-looking, tanned, athletic, joyous young people that anybody would stop and listen to anything they had to say anytime. Not only are they regular Joes and Janes, but they are campus leaders, too, student council presidents and football captains.

"The actual idea for reaching out to the beaches started with Dick Day, who hopped into his MG one day in 1962 and drove down to Newport Beach. Newport is a yachting center of the West and Balboa Island—or 'Bal'—is part of it. During normal times, it has a population of 35,000, but during The Madness it crawls with some 150,000.

"Dick had no specific reason for going there that day, but it didn't take him long to find one. 'Do you know what I found out?' he said recently. 'Those kids thought they were having fun, but most of them were just bored. I knew immediately that they'd welcome the chance to hear what we had to tell them.'

"Forty Crusaders were in prayer. One of the things they were praying about was a banner, the one outside their window saying 'Jesus Is the Answer.' No sooner had it gone up than 15 guys in an apartment across the way put out a banner of their own. It read: 'BOOZE is The Answer.'

"The Crusaders accepted the joke, but they were ready to do battle for the last laugh. For days they prayed for those 15 guys. At last there was a breakthrough. A young man by the name of Steve came across the way, knocked on the door and said: 'How about it? Any of you in there want to live it up a bit?'

ENTHUSIASTIC SPIRITUAL STRATEGY GETS THEM

"Steve was welcomed in—with the eventual result that seven of the fifteen boozers switched sides to learn more about Christ. Steve today calls himself a 'Gung-Ho Christian.'

"Each year Campus Crusade's beach army has grown.

Last year over 400 Crusaders enlisted for 'Bal Week.' Weeks ahead of time they organized sign-in stations, a communications system and a network of meeting places. They had the cooperation of residents who offered their homes and the blessings of the Police Department and such local clubs as Kiwanis and Rotary.

"During Bal Week the Crusaders went to the beaches, conducted seminars. They took over a night club and every evening presented a big, splashy show called 'College Life Classic' with music, campus leaders and a dazzling young magician named Andre Kole. The theme of the evening's entertainment: God and Youth.

"The beach operation is but one aspect of the Campus Crusade's total thrust. For a movement only fifteen years old, it has made spectacular strides, reaching now to campuses throughout the world. The Crusaders believe that the reason so many students protest these days is that they have nothing to proclaim. The Crusaders are tired of college classrooms where Christianity can be openly knocked but no one is permitted to promote it, where there is freedom *from* religion but not *for* it. And so they are urging students to speak out."

And they are increasingly doing just that with intelligence and enthusiasm and effectiveness.

BIG NEWS—SPIRITUAL EXCITEMENT IS HERE

From this and other phenomena, it is clear that the rising tide of spiritual conviction is beginning to show, one that promises the makings of a new day. Everything in life has its cycle and then it runs down and plays out. People get tired of it. A college senior said, "Where do they come with this childish 'beat' stuff? Like a dope I fell for it once, and it nearly threw me. But I've had enough of it. And whether they like it or not, I believe in God, and I'm now really looking into Christ's way of life. Already I've seen enough to know that He has something those fellows never heard of."

Rather plain talk, but that Jesus Christ goes for it I have no doubt at all. He is a pretty tough man Himself and takes life as it comes, dirt and all. And moreover, He knows what to do about it, and does it. The heartening news of our time is that an immense number of young people are going for Him, and with Him. So perhaps it's time to cease condemning the behavior of some young people and start understanding that it's a rebellion against an older generation which has lost its way. It's a flamboyant attempt to find the meaning that was never given them by their parents, their teachers, even the church. Some attack the problem with eccentric dress and long hair. They think an unbathed body is a badge of rebellion. But they will go for a more creative type of rebellion, raised against meaninglessness by those who have found meaning and are terribly excited about their discovery. Their motivation is spiritual enthusiasm that has come of age.

For example, not long ago Dodge City, Kansas, was getting ready to start the day the same way it started days in Dodge City for years when a special train pulled into the Santa Fe Railroad station, with a big sign on it reading *Sing-Out '65 Express!* * The train doors opened and out poured two hundred and seventy-five good-looking, terrifically alive young men and women. Only a short time before they had been idling on the streets of Harlem, on the mountainsides of Appalachia or along the lush beaches of California, but they had come together and found a "new direction."

As they surged out of the train, some were carrying loudspeakers which they set up, others came running with long cords to hook up to electric power, a band assembled and soon the whole group began to play and sing. Several thousand citizens of Dodge City converged upon the railroad station.

They listened astonished as these young people sang. And what singing it was—full of life and power, songs about American freedom, about the future of America, and America under God. And they announced joyously that a new breed of American youth was taking over from the sad sacks who'd had so much free publicity. Then the whistle tooted, the whole joyous company got back aboard, and the long, sleek train pulled out, leaving the citizens of Dodge City with their mouths open and a new light in their eyes. For they had heard something they hardly expected to hear again, songs of faith in the great old American tradition, being sung once again by the nation's youth.

* Clarence W. Hall, "Sing-Out, America!" *The Reader's Digest,* May 1967.

On across the West rode the young people of the *Sing-Out '65 Express*. Some of them took planes to Japan, where seven thousand Japanese students, who had hated the United States, received them and were soon saying that if these are the Americans of the future then they were all for America. They have conviction. They have commitment. Will they take over? What do you think? They are making their lives mean something.

The future belongs always to the believers, who are *for* something, never to those who are only against something.

Who are these for-something new breed of young people, and how did they get that way?

SING-OUTS ARE PUSHING OUT THE FAR OUTS

Clarence W. Hall answers that question. He researched this amazing new phenomenon among America's youth and wrote the exciting story in *The Reader's Digest* under the title "Sing-Out, America!"

"On an early summer's day back in 1965," writes Mr. Hall, "the proceedings of the youth conference at Mackinac Island, Michigan, were going as planned. Sponsored by the Moral Re-Armament movement, the conference aim—'to give youth a goal and purpose for their lives'—was right on the beam.

"Then, suddenly, an interruption. A young college coed stood up. 'It seems to me that some youth leadership is needed right now. I for one am fed up to here with the image of American youth being created by beatniks, Vietniks, draft-card burners, campus rioters and protest marchers.'

"The conference came awake with a rush. From all over the auditorium came cries of 'Yeh! Yeh!'

"The young delegate went on: 'You and I know that such scruffy types don't represent the great majority of us. But does the public? Do the peoples of other countries? We need to do something spectacular to change this image.'

"The response was electric. Said John Everson, a track star from Iowa State University: 'The loud-mouthed, pacifist minority scream about what they're against. Why don't we stage a demonstration of what we're for?' "

Mr. Hall quotes Richard (Rusty) Wailes, an Olympic

gold medalist and one of the conference's directors, who said: "If we're going to debunk the myth of a soft, indulgent and arrogant America and show the world we care about tomorrow, we've got to *sing-out* our convictions, loud and strong."

"That was it—a 'sing-out!' A musical show that would travel across the land, appear on college campuses and military bases or wherever else they were invited, and express in song their commitment to God and country.

"To whip the cast into shape, Henry Cass, famed British producer of 'Old Vic,' was flown over from London. Brought in were the Colwell Brothers, a trio who had lifted folk singing to a fine art, written more than 300 original songs, sung them in 48 languages and dialects around the world. Invited to create 'Sing Out America,' they passed up a fat Hollywood contract to accept, saying, 'We're not interested in orchestrating the moans and groans of a sick society. But if we can help set a generation on the move to build a better world, count us in.'

"From the thousands of young people eager to be in 'Sing Out' a first cast of 130 singers and instrumentalists was selected. It represented 68 colleges and high schools in 41 states, was made up of Whites, Negroes, and American Indians. These, together with a crew of young technicians skilled in staging, sound and light engineering, gave up scholarships, turned down attractive job offers, sold cars, emptied savings accounts to help finance the venture.

"For weeks, Cass and the Colwells drilled both cast and crew, honing their performance into a fast-paced production that the late Walt Disney called the happiest, most hard-hitting way of saying what America is all about that he had ever seen or heard.

"In fourteen months 'Sing Out America' (in some places presented under the title 'Up With People' the name of one of its hit songs) had spread its unabashed patriotism over 300 college campuses, at the four U. S. service academies and 81 military bases in the United States and Canada; had traveled, at the invitation of governments and national leaders, through Japan, Korea, Germany, Austria, Spain, Puerto Rico, Panama, Jamaica and Venezuela; had produced a one-hour TV spectacular seen by 100 million in the U.S., and another seen by 25 million in West Germany and the Eastern Zone. Also, it had grown from one to three full-time traveling casts in the U.S. with 150 exuberant youths in each; had inspired and trained more than 130 regional Sing-Outs, involving 10,000 college and high school youths; had launched an international magazine called *Pace,* with a monthly circulation of 400,000, and inspired the founding of a four-year liberal arts college, Mackinac College, to train young men and women for national leadership in politics, business and the professions.

"From the moment it first hit the road, 'Sing-Out '65' was a smash hit. In Watts, they sang before thousands of Negro teen-agers.

"An example of how deep was the change wrought at Watts was seen in one young Negro who had taken part in the riots. He testified later: 'I measured my life against what these kids represented, and was ashamed. I went to stores I'd looted and offered to pay for the things I'd taken during the riots. Now I want to help show a new image of my community to the world.' He joined with other area students to create their own Sing-Out Los Angeles, a unit still going strong.

"Observers trying to analyze Sing-Out's almost electric appeal ascribe it to two factors: the character and content of its songs, and the enormous gusto of these young people.

"All songs in a Sing-Out repertoire have catchy tunes set to a lively beat, highly singable, with choruses that invite audience sing-alongs. Zestiest favorites with most audiences are two: 'Up With People,' an action song plugging brotherhood and praising the power of ordinary citizens, and the rousing 'Freedom Isn't Free!' with its toe-tapping, memorable chorus: 'You've got to pay a price, you've got to sacrifice for your liberty.'

"Every song makes a tuneful pitch to worthier living or higher national goals. There are songs debunking racial prejudice ('What Color Is God's Skin?'); skit songs satirizing some of modern youth's kookier aspects; a rollicking call to high moral standards ('You Can't Live Crooked and Think Straight').

"At show-time, Sing-Outers don't emerge onto the stage; they explode onto it, race to their places like a football team taking the field, are assembled in ten seconds or less. The sparkling program, like the kids themselves, moves at a fast clip. It shifts so smoothly from one to another of the 30 or more numbers that the audience is scarcely aware of any break. Lights dim, microphones are shifted, a new singing group or combo moves to center stage, spotlights click on—and the scene is changed, all in a matter of seconds. For the show's entire two hours the stage is a scene of constant movement, exemplifying one of its songs, 'Don't Stand Still!' the chorus of which affirms, 'We are moving and we don't stand still; we've got a mighty fine job to fill; the world's awaiting to be remade by every gal and gay young blade! . . .' "

Incidentally, further evidence of the powerful impact these young people are having on the world was demonstrated by a vicious effort against them at Harvard. But before this group of committed young people had finished their thrilling program, even the pickets started joining them. It seems that youth, when shown the truth, goes for the spirit and purpose of the Up-With-People Sing-Out group, even though they had been coached against it by the cynical new-left–new-morality professionals. An account of the attack at Harvard proves it.

"Harvard* was the scene of the most powerful presentation of Up-With-People ever made.

"Prior to the show a crowd of pickets stood outside in the icy weather carrying signs and singing songs protesting against the show. Those who wanted to get into the theater had to fight their way through a line of booing, hissing students.

"Filled with excitement, the cast roared onto the stage as if this was the only show they would ever give. The entire production burst with dynamism, enthusiasm and determination. The applause of the majority of the audience drowned out the smears and hissing of the group of 50 hecklers. Every reference made to God, faith, sacrifice, hard work and the military was hissed by the minority. In many cases, the majority group demonstrated back thunderous applause in support of the cast on stage. The louder the protesters got, the more determined the cast became. Smiles expanded, gestures sharpened and eyes sparkled.

"Olympic gold medalist John Sayre and William Storey of Indio, California, spoke on behalf of the cast, outlining the challenge presented to college America in the modernization of man.

* *Tomorrow's American,* Vol. III, No. 29, March 29, 1967. A Pace Publication.

" 'We do respect the great universities of today, including Harvard, for what they have given to humanity,' they said. 'But if brain power alone were enough to solve the world's problems, it would have been done years ago. We do need economic and social programs but unless university America learns to live the quality of life that grips and captures the wills and hearts of men, we will have failed miserably. College America, equipped with Moral Re-Armament, would be the most revolutionary men and women on earth, able to win both the Communist and non-Communist world.'

"Following the performance the students rushed towards the members of the cast, firing questions at them concerning burning issues of the day and the how and why behind Up-With-People. Many stayed for hours testing the cast to see if they were actually living the quality of life they were demonstrating on stage. Many Harvard and Radcliffe students asked to get application forms to join the show immediately.

A number of the pickets who had protested against the show beforehand, after seeing the demonstration and meeting the cast, said, 'We want to work with you.' "

Clarence W. Hall continues, "Nowhere has Sing-Out been more vociferously received than among the U. S. armed forces. The morale boost imparted was obvious and overwhelming. Said Lt. Gen. Bruce Palmer, Jr., commanding general at Fort Bragg: 'In these days of draft-card burners and Vietniks, sit-ins and teach-ins, how refreshing to discover that the patriotic spirit still burns bright in these United States!'

"At West Point, 2,200 cadets gave the cast a 27-minute standing ovation. At the U.S. Naval Academy at Annapolis, the midshipmen gave Sing-Out a 'hats in the air' salute and a 31-minute salvo of applause. Said one: 'In my four years here I've never seen any response like it. You show the thing in America worth defending.'

"But if Sing-Out '65 set Americans cheering, it caused a sensation when it went abroad. To show Asians what young Americans live for, they proved that a large segment of youth everywhere has the same hunger for positive purpose as those in the United States.

"In Japan, Sing-Out performed before standing-room-only crowds of Japanese youth at universities, in the famous Kabuki theater, at the Tokyo Olympic Gymnasium (with Prime Minister Eisaku Sato, U. S. and Soviet ambassadors present), and at Japanese and American Army posts.

"In Korea, their platform, a flag-bedecked railway car was only a few miles from the Communist lines. 'Thank God you came,' said a U. S. Army colonel. 'You've totally erased a very bad impression of American youth we were getting over here.'

"In West Germany, acclaim was even warmer. Wrote the mass-circulation daily *Bild Zeitung:* 'A musical tornado has gone through the city of Hamburg with gold and dynamite in their voices. Their singing is like an explosion, and the idea behind it shakes you up.' In Munster, the *Westphalischer Nachrichten* reported: 'Citizens of this town, normally known as sober and reserved, rose from their places in a public demonstration and sang and danced.' In the opinion of *Die Welt*, West Germany's national daily, ' "Freedom Isn't Free" could well become the theme song of our Western World.'

"The spread of the 'Sing-Out explosion,' at home and abroad, has been little short of phenomenal. In almost every place where the traveling casts have appeared, local and regional Sing-Outs have formed. Nation-ranging casts sprang up in Japan, Korea, Germany, East Africa, Australia, Latin America. Patterned carefully after the American format, national versions travel full-time through their countries, sparking, as in the U.S., the proliferation of innumerable local Sing-Outs. Following the visit of the U. S. group to Caracas, for example, casts totaling 400 sprang up in Venezuela; in Puerto Rico, 'Sing-Out San Juan' recruited more than 1,000.

"Notably zooming is Japan's own Sing-Out called 'Let's Go '67.' Having recruited more than 500 members, 'Let's Go '67' early this year sent a traveling cast to the Philippines and Indonesia, inspired the formation of similar groups in Taipei and Seoul, announced plans to take the program 'to every corner of Southeast Asia.'

"Another observer got close to Sing-Out's secret when he declared: 'This is vastly more than a show. It dramatizes a philosophy and a way of life once familiar to this nation's pioneers, but which has somehow been lost in our affluent society. Call it a revolt against the cynicism and moral relativism which have diluted the country's traditions, and in favor of bold new standards and purposes for us all.'

"Sing-Outers speak with disarming frankness about their acceptance of these new standards and purposes. A good example is Esther Diaz Lanz, an attractive young refugee from Castro's Cuba who, when Sing-Out came to Florida, had just graduated from a Miami high school. Impelled to join the group as a singer, she first went to her school principal to say: 'I don't deserve my diploma. I cheated on the final exam'—and insisted upon being given a new test, which she passed with better grades than before. Another is William Storey, a handsome young Negro who before joining Sing-Out was the leader of one of the toughest youth gangs on Chicago's West Side. Says Storey: 'The kids in Sing-Out seemed to have an answer to the hate and violence in the world. I decided to do something to help spread that answer. Now I find it takes more guts to stand up for what is right than it did to take part in the gang fights.'

"One father declared, 'I can't recognize my son since he joined this Sing-Out thing. Formerly he was wild and shiftless, with no purpose or goal. Now he's got more of both than I can comprehend!'

"Sing-Outers themselves find their aims not at all incomprehensible. As one of them wrote recently in their publication *Pace:* 'Our generation is looking for ideas we can believe in, fight for, demonstrate. We want peace, but not at the price of freedom. We'd rather be challenged by hard work and sacrifice than mothered by society. Ours is a generation on the move, ready to be disciplined and to dare. It wants to cure poverty, immorality and division— and do it with a revolution of character far more effective than hate-propelled violence.'

"Witness, for example, what Indonesia's youth did to save their country recently—and what China's Red Guards are doing to wreck theirs. Don't knock what these kids are doing with their Sing-Out. And above all, don't underestimate it!" So concludes Clarence W. Hall's appraisal of American youth who know the score, the very different new generation.

We are still a young country. Our original basic strength came from the principles we believed in, not only religious and political freedom, but a sense of compassion toward each other which was foreign to the old countries. We wanted to treat our neighbor as we would have him treat us. Having belief and faith and the marvelous enthusiasm that is the birthright of the young, we established a nation unique in the history of our civilization. It is heart-warming to find a resurgence of those basic strengths in a vast group of our young people. Their extraordinary action reminds us that enthusiasm is a *young* trait. It belongs to those young in heart and spirit and need not be hampered by chronological age.

I've known men of eighty who were young—among them my dear late friend, Dr. Smiley Blanton—and I have known boys of eighteen who were old. If youth is a state of mind, then enthusiasm is a part of it. And if you have enthusiasm, you'll have no need of hormones, face lifts, hair dyes and other artificial rejuvenators. Enthusiasm brings sparkle to the eyes, color to the cheeks and a joyous life to the heart.

So make enthusiasm your contribution not only to your own well-being but to this exciting pro-American counter-revolution that is being born in our country. If there is one trait the young will accept from their elders, it is enthusiasm. They long for dynamic action. They want a positive platform. We can make it possible by our mature wisdom and positive help, to aid the new crusaders. Fill your heart with faith, your spirit with enthusiasm and join the youth, the middle-aged and the senior citizens in a rich rewarding spiritual crusade. God will be with you.

TWELVE

ENTHUSIASM
MAKES THE DIFFERENCE

S. S. Kresge, founder of the immense empire of nearly a thousand retail stores bearing his name, had the cool quiet enthusiasm that smashes barriers and achieves spectacular results. This remarkable man lived for ninety-nine and one-half years and his philanthropic gifts have benefited thousands.

The Kresge story is in the tradition of the American saga; up from poverty to achievement, fostered by the proud Pennsylvania Dutch virtues of hard work, thrift, scrupulous honesty, faith and enthusiasm. S. S. Kresge was a devout Christian, a down-to-earth person and a keen thinker. He had a dry sense of humor. When Harvard bestowed an honorary degree upon him and he was to respond with a speech, he stood up and said, "I never made a dime talking." And sat down. It was probably the shortest speech ever delivered at that university, maybe one of the most sensible. He made some $200,000,000 in his lifetime, but gave most of it away. He never lost sight of God or the dignity of people. To use his own words, "I tried to leave the world a better place than I found it."

I once asked him the secret of his amazing life. "I have a simple philosophy," he said, "go early to bed; get up early; don't eat too much; work hard; help people; don't let anything get your goat; tend to your own business; be

202

enthusiastic; and always keep God in mind." With this simple philosophy, he went through life building, always building, with enthusiasm and faith.

"When one begins at the bottom and learns to scrape, everything becomes easy," Mr. Kresge declared. Certainly it does if you have the character and courage, the faith and enthusiasm to keep scraping. Such ability is greatly aided and abetted by built-in enthusiasm, the kind that overcomes barriers. What barriers? Why, of course, everything that gets in the way of a better life, of real success, of your God-given motivation to do the best possible with the capacities you possess.

A woman came up to me recently after I had made a speech. She turned out to be a high-school classmate of mine whom I had not seen since graduation. "Norman," she said, "I've been studying you as I listened to you. You've really done quite a lot with the little you had to start with." At first I felt let down. Then I realized that her remark was really a compliment. If you have only a little to start with but you do the best you can with that little, it is astonishing how much it may become.

HAVE A MADE-UP MIND AND MOVE ON UP

Enthusiasm develops and maintains the quality of determination which is vitally important in overcoming barriers to a better life. I have been tremendously moved by the story of Mahalia Jackson, one of the most outstanding singers of gospel songs this country has ever known. Barriers she had aplenty, but she also had "a made-up mind," enthusiasm, and faith in God. So she had what was required to "move on up."

Mahalia Jackson, up from poverty, has sung to vast and enthusiastic crowds in Berlin's Sportspalast, in London's Albert Hall and in many other great concert halls of the world. She was reared in New Orleans where her father worked on the river docks during the week and was a preacher on Sunday. Her people were very poor. She had little schooling, not even a formal musical education. But she heard the showboat music along the lower Mississippi. She listened fascinated to the great jazz bands. She felt something expanding in her and came to realize that she had been given a truly great voice. From the early thrill of

singing in the choir in her father's little church, where she
would lift her magnificent voice in moving gospel songs
like *How Wonderful That Jesus Lifted Me,* she went on
step by step to great success. One of her recordings, *Move
On Up a Little Higher,* sold eight million copies.

"What do you want to be?" she asks. "Where do you
want to go? God will lift you up." But there is a condition: "You've got to have a made-up mind."

She says that if God could lift her out of the washtubs
on the levee in Louisiana, if He could take her knees off
the floors she used to scrub, if He could lift her above the
sorrow which her race suffers, then, says Mahalia Jackson,
"He can lift you up too." And this is a fact. There isn't
anybody whom God cannot lift far above any goal he ever
hoped for or even imagined. But you must have a "made-
up mind." You've got to want it and you've got to let
Jesus Christ lift you up. Then you achieve victory over
weakness, over troubles, over yourself. So be wise; be one
of those who takes hold of life which is life indeed. Mahalia Jackson's story is another demonstration of an inspiring
fact. You can have what you want from life provided
you've got the enthusiasm that pushes barriers aside. You
can indeed "move on up" with faith.

TIRED SICK COUPLE FIND REJUVENATING ENTHUSIASM

I saw a run-down, middle-aged couple develop enthusiasm for life, an enthusiasm of such power and vitality
that they literally smashed the barriers of sickness and
dullness that had been blocking their way to a happy and
creative life.

This exciting human experience occurred one memorable May morning at our farm in Dutchess County, New
York. In a meadow on our property is an old, weatherbeat-
en, uninhabited house, which we use for storage. Hard by
this house is an enormous stand of lilac bushes. The grass
was deep and in the mist of the morning there was mystery and beauty around that old weather-beaten house.
The lilacs themselves were heavy with great globules of
dew. When you put your face into them the water was
cool and fresh, the fragrance was lovely, and it felt very
clean. Two Black Angus steers came up and looked at me
through the fence. And I looked at them. There seemed an

interesting, friendly expression on their big placid faces. I liked them, so I said, "Hi, boys. How are you?" But all they did was to blow long streamers of steam out of their nostrils.

Then the morning mist began to roll away. Long shafts of sunlight fell upon the lavender of the lilacs. The morning became dazzlingly bright. There came to mind from across the years something my father used to say of a happy and enthusiastic person. "He's as bright as a May morning." I stood in the deep grass thinking how many May mornings I'd lived, and I was happy because it still excited me the same as when I was a boy. I offered a prayer there by the lilac bushes that my up-beat spirit would never become eroded, that always, every day, life would be full of wonder, mystery and glory, full of tremendous excitement and enthusiasm.

The Bible offers intriguing advice, "Take hold of the life which is life indeed." We are told that Jesus came that we might have life "more abundantly." For it isn't the natural world, charming as it is, that gives the greatest excitement or joy or makes life most deeply meaningful and satisfying; rather it is the experience of the enhanced spirit, of revitalized sensitivity and boundless enthusiasm that gives it meaning.

So many people become jaded, old and tired before their time. They grow cynical and take on a condition of mind they call sophistication. But actually it isn't sophistication at all, for the real meaning of the term is "to be smart or wise in the ways of the world." And it is hardly smart to grow dull and to lose excitement. But it is a part of wisdom to come alive so that emptiness and deadness fall away.

Well, on this particular May morning, a couple drove to my farm to see me. I knew them as typical, bored sophisticates from the city. They were nice people, but they'd had it. Life had run down. The man said, "Helen isn't well and I'm terribly worried about her. And," he added, "I'm not well either."

"You look pretty husky to me," I remarked.

"Maybe so, but I'm not well in my thoughts, and I've lost the creative ability I had." This man is a music writer and an editor of distinction. "Something has left me," he said. "I've lost enthusiasm and the sense of being thrilled that I have always had. I want to know how to get it back again. Life is no good without it."

"Now look, Bill, you've come to the wrong person," I said, "I am a minister of the Gospel and you are one of our super-modern sophisticates. How come you're asking me how to get the thrill of life back again? You've made a mistake in coming to me about this problem, because I will give you a simple answer, one that is on the spiritual side. I'm not hopeful because you probably aren't simple enough to accept a simple answer. You are too complex, or shall we say too advanced for that—or at least you make out that you are. But if you will come down off that complicated, sophisticated perch of yours and show some humility, I can give you a real answer that will really answer."

"Boy," he said, "you're being a little rough on me, aren't you?"

"Maybe that will do you good," I replied, grinning. But we understood each other.

"You name it, I'll take it," he said. And I got the distinct feeling he was really reaching for something this time.

"Okay, come inside." I took Bill and Helen into the house and went into the library. "Now," I said. "See that rug? It is a good Chinese rug that my wife is still paying for. It's thick and will cushion your knees, which doubtless haven't been on the floor in prayer in years. So get yourself down by this chair on your knees."

They both knelt, and we prayed. I found that I had misjudged these people. He really poured his heart out, and she did, too. They didn't mince words, but came right out and asked the Lord Jesus Christ to re-create them. And, believe it or not, right there in my library on that May morning, I witnessed that tremendous phenomenon where a man is re-created. And a woman, too. Presently they walked out with a spring in their step and a new light in their eyes.

A year later, Bill wrote me a letter, and evidently the enthusiasm still held. It was poetically expressed, for Bill tends to be poetic, and it says: "The skies were never more blue; the grass was never more green; the fragrance of the flowers has never equalled that of this year; the song of birds has been positively ecstatic. We never knew that life could be so wonderful. Helen is better, and I've been released." They kept the revitalized enthusiasm they found on that picture postcard May morning; it has never dimmed. They discovered the enthusiasm that smashes all barriers to a worthwhile and joyful life.

ENTHUSIASM KNOCKS OUT BARRIERS TO BETTER LIFE

Barriers to better life are many and varied. There is, of course, fear. That is a big barrier, indeed. And along with fear goes caution. Proper caution is wise and prudent, but don't be too cautious. The fearful, the timorous, the extra-cautious never surmount the barriers beyond which lie the really wonderful values of this world. Too much caution is actually bad for you.

At our farm one day, an oil truck came to make a delivery. But presently I noticed that the driver did not get out of the cab. I walked over and asked, "What's the matter?"

Nervously the man answered, "Look at that dog." Now, we have a big dog of no recognizable breed, just a plain dog, who has an enormous bark and mean look to go with it. But actually he is a fake. Mean look and bark are all he's got. "Why, that dog wouldn't hurt a fly," I said.

"I'm not interested in flies," the man retorted. "I'm interested only in not being bitten."

"Look," I said, "if you will just get out of that cab and walk right at this dog, he will fade."

But he was taking no chances. "Look at his eyes," he said. "No thanks." And he sat right where he was.

I turned to the dog. "Go away, Petey!" I commanded. "Go away!" But to my surprise and embarrassment he came at me instead with a mouthful of barks. I almost jumped aboard the truck myself!

Petey knew he had this delivery man buffaloed and he was going to see if he could scare me too. "As long as you're afraid of this dog," I told the man, "he knows it and is determined to keep you sitting in that cab."

Finally my assurances prevailed. The cautious fellow climbed out. Together we walked straight toward the dog. When Petey saw he was not scaring anybody he retreated, and fast. After that he just hung around the edges growling while the man went about his business.

Well, it's no news that an animal, sensing your fear, will

often do its best to intimidate you all the more. The longer you permit yourself to be cowed by anything, the more scared of it you become.

A person who has been in an automobile accident is likely to feel shaky the next time he rides in a car. But the sooner he does so, the better. If he puts it off, he may develop a fear of cars that can develop into a phobia against all modes of travel. Fear sometimes increases with the passage of time and also undergoes "generalization"—that is, it spreads from the original threat to other areas.

So it is plain that too much caution is bad for you. By avoiding things you fear, you may let yourself in for unhappy consequences. It is usually wiser to stand up to a frightening experience, meet it head-on, risking bruises or hard knocks. You are likely to find that it is not as tough as you had anticipated. Or maybe you will find it plenty tough, but also discover that you have what it takes to handle it—and thereby become a stronger person.

John Ruskin in his early twenties became painfully aware of being extremely timid. During a stay at Chamonix in the French Alps this tendency caused him acute distress. Having watched other young men climbing the mountains, he tried a few of the lesser peaks himself; but fear made him physically ill and he almost gave up mountain climbing.

In the stress of this difficulty he wrote: "The question of the moral effect of danger is a very curious one; but if you come to a dangerous place and turn back from it, though it may have been perfectly right and wise to do so, still your character has suffered some slight deterioration; you are to that extent weaker, more lifeless . . . whereas if you go through the danger, though it may have been apparently wrong and foolish to encounter it, you come out of the encounter a stronger and better man, fitter for every sort of work and trial."

The essence of the matter is summed up in advice which Henry J. Taylor, well-known news correspondent, received years ago from his father: "Don't worry too much about yourself and about getting hurt. People who go through life being cautious miss a great deal. Take your chances wherever you have to. It's better luck, you'll see more, and you'll probably live as long anyway."

Then another barrier that needs smashing is resentment. Have you ever realized that the term resentment is derived from a word which means to re-hurt? This may explain the mental soreness and pain felt when you resent, for you are actually re-hurting yourself, keeping the old wound open. The expression "sorehead" rather graphically pictures the pain in the mind caused by resentment, for mental soreness is continually activated. Resentment is indeed a big barrier to real life, but enthusiasm can get you over that hurdle too.

Still another barrier is self-isolation that avoids concern about other people. It could be that much of today's unhappiness and lack of enthusiasm may be attributed to an acute self-interest that refuses to become involved in any human need. It was estimated that at least thirty-nine people heard the screams of a woman being stabbed to death in New York City, and incredibly, these people shrugged it off as no business of theirs.

"Why should I get mixed up in this?" they tried to reason. "It isn't my funeral." But it was their funeral. The poor woman lost her physical life. They lost life in their souls. How can they ever forget those agonizing cries to which in their dull selfishness they failed to respond? Their non-involvement will forever haunt them. This desire not to be involved in the sorrow, pain and tragedy of other people is a huge barrier to top-quality life. But real enthusiasm for human beings smashes such indifference and produces a quality of happiness that can hardly be found in any other way. As Arthur Gordon puts it, "Enthusiasm is the state of caring—really caring."

DRAMA IN THE SUBWAY

Take, for example, the way Sal Lazzarotti, Art Director of *Guideposts* magazine, rose to the challenge of a potential tragedy in which he allowed himself to become involved one morning in a New York City subway on his way to work. A few feet from where he was sitting stood a nice, clean-cut looking boy of about eighteen holding onto one of the center posts in the swaying train. And seated across from Sal was a well-dressed young woman of perhaps twenty-five years of age, reading a paperback. As the train stopped at a station, this girl arose and walked past the boy toward the door. Then suddenly she screamed, "You fresh punk! Don't look so innocent! I know you touched me!" And she flew at him, scratching at him like a tigress. The boy, astonished, threw up his hands to protect himself and in so doing apparently touched her face, for suddenly there was a speck of blood on her lip. Then, breaking free, he ran from the car down the platform—she after him, high heels clicking, crying, "Police! Police!" The train doors closed. The startled passengers shrugged their shoulders and went back to their newspapers. To them, it was just one of those things.

Now from where Sal sat he had seen quite clearly that there had been no contact between the boy and the girl before she screamed. The boy was completely innocent. Sal wondered what would happen to the boy and whether some witness—himself—ought to get in touch with the police. He tried to persuade himself that it was none of his business, that the boy had probably got away anyway, and that he had better stay out of it. He was too busy to get involved in somebody's trouble. But he couldn't get the boy out of his mind.

What he did then completely ruined his day's work. To begin with, it took four telephone calls to locate the police precinct to which the boy would have been taken had he been caught. The desk sergeant told him yes, the boy had been brought in and had been sent from there to Juvenile Court. Sal called Juvenile Court and got the boy's name —Steve Larsen—and his parents' name and address; got Steve's mother on the phone; learned that the family had no money for legal help; took upon himself the job of finding the boy a lawyer; and along with the lawyer and mother, Sal went to the courtroom as a witness.

When questioned by the judge, the girl gave an impressive story of how she had been attacked. Sal listened in amazement, knowing that nothing she was saying had occurred. At one point the judge interrupted to tell the girl, "There is a witness to the incident present, so be sure of what you say." The girl looked around the room, saw Sal, recognized him, stared at him incredulously and went completely to pieces. She fumbled her words, contradicted herself, made a spectacle of herself. The judge called the girl's lawyer and Steve's into a huddle, decided the girl was in need of psychiatric help, and dismissed the case.

If Sal Lazzarotti had decided that the incident was none of his business and had avoided getting involved, the boy would undoubtedly have been convicted; he would have gone to jail, a blot on his record, he might consequently have become a criminal. He was saved from catastrophe by the presence in that subway car of a man who felt a responsibility toward a human being he didn't even know.

But Sal had a burning enthusiasm for people—he really cared, and his enthusiasm smashed the barrier of non-involvement which stands across the path to happy life.

HARD HITTING SURPRISE FOR GANG OF HOODLUMS

Still another enthusiastic barrier smasher of the paralyzing attitude of non-involvement was Naval Reserve Airman James R. George, age 23, from Georgia, on leave in Philadelphia and intent on seeing the historical sights of that city. In the subway station at the corner of Race and Vine, he was confronted with a sight he hadn't expected to see in Philadelphia, cradle of human liberty. Fifteen or twenty young hoodlums had cornered a young girl and were about to rape her. Six men were just watching, making no move to intervene. George called to them, "Come on! You're not going to let them get away with this, are you?"

But they shrugged their shoulders. "None of our business," was their attitude. "Don't want to get mixed up in it. Not our fight."

But this boy was made of sturdier stuff. It was his fight. He threw off his jacket and sailed all by himself into that vicious gang of punks. He threw them right and left, sent them sprawling all over the platform. They came back at him, beating him up, but he finally drove them off and saved the girl. The six men, meanwhile, just stood idly by.

The Mayor of Philadelphia held a public ceremony in George's honor, cited him for his courage and sense of responsibility and made him an honorary citizen of the city. When it came time for George to respond with a few words before the microphone, the first thing he said was, "I have enjoyed my stay in Philadelphia . . ." Of course, he had, not withstanding his bruised face and other marks of violence. Why had he enjoyed himself? Because his conscience was clear. Because when decency demanded, he had given himself for one of God's defenseless children. He had what it took to get involved. He had enthusiasm for people, especially for the helpless and defenseless.

Still another barrier to happiness that spiritual enthusiasm overcomes in a victorious way is the fear of illness, the fear of losing a loved one. This is a matter of deep and anguished concern, one of the profoundest anxieties of life, but the person who has found spiritual answers develops a positive, powerful and enthusiastic faith that carries him over this, one of the greatest of all human problems.

BOY SAVED BY LETTING GO AND LETTING GOD

One noonday while speaking at a luncheon meeting in a Chicago hotel, I noticed at the back of the hall a number of waitresses standing and listening. Afterward, hurrying through the lobby to catch a plane, I heard my name called. There was a young woman perhaps thirty years of age, in a waitress's uniform, her face all alight. She rushed up to me and, taking both of my hands in hers, surprised me by saying, "Doctor Peale, I just love you!"

"Well, don't announce it so loudly!"

"Oh," she repeated, "I just love you."

Touched by her candor and sense of joy, I said, "Do you know something? I love you too. But please enlighten me. Why do we love each other?"

"I'll tell you," she answered. "I have a little boy. His father deserted us, but I thanked God all the more that He'd given me this wonderful child. Then when my boy was five years old he became sick. The doctor told me it was very serious. And one day he said, 'Mary, you've got to be strong. I don't know whether we can save your boy or not.' He was preparing me for the worst. I was so terribly distraught, I felt my whole world would go to pieces if I lost my boy. I loved him so much. He was my entire life.

"Then a neighbor gave me one of your sermons in which you said 'If you have a loved one who is ill or about whom you are worried, don't hold this loved one too closely. Give the loved one to God. God gave him to you. He isn't yours, really; he is God's. So give him to God, for God is good, He is loving, He is a great kind Father who holds each child in His love. Let go and let

God care for him. No harm, only good can come to him when he is in God's hands.'

"Well," she continued, "I'd never heard anything like that before. It seemed awfully hard to do. But something inside my heart told me that it was right. So I prayed like you said and I put my boy in God's hands." And she put her hands out as though handing a child up into the great hands of God.

"Yes, and what happened?" I asked gently.

Smiling through tears of joy, she said, "Isn't God good? He let me keep my boy. And now God and I are raising him together."

Several other waitresses, Mary's friends, had come and stood listening. There were tears in everyone's eyes, including mine. And I said, "Mary, I want to tell you something. You're really a great mother, that is what you are. And you're one of the strongest and wisest human beings I ever met."

The other waitresses agreed, "She's everything you say!" So we separated. And I went my way refreshed by yet another wonderful human drama. That young woman really had the power of enthusiastic faith, and with it she had overcome one of the toughest of all human problems.

A familiar barrier to going ahead is the tendency to exaggerate obstacles. How many years I have listened to people trying to explain why they can't! If they would utilize half of the time consumed in telling why "they can't," to doing what they could, they would find that they can after all!

My old fifth-grade teacher George Reeves, a huge man physically, and even bigger in faith, left a lasting impression on his students. He had the curious habit of suddenly writing the word CAN'T in big letters on the blackboard. Then, eraser poised, he would ask, "What can we do about that word?" And the well-trained class would chant, "Knock the T off the CAN'T!"—which he would do with a wide sweeping stroke of the eraser. "See that you go through life knocking the Ts off the CAN'Ts," he would admonish, adding, "You can if you think you can!"

NEVER BUILD A CASE AGAINST YOURSELF

I first heard that statement of power-packed truth in a

conversation with my old friend, Robert Rowbottom, up in Berkeley, Rhode Island, where I had my first church; and it hit me, "like a ton of bricks." For you see, that was exactly what I had been doing—building a case against myself. But with Rob's positive concept working in my mind, I began to realize I was going at life with an entirely wrong attitude, one that could only end in a negative result. Therefore, I decided to do a mental about-face. I asked God to change me and give me a more positive attitude, and I meant it with all the strength I could summon.

Fortunately, God heard my desperate prayer, for believe me, it is miserable to live with that painful state of mind called an inferiority complex. Being freed from it was one of the greatest things ever to happen to me. So I began to experiment with this powerful technique. With insight came new concepts that made a terrific difference in my life—the power of positive thinking and of enthusiasm. But these two tremendous mental and spiritual qualities must be learned and mastered, a discipline that does not come easily. But once they do take over fully, then you can smash barriers which otherwise would surely defeat you and could result in the ruin of your life plan.

Of course, it might not be that drastic a result for you. But I knew that it would be for me. In my case, it was a matter of survive or perish, so deeply rooted were my insecurity and inferiority feelings. Therefore, I grasped for the mastery of positive thinking and enthusiasm, and relying upon the help and guidance of our Lord Jesus Christ, went to work to build my life on that foundation.

Positive thinking is how you think about a problem. Enthusiasm is how you feel about a problem. And the two together determine what you do about a problem.

TURN TYPHOONS INTO TAIL WINDS

I was sitting at one time in the copilot's seat of a DC-6 airplane in the Far East, in the area where typhoons, a big blow with a sinister name, roam violently over land and sea. I asked the pilot about the problem of flying in typhoon territory. "Well," he drawled, "they're not exactly anything to fool with. They may cover an area of three to five hundred miles and consist of circular high winds rotating counterclockwise."

"Well, what do you do when you encounter a typhoon?" I asked.

"Oh," he replied, "one thing is sure. I don't try to buck it. I just get on its edge and go the way it's going. In that way I turn typhoons into tail winds."

Positive thinking and enthusiasm do just that. They turn problems and difficulties into tail winds, so that you can ride them to successful outcomes.

There is, of course, always a danger, in advocating the development and use of enthusiasm, that it may result in overtension. Even enthusiasts need to practice the easy-does-it principle, lest they fall victim to the tendency to overpress or become unduly excited. Enthusiasm is not necessarily a flashy or heated phenomenon, but rather a strong, controlled motivation, and may be present in the quiet and restrained person, as well as in the vigorous extroverted individual. The world belongs to the enthusiast who can keep cool.

Of the people whom I have observed who fit this description, the late Calvin Coolidge comes to mind. He was such a quiet man that he was referred to as "Silent Cal." But he had a personality in which enthusiasm operated under cool control. He was one of the few politicians to use words sparingly. His speeches were short and succinct. He said what he wanted to say and no more. He won the liking of a great many people simply by not talking too much.

A college student and I were received at the noonday reception the President had in his office at the White House for members of Congress who wanted to introduce their constituents to the Chief Executive. Brashly, I gave him the Phi Gamma Delta fraternity grip. He returned the grip and said, "I belong to the Amherst chapter."

"I know that, Mr. President," I replied. That was the end of the conversation.

Before his career as a public servant, Coolidge was a lawyer in Northampton, Massachusetts. He had a downtown office and his home was up the street. Coolidge never drove to his office; that would have been expensive. He believed in being economical. He used to walk from home to office every morning at precisely the same time. This route took him past a house where lived a friend by the name of Hiram. Every morning when Coolidge came along, Hiram would be leaning over the fence. And for twenty years the daily conversation ran something like this.

"Hi, Cal," said Hiram.

"Hi, Hiram," said Cal.

"Nice morning," Hiram added.

"Nice morning," agreed Cal.

That was the way it went for twenty years. Then Coolidge was elected Lieutenant Governor, then Governor, then Vice-President of the United States. And then he became President. He was gone from Northampton for quite a few years. His Presidency ended, Coolidge returned to Northampton and to law practice. He dusted off the furniture, got his office ready, and one morning not long afterwards, he walked once again from his house to his law office. And sure enough, there leaning on the fence was his old friend, Hiram.

"Hi, Cal," said Hiram.

"Hi, Hiram," said Cal.

Hiram said, "Nice morning."

Cal said, "Nice morning."

Just like it had always been. But then the heavens fell. Hiram, this taciturn New Englander, added, "Ain't seen you around lately, Cal."

"Nope, been away a spell," Cal replied. All the business of being Governor and President was over. Life was what it was now. Calvin Coolidge took it as it came. He had enthusiasms of the quiet kind and they ran deep. He was enthusiastic about the United States, and to him it stood for something. But as to himself, he did not take Cal Coolidge too seriously. He was a quiet, relaxed enthusiast. The drive was there, but it was controlled.

The purpose in writing this book is to point out the incalculable value of enthusiasm, especially to the individual who has the urge to accomplish something worth accomplishing in life. I agree with the publisher, B. C. Forbes, who said, "Enthusiasm is the all-essential human jet propellor. It is the driving force which elevates men to miracle workers. It begets boldness, courage; kindles confidence; overcomes doubts. It creates endless energy, the source of all accomplishment."

I have sought to show by various examples how enthusiasm has made an immense difference in the lives of many people. By now you are aware that in my opinion the chief importance is spiritual enthusiasm, for it makes you a new person with new spirit, new energy and new know-how. Now you have guidance. As a result, you develop the enthusiasm that smashes barriers, those you have erected in your mind, as well as barriers on the outside.

LISTLESS CARL REACTIVATED BY ENTHUSIASM

I was scheduled to speak to a sales convention of a certain industry, and before the meeting, a businessman approached me and said, "Dr. Peale, I have one salesman who wouldn't have the initiative to come to this convention on his own, so I invested two hundred dollars to bring him. Having read your *Power of Positive Thinking*, I expect you to get him activated so I get my money back through his increased sales. I have gotten him a front seat. I recall reading in one of your books how you built a fire under another sleepy guy in similar circumstances."

"The fire was built in him, not under him," I replied. "I'll do what I can for your man."

He pointed the man out to me. As I was talking, I looked at this salesman now and then. He had a kind of blank, aimless expression on his face; showed no sign of reacting to anything.

However, after the meeting, he came up to me. "My name is Carl," he said. "I'm the dull salesman Mr. . . . . invested money in to bring me here to this convention and to get me motivated."

"You know about it then?"

"Sure, how could it be otherwise? He has been telling everyone about me." He said this without bitterness; in fact, he did not seem to care.

I asked him to my room that we might talk. "What's the matter with you, Carl?" I asked.

"I don't know. I just don't know."

I tried a few exploratory questions to get acquainted.

"Did you go to college? Did you do all right there?"

"Well, I got by."

"And how have you been doing in business?"

"Oh," he answered, "I get by."

"Boy, you're not getting by very far, if you ask me," I said. "Your boss is really upset about you. He says you're not producing, yet he thinks you've got what it takes to be a real salesman if only you get motivated."

"But I haven't any energy. I'm clean out of enthusiasm. In this competitive work, you've got to be alert, you've got to be on the ball, you've got to get out and after them. Drive is what you must have, and lots of it."

"Where did you hear all that sort of thing?" I asked.

"In the sales meetings. And," he added, "it wears me out to hear them talk that way. It all seems stupid, but I just have no interest in anything."

"Do you go to church?" I asked, trying a new tack.

"Oh, once in a while. But it leaves me cold."

"Do you belong to any clubs or associations?"

"No, nothing. What the heck—I have no interest in that stuff."

He seemed completely apathetic and listless. Yet he was gifted with a rather nice personality, or it could be if he had some force.

"Carl, I want to ask you something. Do you believe in God?"

He said of course he did.

"What are we to learn from Jesus?" I asked.

"Well, He teaches us to be good," Carl replied uncertainly.

"That's true," I agreed, "but did it ever occur to you that Jesus Christ is also energy, that He is vitality, that He is life, and that if you get Him in your mind you will come alive? Fill your mind with thoughts of God and Christ and you will have boundless enthusiasm and energy."

The man looked at me with interest, the first I had seen in him. "You really believe that, don't you?" he asked. "Well, that makes sense. I'll try it if you will help me."

"Let's pray about you," I suggested. "What do you say?"

He said, "I'd like that. Maybe that's what I need." So I offered a prayer, then asked, "Now, Carl, how about you saying a few words?"

I cannot remember Carl's short prayer word for word. I wish I could for it was one of the best I ever heard. It was most affecting. It went something like this: "Lord, I'm a dull, sleepy, no-account guy. But I really don't want to be that way. Honestly, I don't. I'm sick of being the way I am. I just don't amount to anything, and I'm asking, please revitalize me, Lord. Amen." Then he looked at me, and after a long silence said, "You know something? I think the Lord is going to answer that prayer."

"I think so, too," I replied, for I felt sure of it.

Before we parted, I told Carl something I had heard when I was a very young man which gripped me and had meant much to me all across these years. I heard a man say, "You can become strongest in your weakest place." He was referring to weakness of character or personality. I recalled how this man used as an illustration the process of welding, in which two pieces of metal are fused under intense heat. He asserted that if an effort should be made later to break the joined metal, it would probably not break at the welded place since, due to molecular fusion under heat, that had become the strongest part.

"That is for me," said Carl, "for apathy is sure my weakest place. I promise you I will follow your advice and try to get spiritually welded." But I did not leave it to him altogether. I contacted a minister in his city whom I knew to be a vital, enthusiastic man of faith. He took Carl on and got him related to a group of business men, all of whom had experienced changes in their personal life. In the positive atmosphere of that fellowship, Carl's apathy began to give way. The intense heat of real faith and prayer and joyous release fused his conflicted personality until he did indeed become strongest at his weakest place. In fact, he became positively dynamic and alive in the fullest sense.

He became active in his church; he joined one of the service clubs in town and really got into its work. Within three years, he was president of the local chamber of commerce. It seems eventually, according to many, that he did more for his town to build it up than any man in a decade. People used to come and tell me, "Carl is a ball of fire." And that was an understatement. At Carl's request I went to his town to make a speech. He met my plane.

I said, "Carl, I've been on the go steadily. I want to go to my hotel room and lie down and rest before my speech."

"Rest?" he echoed. "Why should you rest? Where's that energy and enthusiasm you're always talking about?"

I gave in sheepishly. "All right, let's forget the hotel. Where do we go next?" He really showed me around, and his enthusiasm so rubbed off on me that I forgot all about being tired.

Carl is only one of the hundreds of people across the years in whom I have seen the marvelous process of spiritual change take place, whereby the dead (the alive dead) learn to live again. Listless, de-energized, even cynical, those men have in one way or another got into proximity with the dynamic Person who said, "I am come that they might have life, and that they might have it more abundantly."

And then something happened in each case, some emanation of stepped-up vitality and energy passed into them, so that no longer were they the same men. They became completely different from what they had been. The new spirit showed in their eyes, in their step, indeed, in their entire demeanor. And it showed also in the amazing results that came to them in the form of up-graded creativity. The New Testament says, "All things are become new." These men had their lives changed. Bursting now with eagerness and aliveness, with a grip on their lives and their jobs, they know for a fact—for a wonderful fact—that enthusiasm makes the difference.

INDEX